Garfield hangs out

BY: JIM DAVIS

BALLANTINE BOOKS · NEW YORK

Published in the United States by Ballantine Books, a division of Random House, Inc., New York, and simultaneously in Canada by Random House of Canada Limited, Toronto.

Library of Congress Catalog Card Number: 89-92608

ISBN: 0-345-36835-5

Manufactured in the United States of America

First Edition: October 1990

10 9 8 7 6 5 4 3 2 1

PET PICKS & PANS

PET EXPERT GARFIELD ON CATS AND THEIR COMPETITION

RABBITS: BUY TWO CHOCOLATE ONES AND HOPE THEY MULTIPLY.

HAMSTERS: BIG DUMB COUSINS OF MICE.

GOLDFISH: NEAT, QUIET, DON'T NEED WALKING, AND IN A PINCH THEY MAKE A TASTY HORS D'OEUVRE.

SPIDERS: THAT'S NOT A PET; THAT'S A NIGHTMARE.

MICE: SURE, THEY'RE CUTE, BUT THEY ONLY LOVE YOU FOR YOUR CHEESE.

BOA CONSTRICTORS: RIGHT. NOTHING LIKE A PET THAT WILL HUG YOU, THEN EAT YOU.

PARROTS: PRETTY BIRDS. A GOOD ACCESSORY WITH AN EYE PATCH AND PEG LEG.

DOGS: LOVING, LOYAL, OBEDIENT, AND BREATH THAT WOULD STUN A YAK.

CATS: NATURE'S MOST PERFECT PET. NEED I SAY MORE?

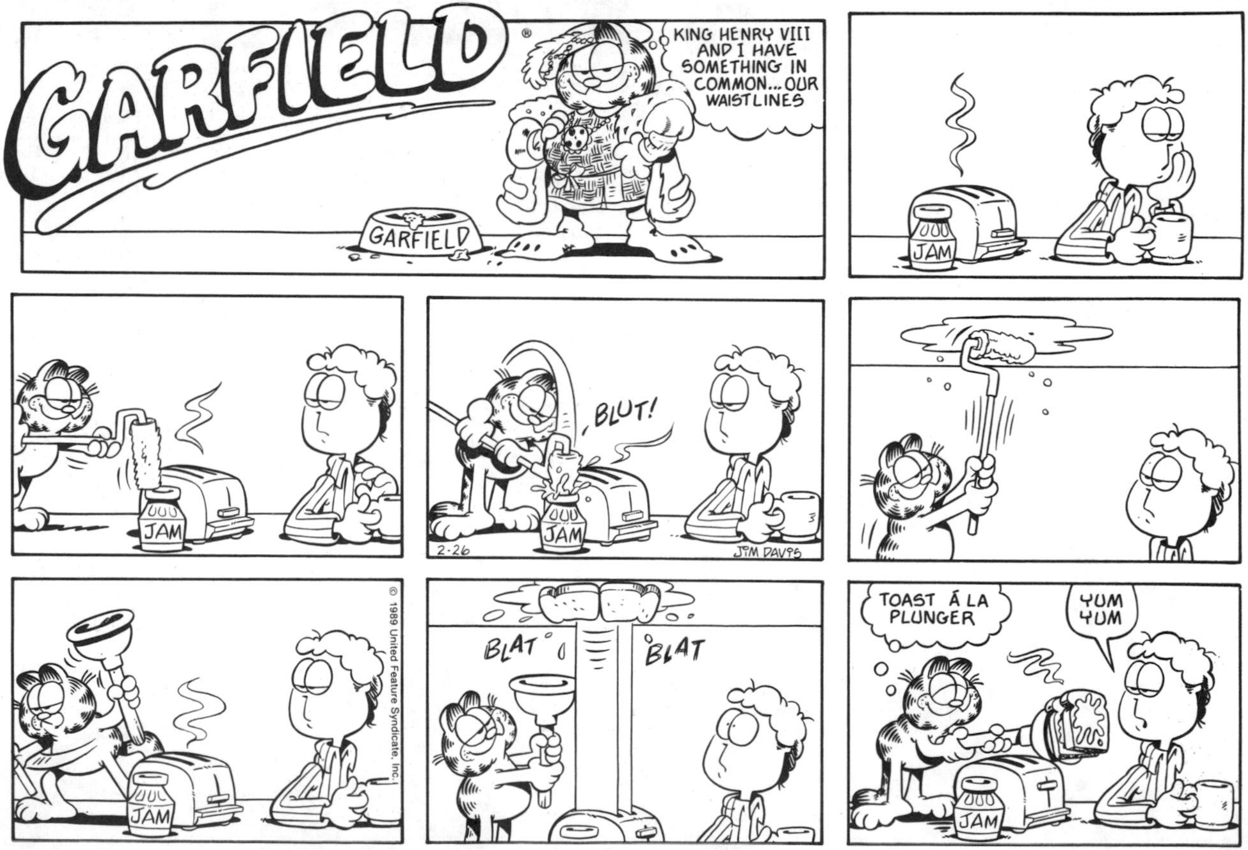
GARFIELD®
KING HENRY VIII AND I HAVE SOMETHING IN COMMON... OUR WAISTLINES
GARFIELD
JAM
JAM
,BLUT!
JAM
2-26
JIM DAVIS
© 1989 United Feature Syndicate, Inc.
JAM
BLAT
BLAT
TOAST Á LA PLUNGER
YUM YUM
JAM

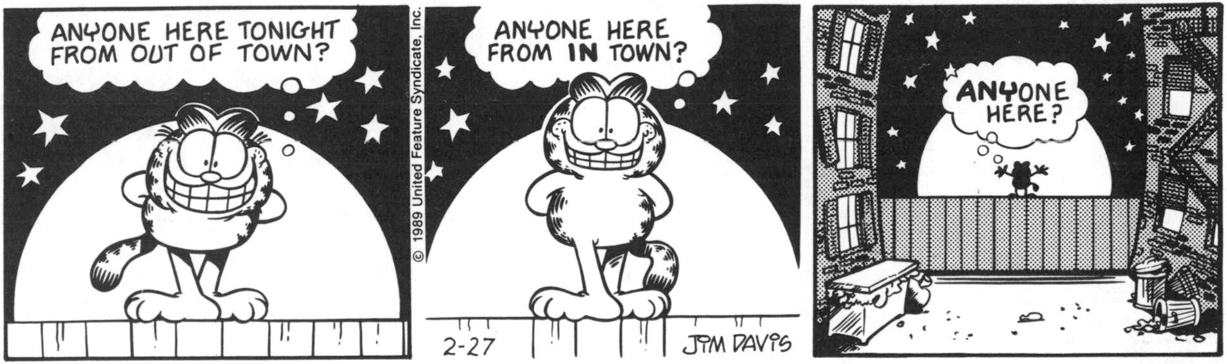
ANYONE HERE TONIGHT FROM OUT OF TOWN?
© 1989 United Feature Syndicate, Inc.
ANYONE HERE FROM **IN** TOWN?
2-27
JIM DAVIS
ANYONE HERE?

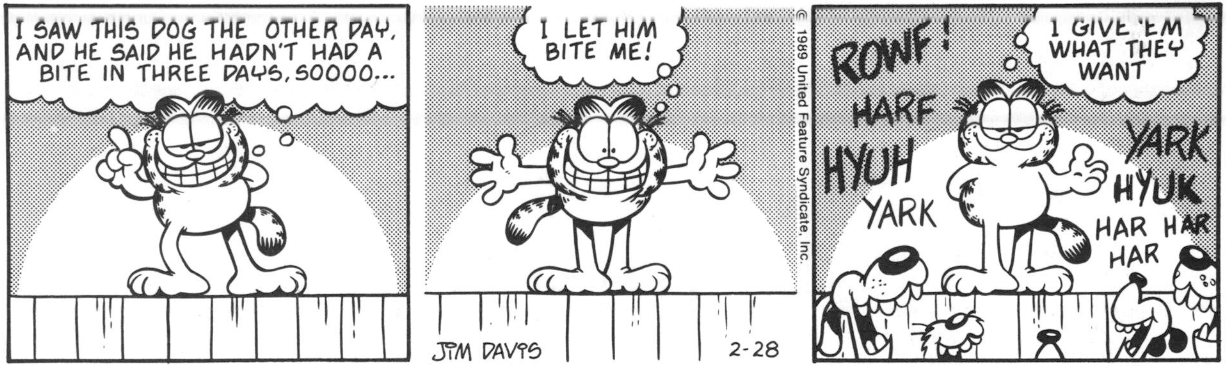
I SAW THIS DOG THE OTHER DAY, AND HE SAID HE HADN'T HAD A BITE IN THREE DAYS, SOOOO...
I LET HIM BITE ME!
JIM DAVIS
2-28
© 1989 United Feature Syndicate, Inc.
ROWF!
HARF
HYUH
YARK
I GIVE 'EM WHAT THEY WANT
YARK
HYUK
HAR HAR HAR

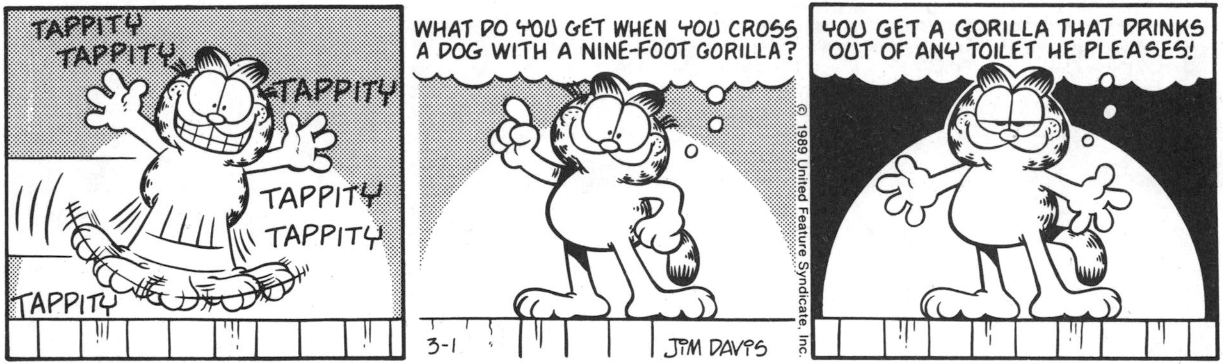
TAPPITY
TAPPITY
TAPPITY
TAPPITY
TAPPITY
TAPPITY
WHAT DO YOU GET WHEN YOU CROSS A DOG WITH A NINE-FOOT GORILLA?
3-1
JIM DAVIS
© 1989 United Feature Syndicate, Inc.
YOU GET A GORILLA THAT DRINKS OUT OF ANY TOILET HE PLEASES!

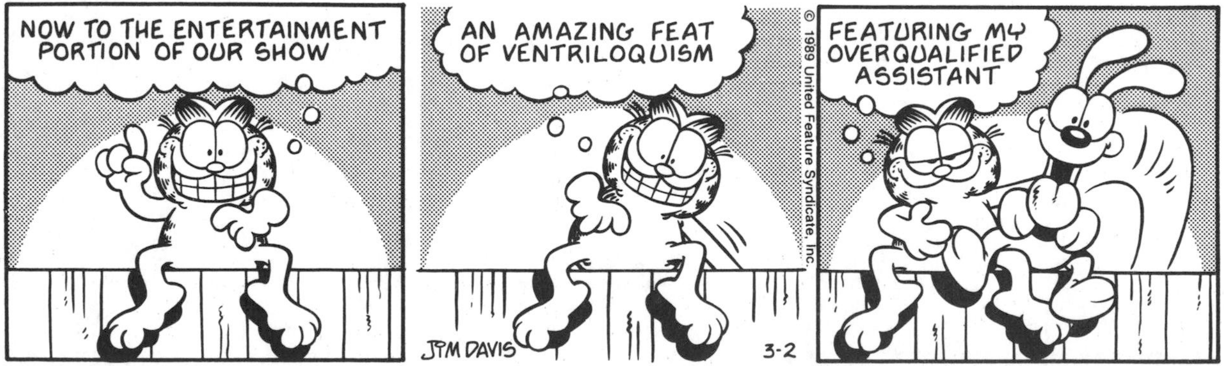
NOW TO THE ENTERTAINMENT PORTION OF OUR SHOW
AN AMAZING FEAT OF VENTRILOQUISM
JIM DAVIS
3-2
© 1989 United Feature Syndicate, Inc.
FEATURING MY OVERQUALIFIED ASSISTANT

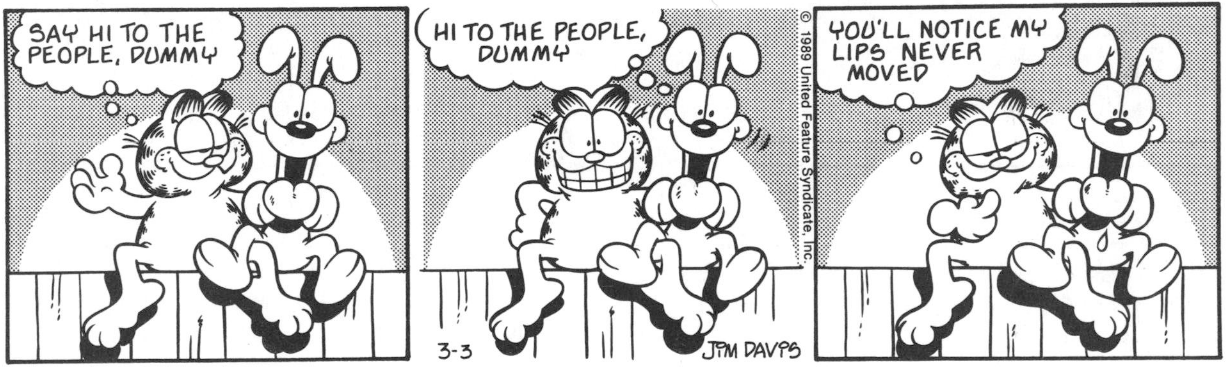
SAY HI TO THE PEOPLE, DUMMY
HI TO THE PEOPLE, DUMMY
YOU'LL NOTICE MY LIPS NEVER MOVED
3-3
JIM DAVIS
© 1989 United Feature Syndicate, Inc.

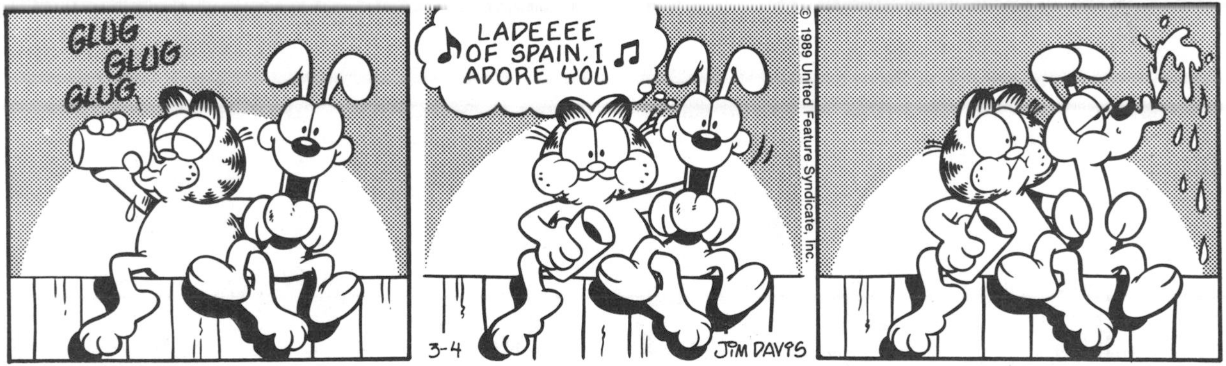
GLUG GLUG GLUG
LADEEEE OF SPAIN, I ADORE YOU
3-4
JIM DAVIS
© 1989 United Feature Syndicate, Inc.

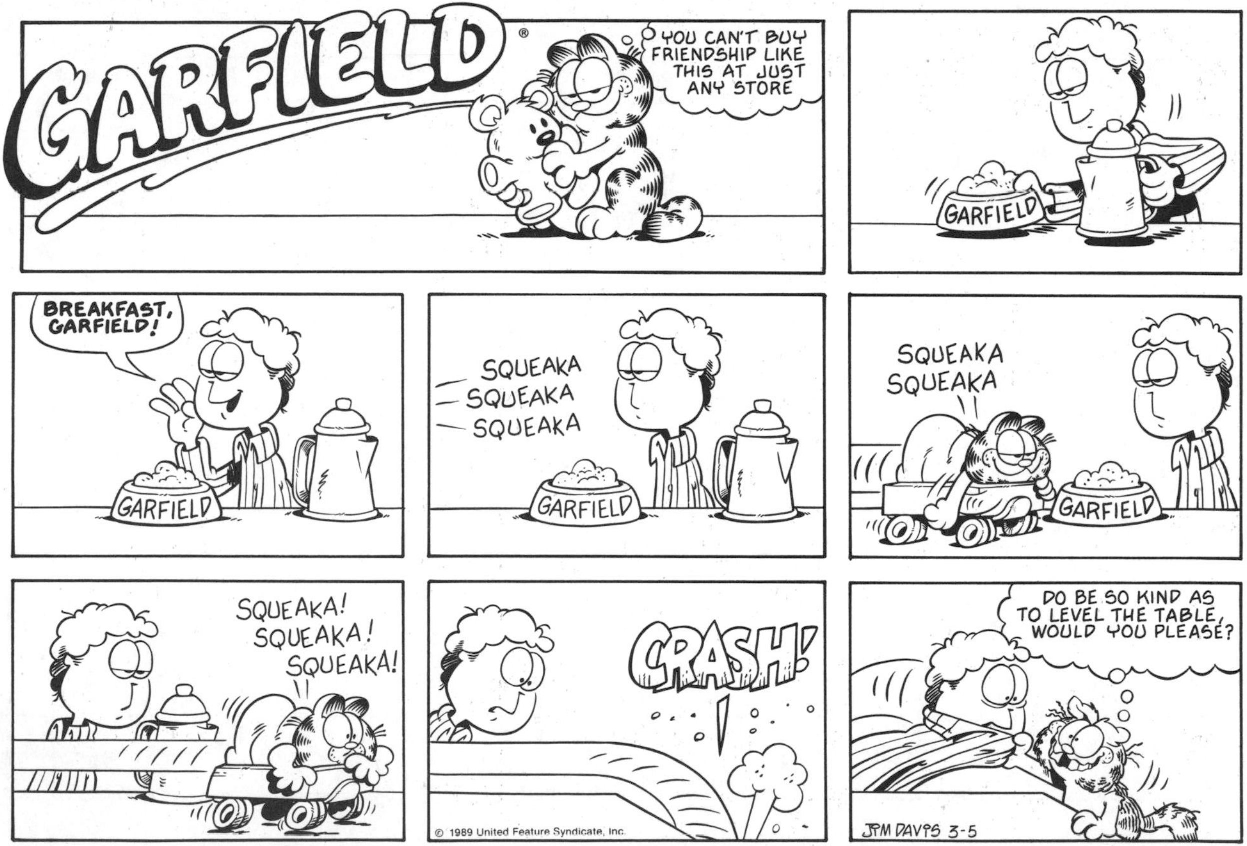
GARFIELD®
YOU CAN'T BUY FRIENDSHIP LIKE THIS AT JUST ANY STORE
GARFIELD
BREAKFAST, GARFIELD!
GARFIELD
SQUEAKA
SQUEAKA
SQUEAKA
GARFIELD
SQUEAKA
SQUEAKA
GARFIELD
SQUEAKA!
SQUEAKA!
SQUEAKA!
CRASH!
© 1989 United Feature Syndicate, Inc.
DO BE SO KIND AS TO LEVEL THE TABLE, WOULD YOU PLEASE?
JPM DAVIS 3-5

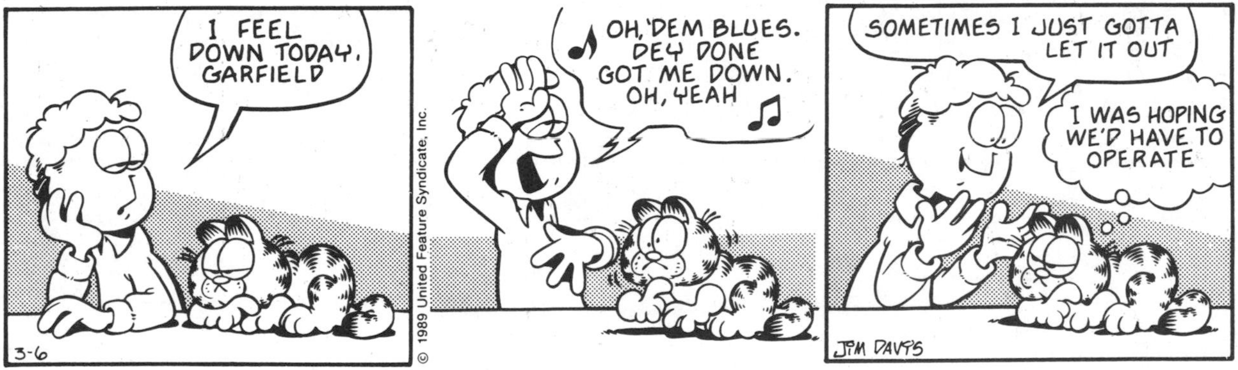

I FEEL DOWN TODAY, GARFIELD
OH, 'DEM BLUES. DEY DONE GOT ME DOWN. OH, YEAH
SOMETIMES I JUST GOTTA LET IT OUT
I WAS HOPING WE'D HAVE TO OPERATE
3-6
JIM DAVIS
© 1989 United Feature Syndicate, Inc.

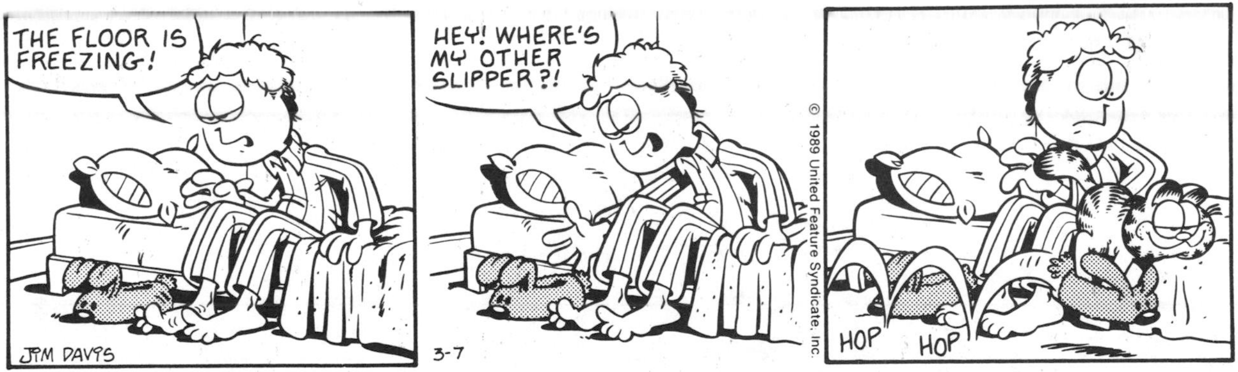

THE FLOOR IS FREEZING!
HEY! WHERE'S MY OTHER SLIPPER?!
HOP
HOP
JIM DAVIS
3-7
© 1989 United Feature Syndicate, Inc.

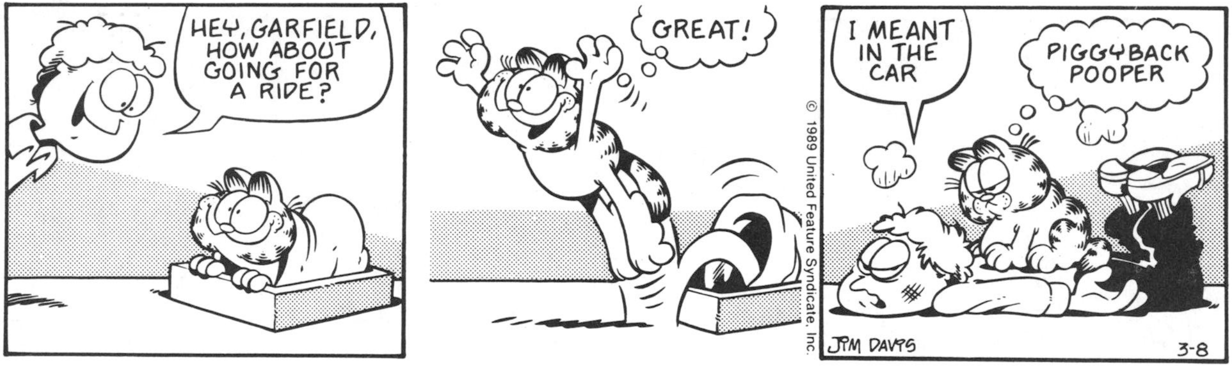
HEY, GARFIELD, HOW ABOUT GOING FOR A RIDE?
GREAT!
I MEANT IN THE CAR
PIGGYBACK POOPER
© 1989 United Feature Syndicate, Inc.
JIM DAVIS
3-8

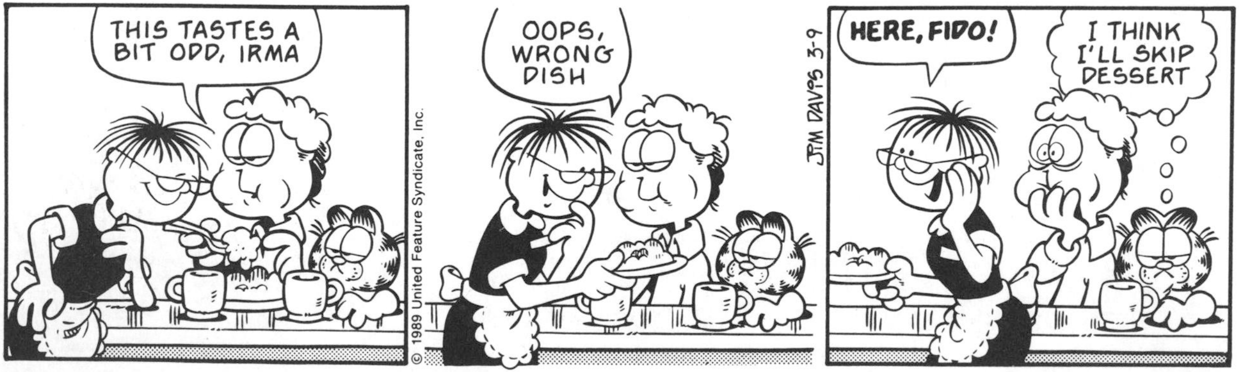
THIS TASTES A BIT ODD, IRMA
© 1989 United Feature Syndicate, Inc.
OOPS, WRONG DISH
JIM DAVIS 3-9
HERE, FIDO!
I THINK I'LL SKIP DESSERT

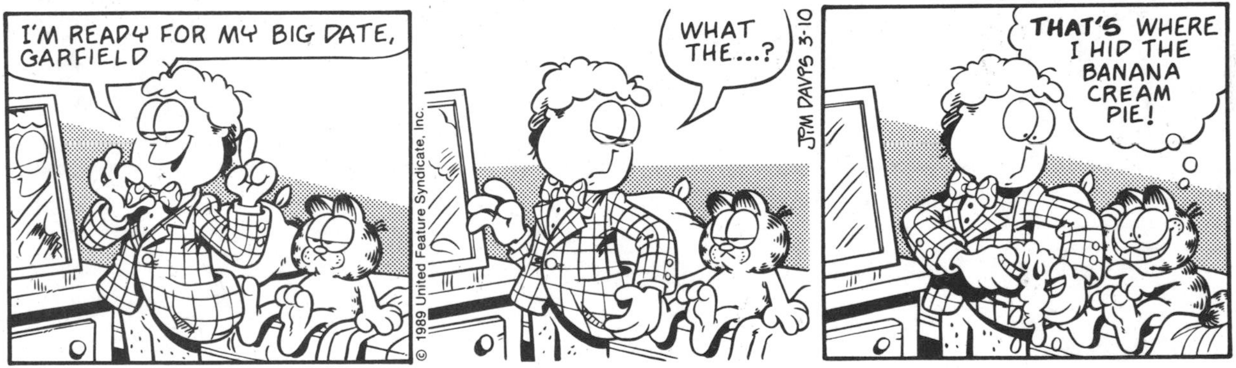
I'M READY FOR MY BIG DATE, GARFIELD
© 1989 United Feature Syndicate, Inc.
WHAT THE...?
JPM DAVPS 3-10
THAT'S WHERE I HID THE BANANA CREAM PIE!

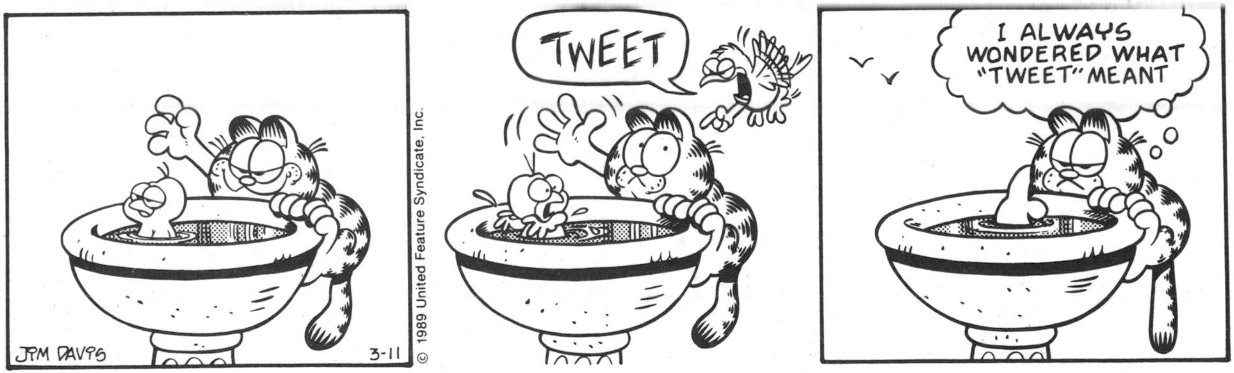
JPM DAVPS
3-11
© 1989 United Feature Syndicate, Inc.
TWEET
I ALWAYS WONDERED WHAT "TWEET" MEANT

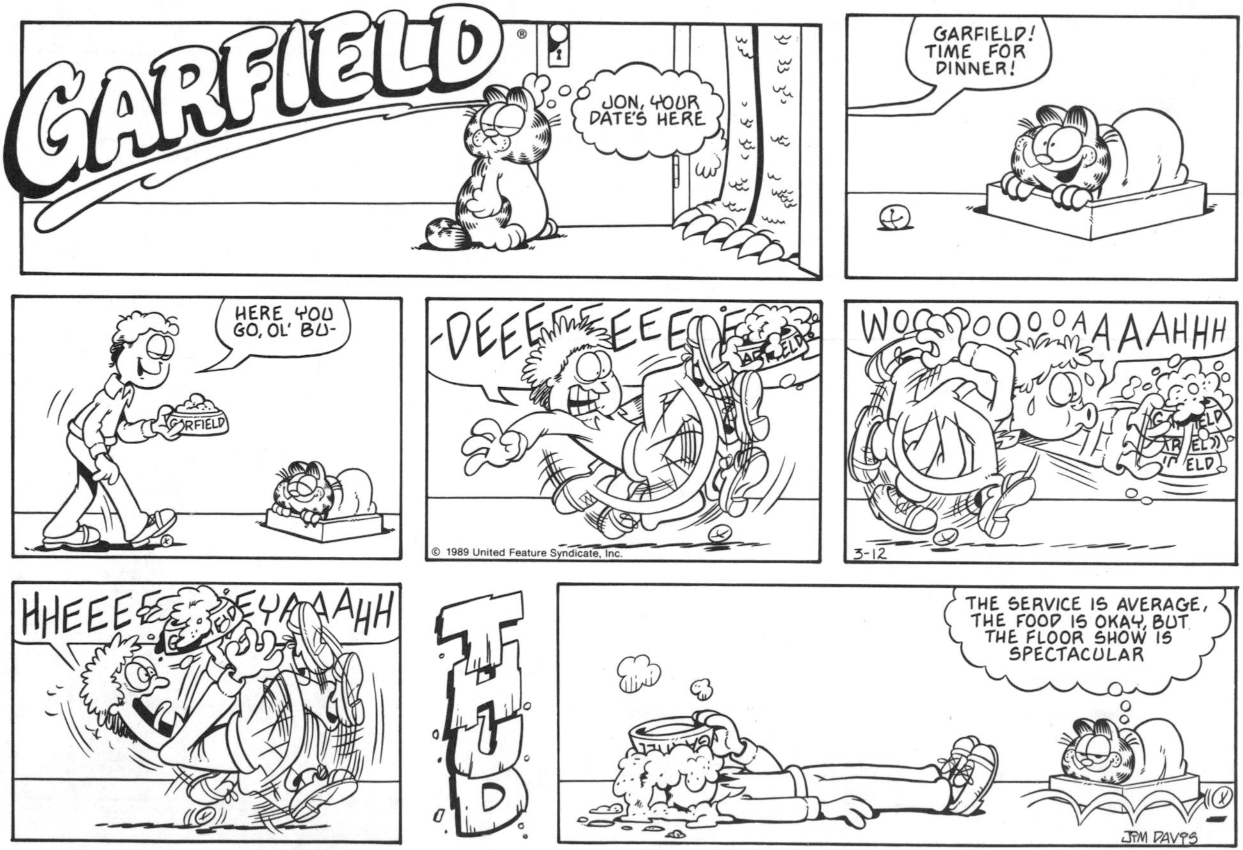
GARFIELD®
JON, YOUR DATE'S HERE
GARFIELD! TIME FOR DINNER!
HERE YOU GO, OL' BU-
-DEEEEEEEEEEE
GARFIELD
WOOOOOOOOAAAAHHH
3-12
HHEEEEEEEYAAAHH
THUD
THE SERVICE IS AVERAGE, THE FOOD IS OKAY, BUT THE FLOOR SHOW IS SPECTACULAR
JIM DAVIS

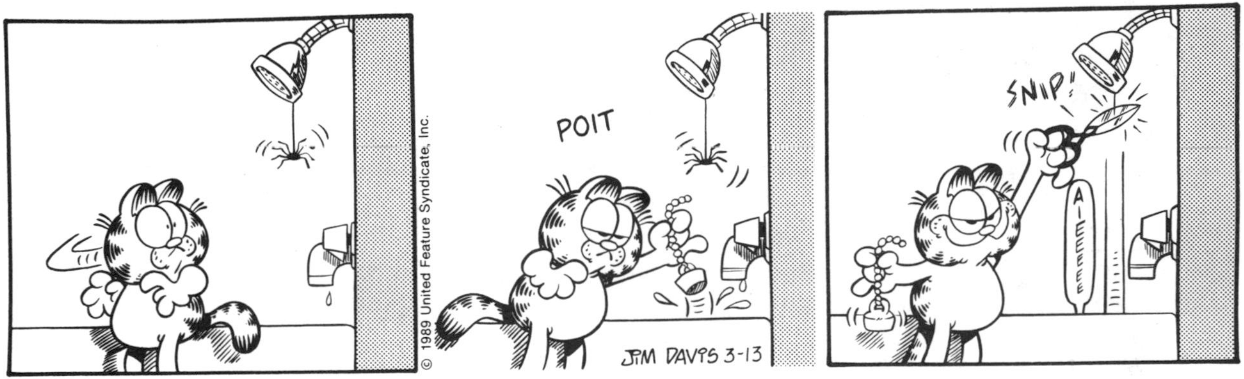
POIT
SNIP!
AIEEEEE
JIM DAVIS 3-13
© 1989 United Feature Syndicate, Inc.

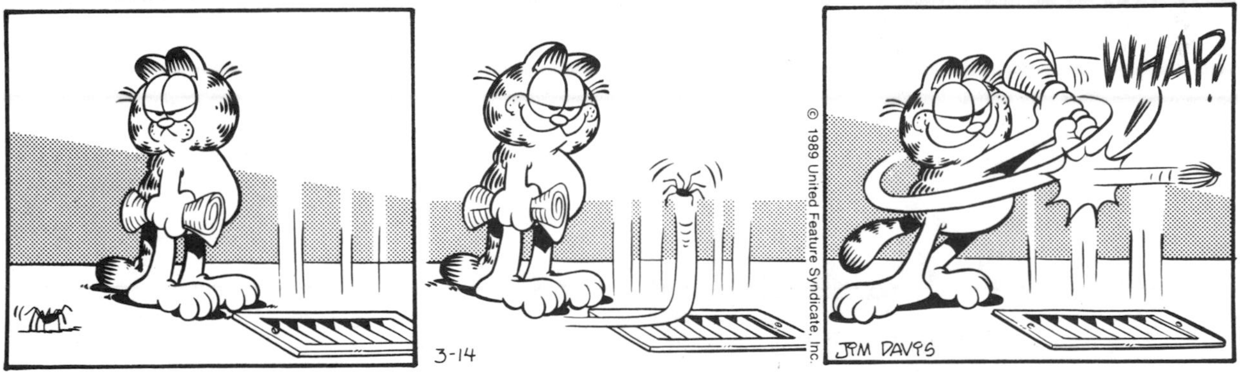
WHAP!
3-14
JIM DAVIS
© 1989 United Feature Syndicate, Inc.

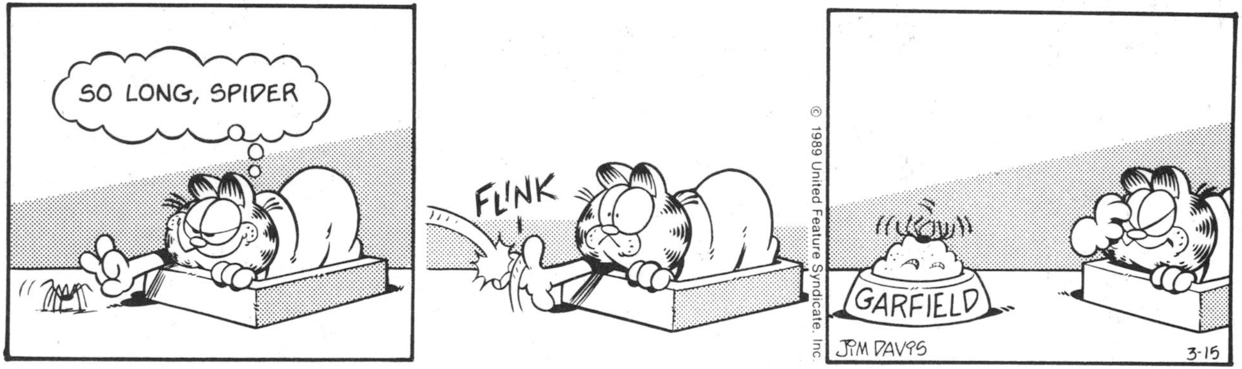
SO LONG, SPIDER
FLINK
GARFIELD
© 1989 United Feature Syndicate, Inc.
JIM DAVIS
3-15

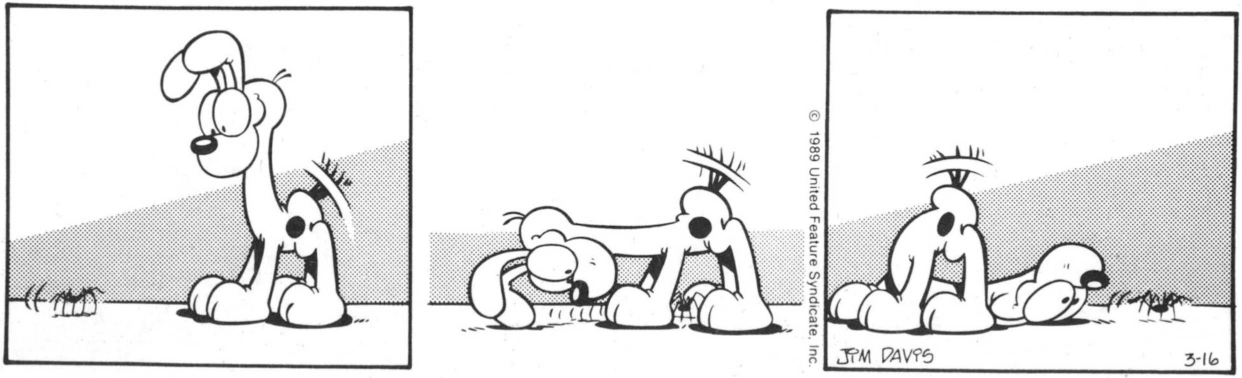
© 1989 United Feature Syndicate, Inc.
JIM DAVIS
3-16

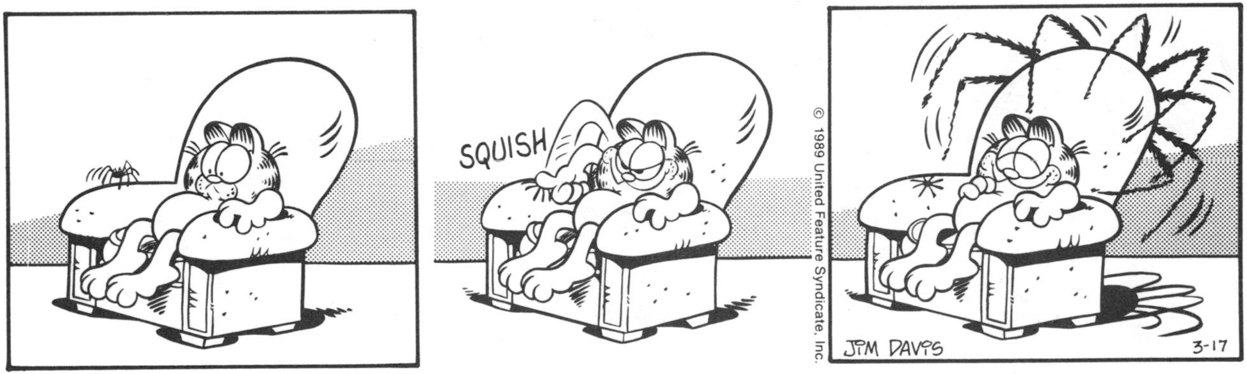
SQUISH
© 1989 United Feature Syndicate, Inc.
JIM DAVIS
3-17

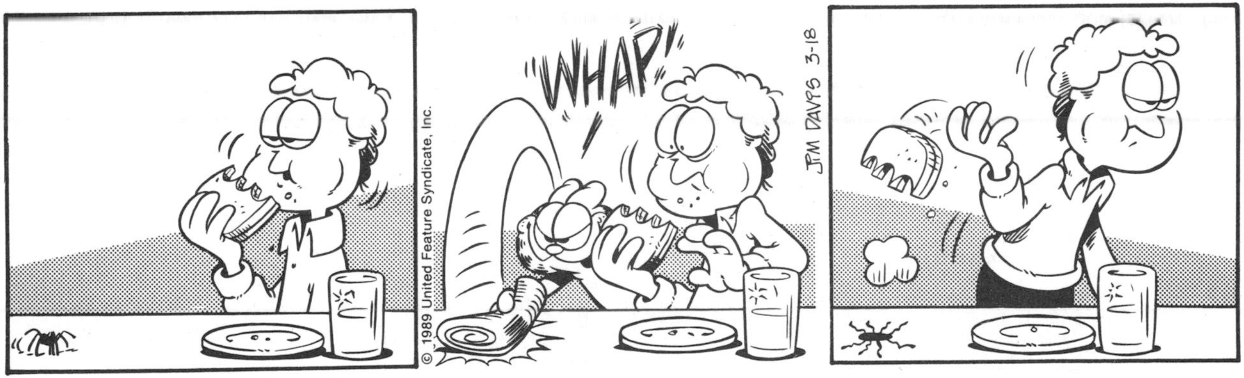
© 1989 United Feature Syndicate, Inc.
WHAP!
JIM DAVIS 3-18

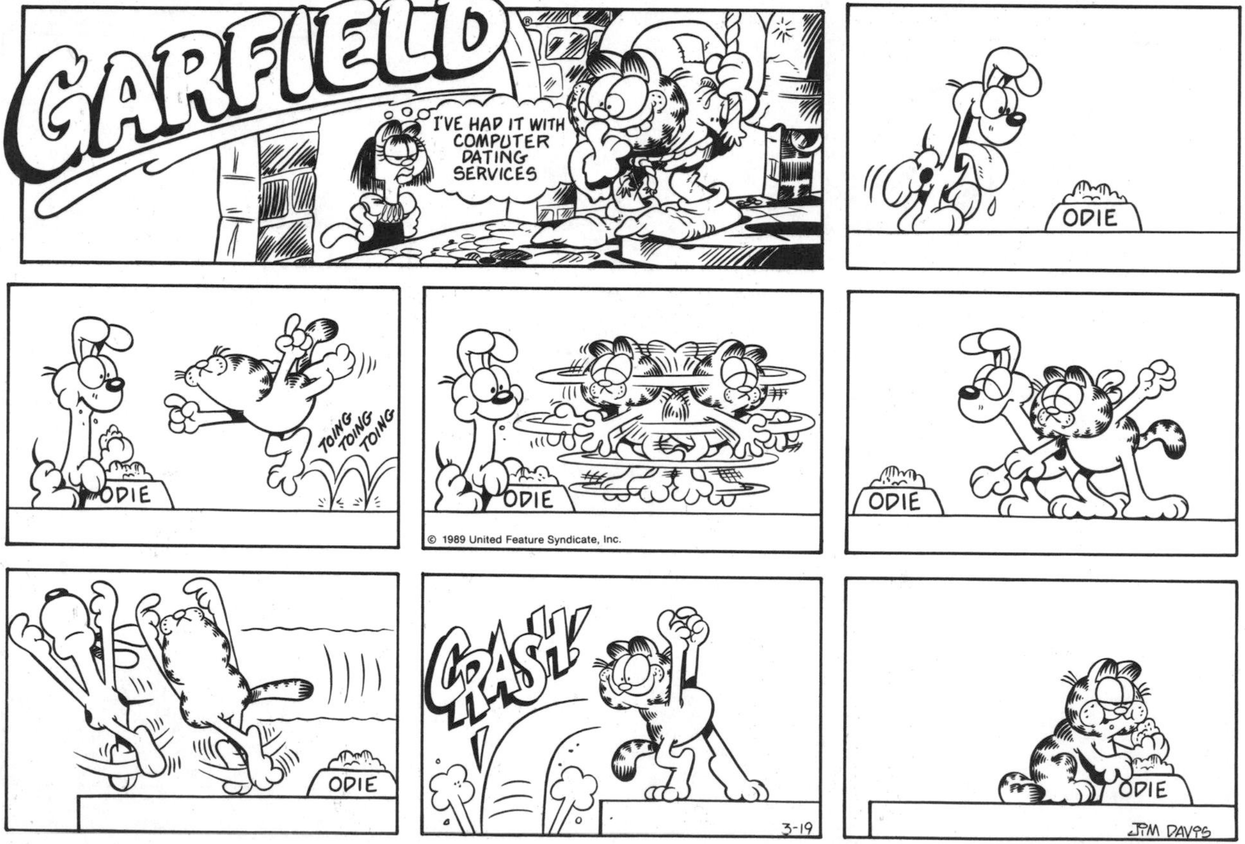
GARFIELD
I'VE HAD IT WITH COMPUTER DATING SERVICES
ODIE
TOING TOING TOING
ODIE
ODIE
© 1989 United Feature Syndicate, Inc.
ODIE
ODIE
CRASH
3-19
ODIE
JIM DAVIS

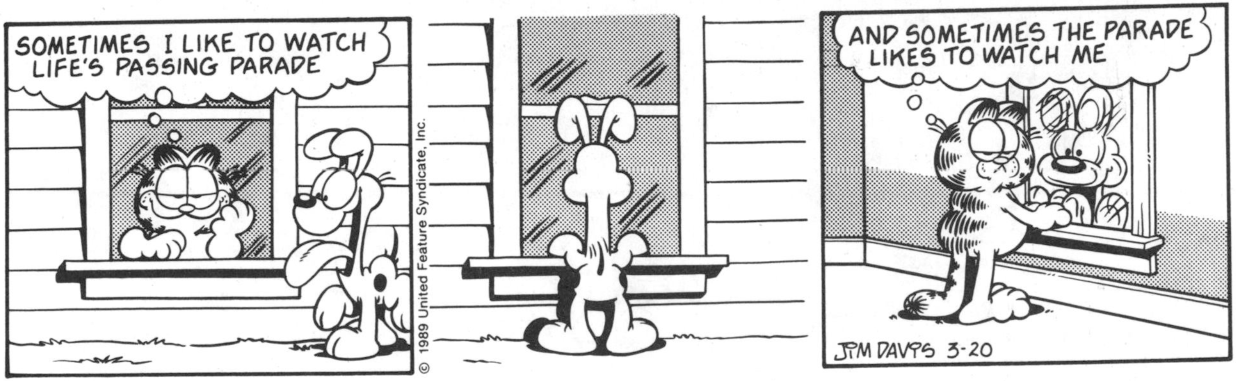
SOMETIMES I LIKE TO WATCH LIFE'S PASSING PARADE
© 1989 United Feature Syndicate, Inc.
AND SOMETIMES THE PARADE LIKES TO WATCH ME
JIM DAVIS 3-20

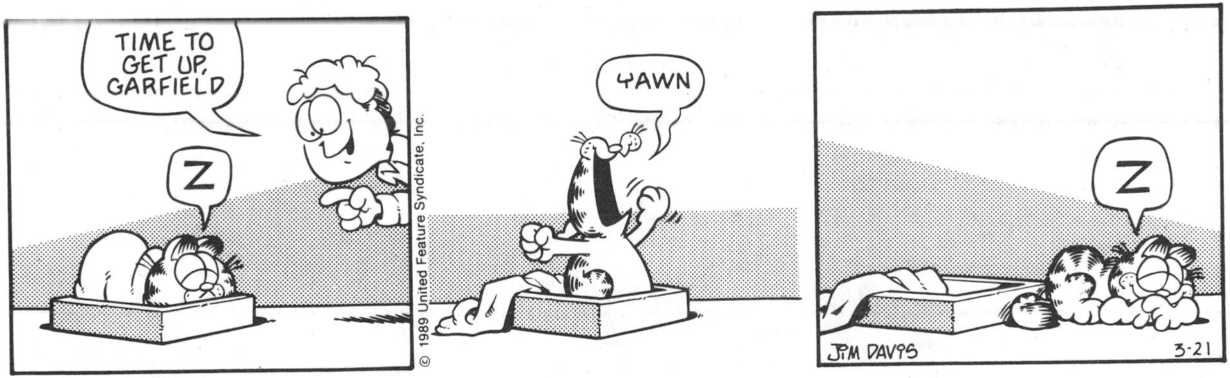
TIME TO GET UP, GARFIELD
Z
© 1989 United Feature Syndicate, Inc.
YAWN
Z
JIM DAVIS
3-21

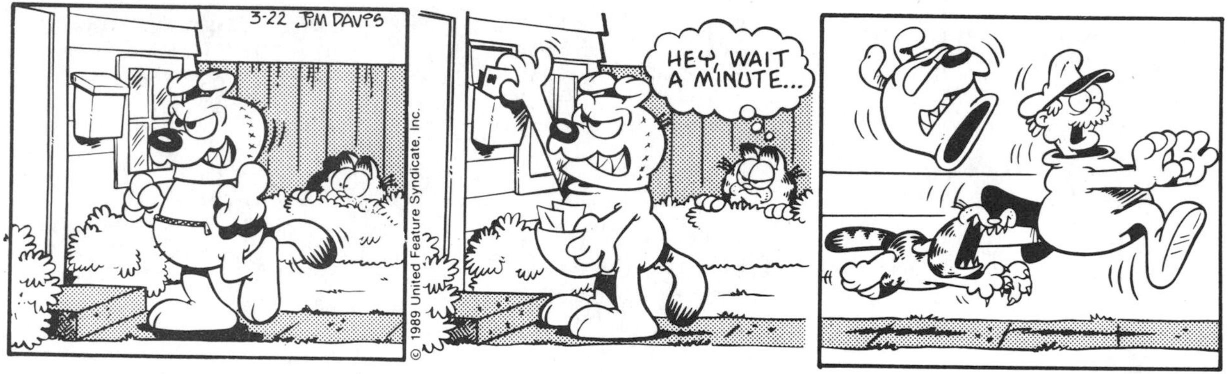
3-22 JIM DAVIS
© 1989 United Feature Syndicate, Inc.
HEY, WAIT A MINUTE...

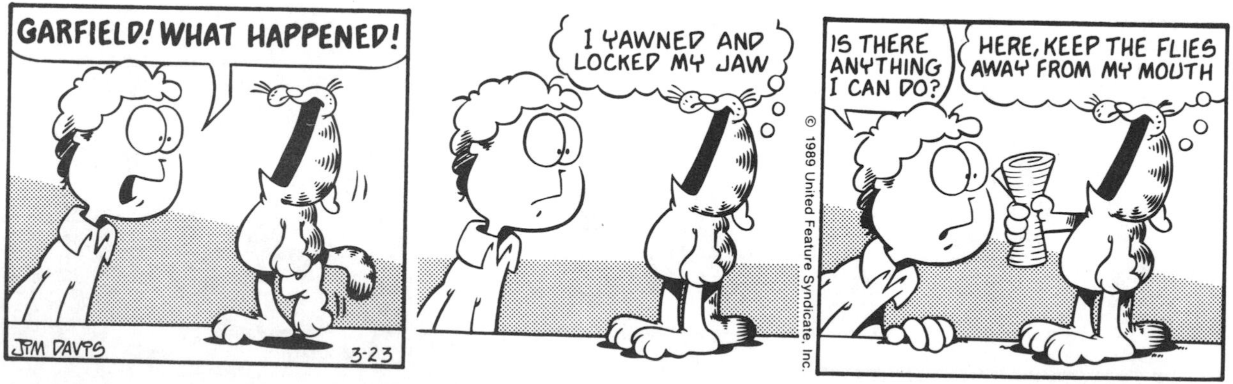
GARFIELD! WHAT HAPPENED!
JIM DAVIS
3-23
I YAWNED AND LOCKED MY JAW
© 1989 United Feature Syndicate, Inc.
IS THERE ANYTHING I CAN DO?
HERE, KEEP THE FLIES AWAY FROM MY MOUTH

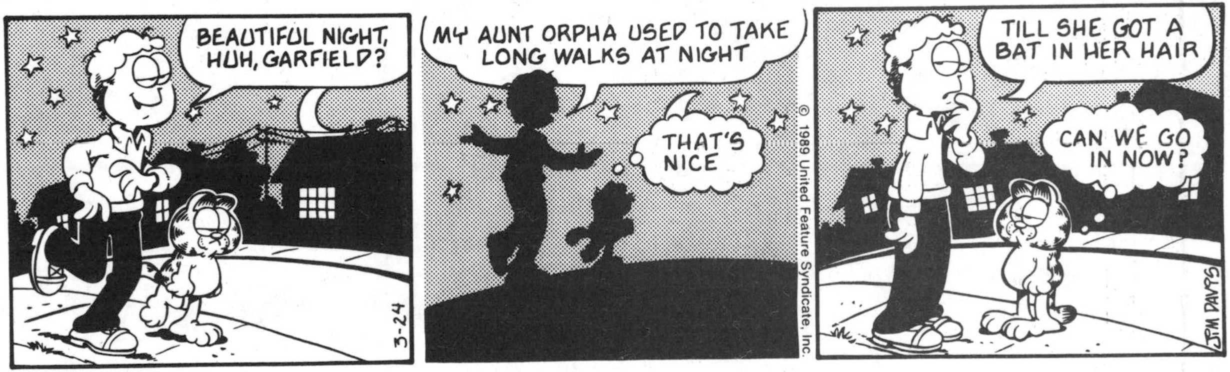
BEAUTIFUL NIGHT, HUH, GARFIELD?
3-24
MY AUNT ORPHA USED TO TAKE LONG WALKS AT NIGHT
THAT'S NICE
© 1989 United Feature Syndicate, Inc.
TILL SHE GOT A BAT IN HER HAIR
CAN WE GO IN NOW?
JIM DAVIS

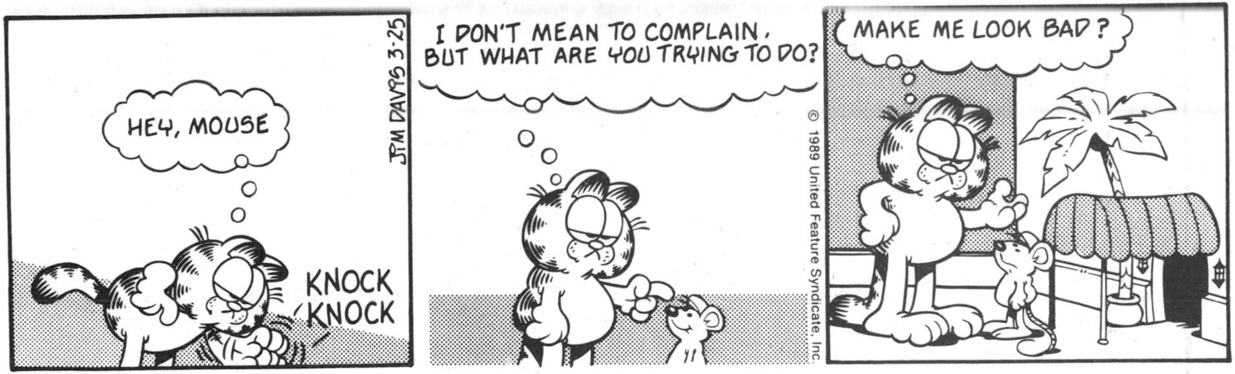
JIM DAVIS 3-25
HEY, MOUSE
KNOCK KNOCK
I DON'T MEAN TO COMPLAIN, BUT WHAT ARE YOU TRYING TO DO?
© 1989 United Feature Syndicate, Inc.
MAKE ME LOOK BAD?

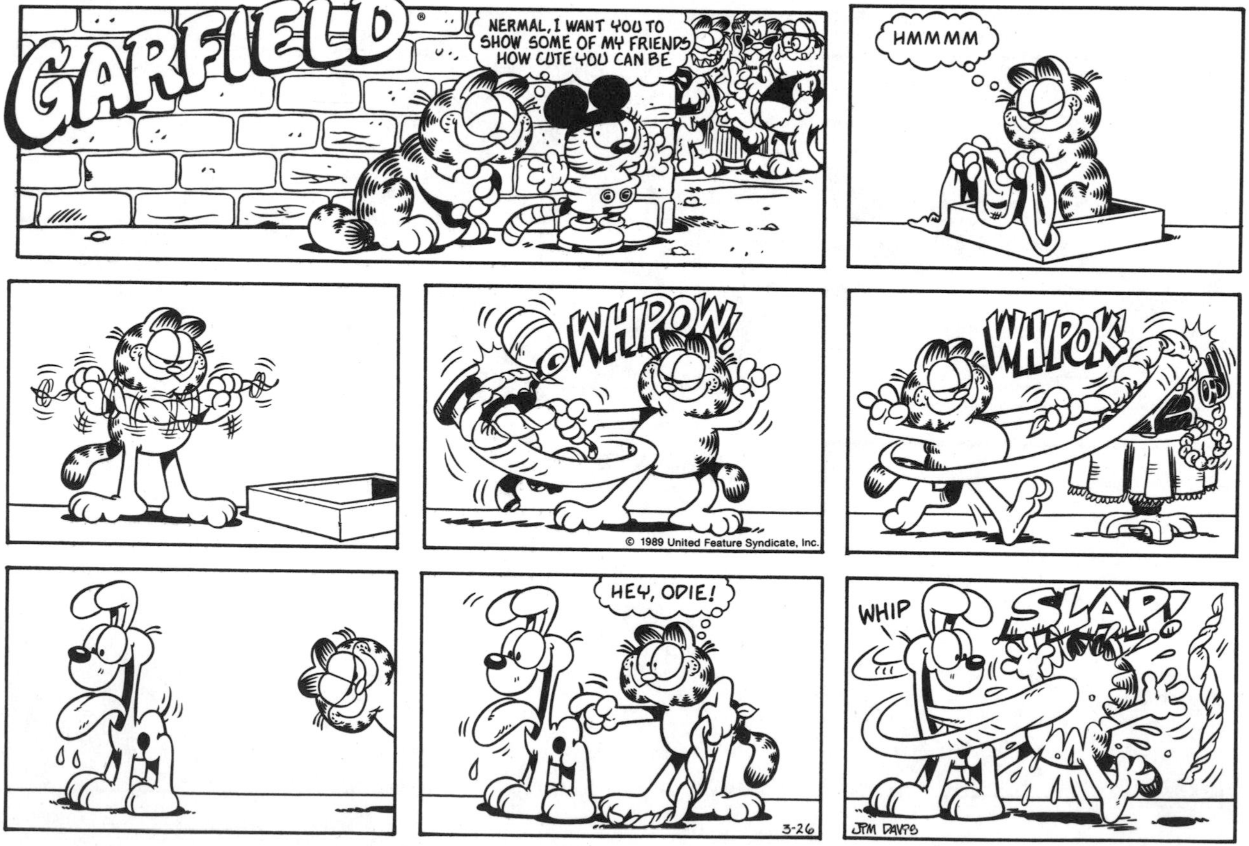
GARFIELD
NERMAL, I WANT YOU TO SHOW SOME OF MY FRIENDS HOW CUTE YOU CAN BE
HMMMM
WHPOW!
WHPOK!
© 1989 United Feature Syndicate, Inc.
HEY, ODIE!
3-26
WHIP
SLAP!
JPM DAVPS

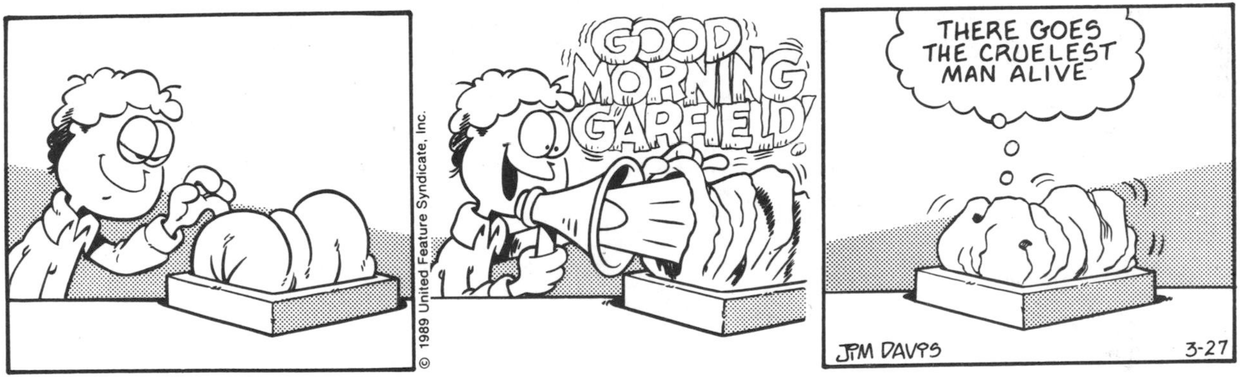
GOOD MORNING GARFIELD!
THERE GOES THE CRUELEST MAN ALIVE
© 1989 United Feature Syndicate, Inc.
JIM DAVIS
3-27

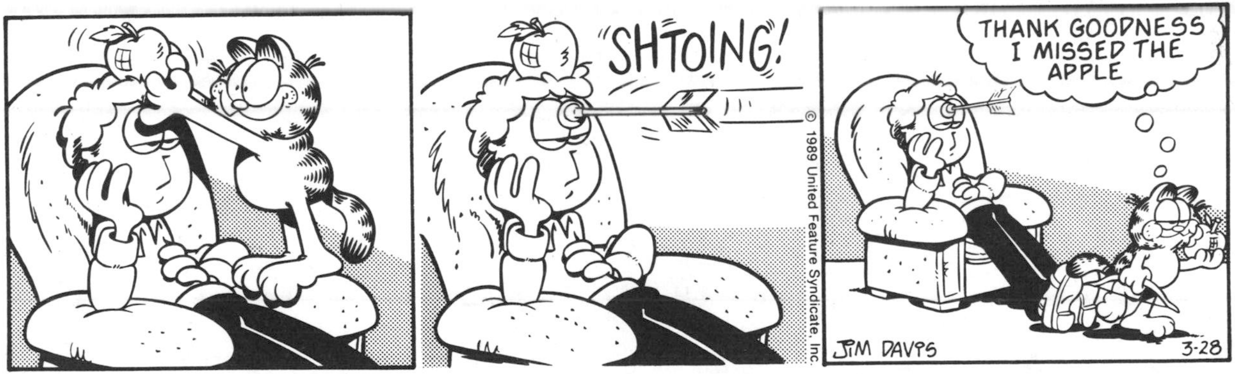
SHTOING!
THANK GOODNESS I MISSED THE APPLE
© 1989 United Feature Syndicate, Inc.
JIM DAVIS
3-28

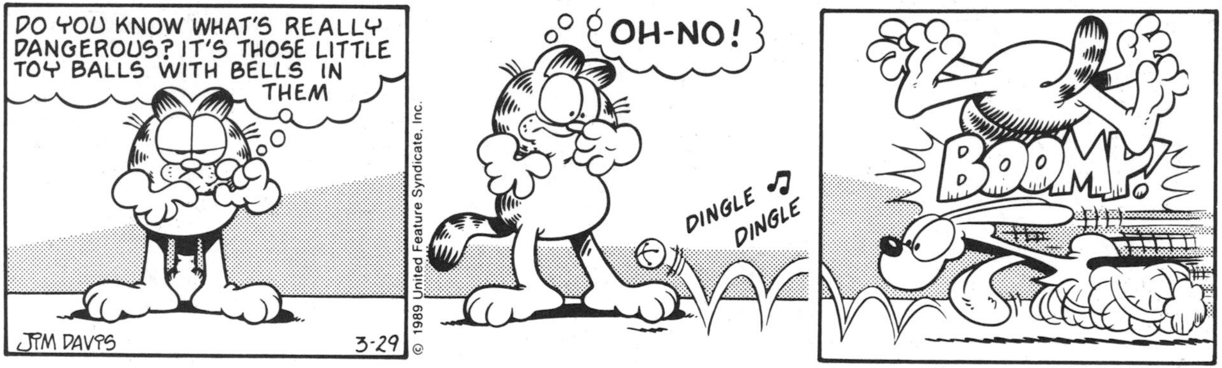
DO YOU KNOW WHAT'S REALLY DANGEROUS? IT'S THOSE LITTLE TOY BALLS WITH BELLS IN THEM
JIM DAVIS
3-29
OH-NO!
DINGLE ♫ DINGLE
BOOM!
© 1989 United Feature Syndicate, Inc.

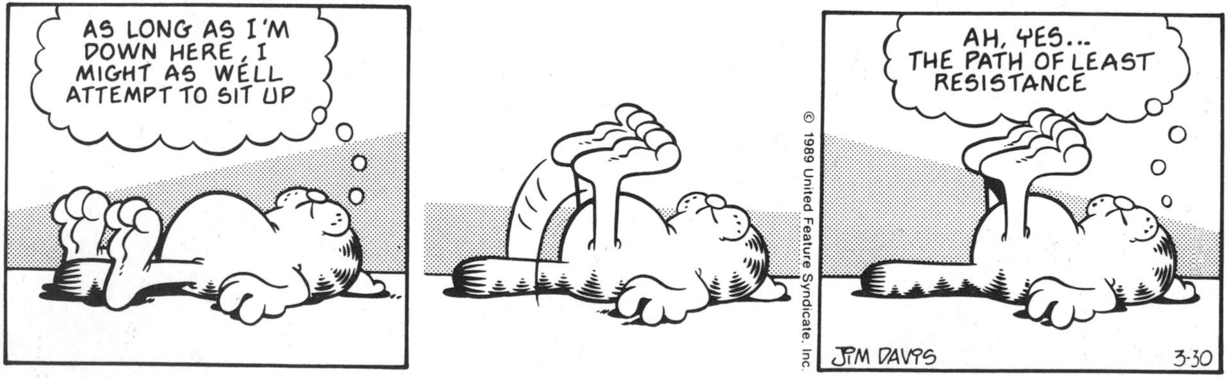
AS LONG AS I'M DOWN HERE, I MIGHT AS WELL ATTEMPT TO SIT UP
AH, YES... THE PATH OF LEAST RESISTANCE
JIM DAVIS
3-30
© 1989 United Feature Syndicate, Inc.

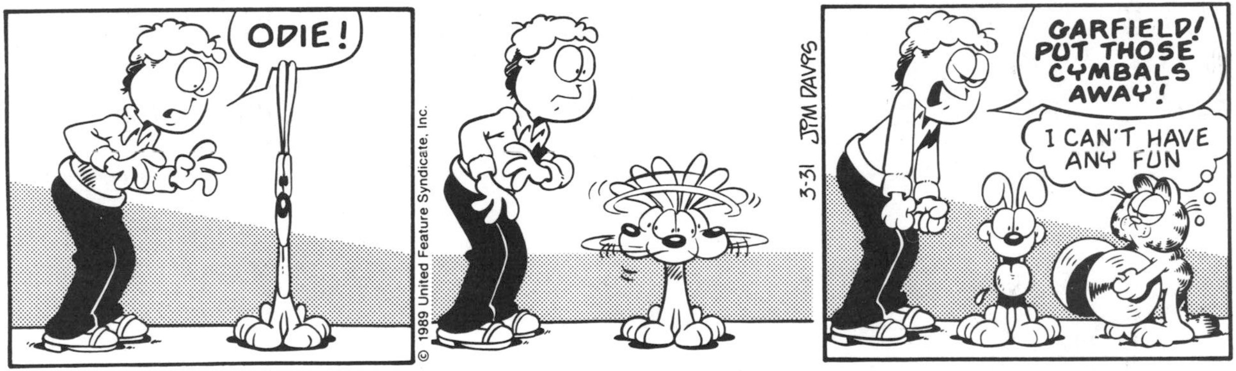
ODIE!
GARFIELD! PUT THOSE CYMBALS AWAY!
I CAN'T HAVE ANY FUN
JIM DAVIS 3-31
© 1989 United Feature Syndicate, Inc.

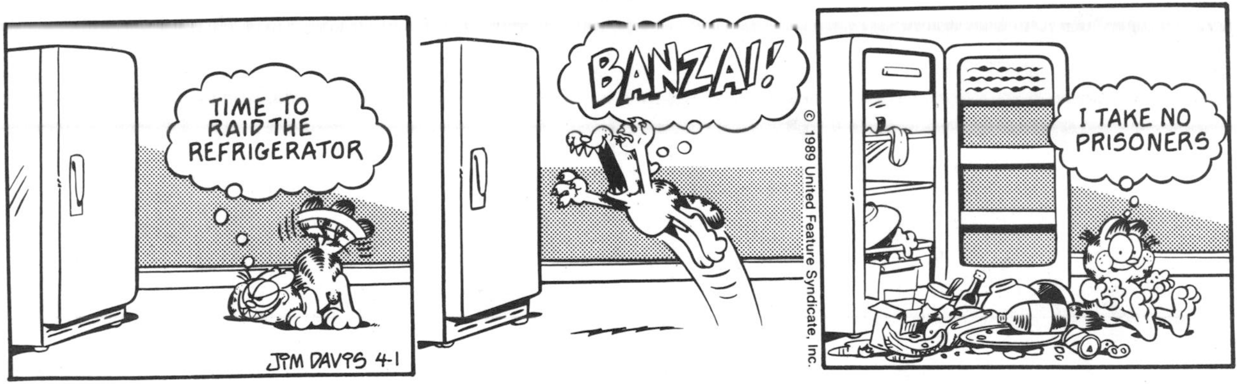
TIME TO RAID THE REFRIGERATOR
BANZAI!
I TAKE NO PRISONERS
JIM DAVIS 4-1
© 1989 United Feature Syndicate, Inc.

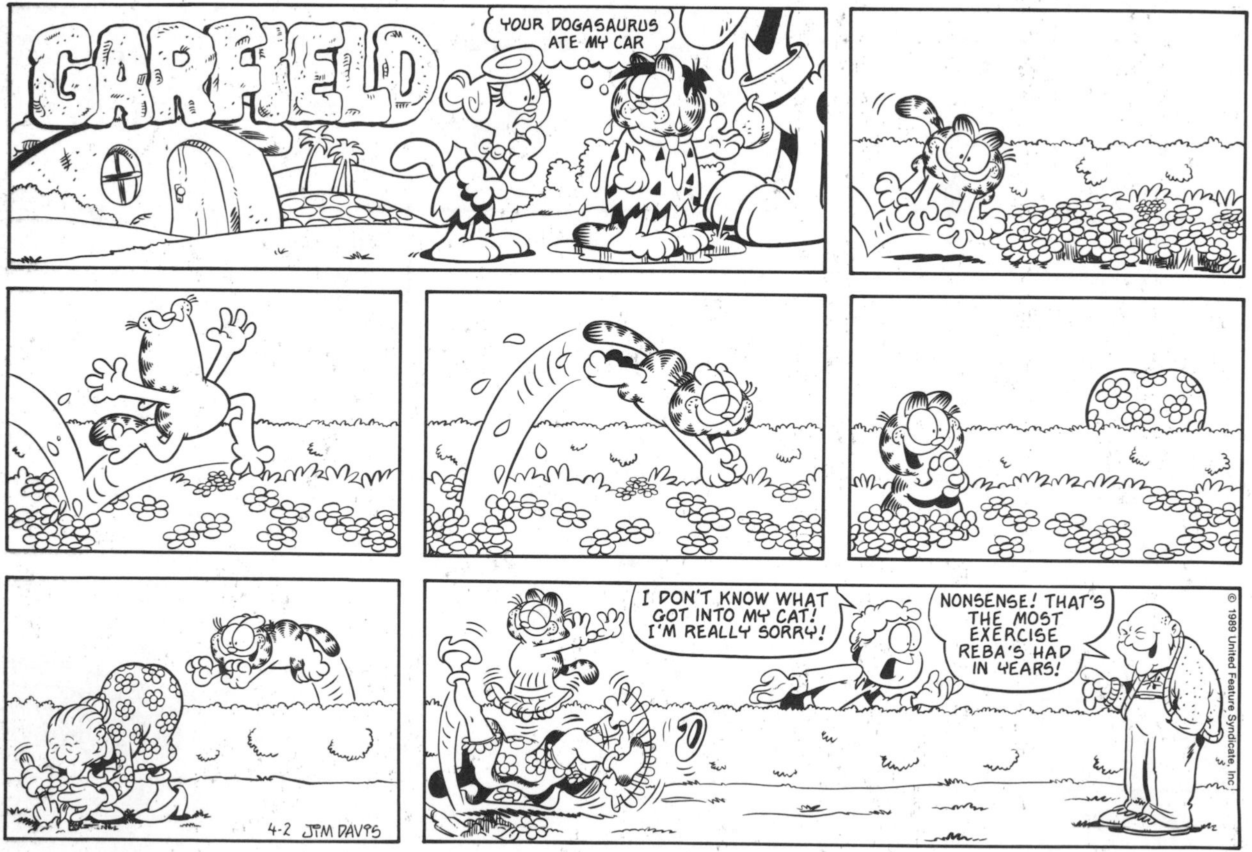
GARFIELD
YOUR DOGASAURUS ATE MY CAR
I DON'T KNOW WHAT GOT INTO MY CAT! I'M REALLY SORRY!
NONSENSE! THAT'S THE MOST EXERCISE REBA'S HAD IN YEARS!
4-2 JIM DAVIS
© 1989 United Feature Syndicate, Inc.

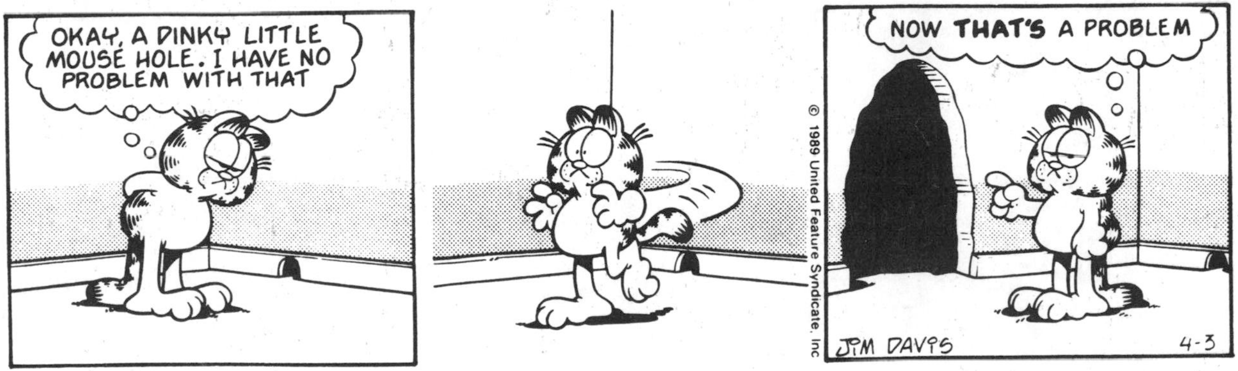
OKAY, A DINKY LITTLE MOUSE HOLE. I HAVE NO PROBLEM WITH THAT
NOW THAT'S A PROBLEM
JIM DAVIS 4-3
© 1989 United Feature Syndicate, Inc

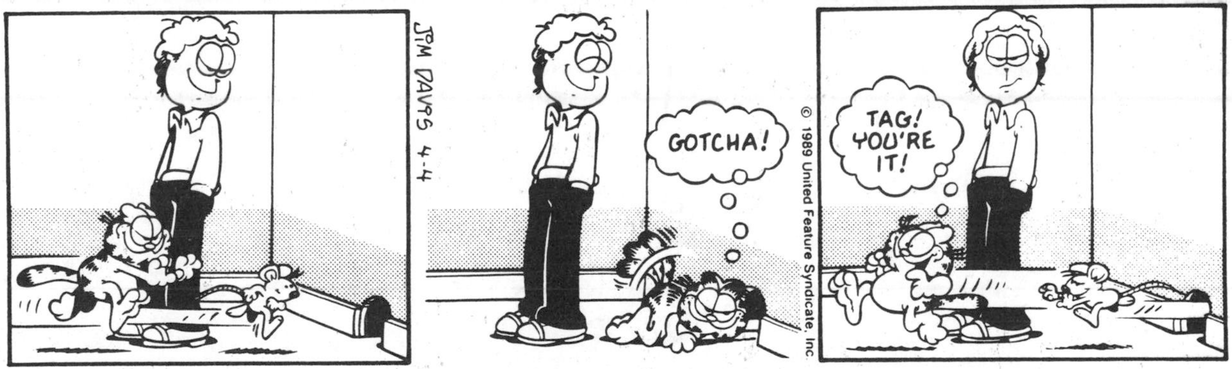
JIM DAVIS 4-4
GOTCHA!
TAG! YOU'RE IT!
© 1989 United Feature Syndicate, Inc

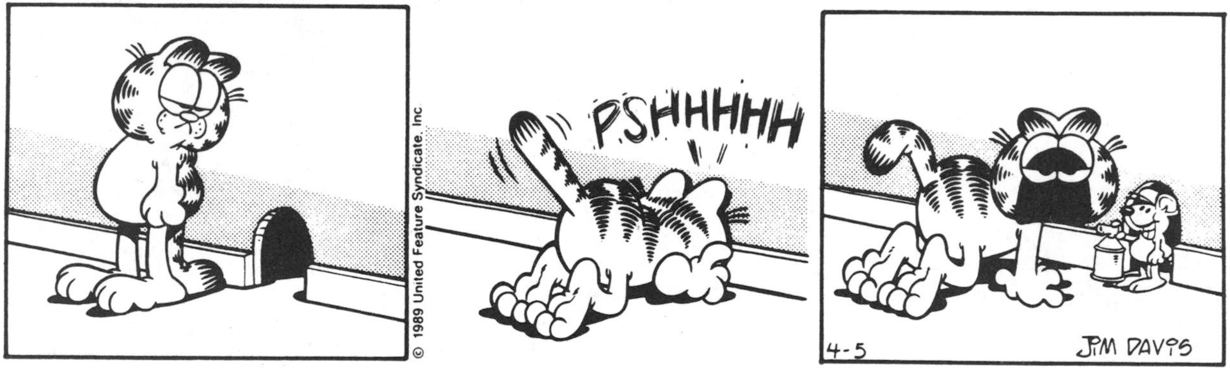
© 1989 United Feature Syndicate, Inc.
PSHHHHHH
4-5
JIM DAVIS

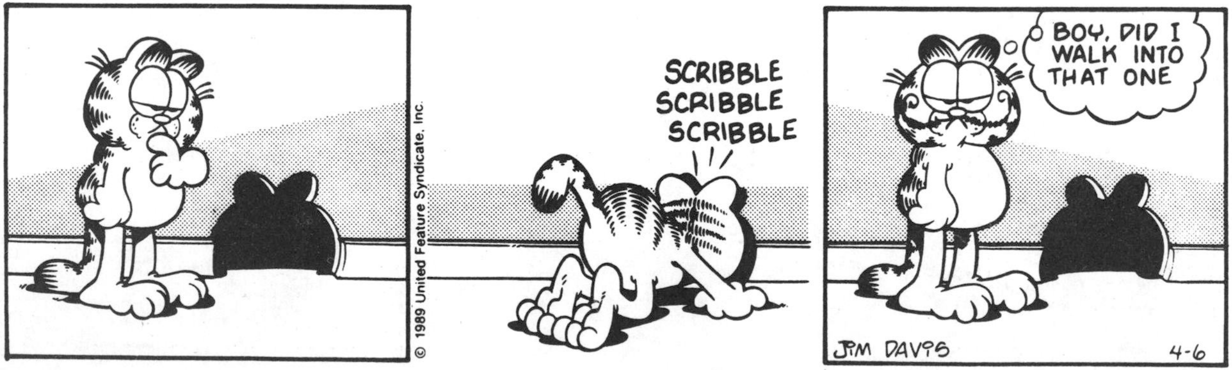
© 1989 United Feature Syndicate, Inc.
SCRIBBLE SCRIBBLE SCRIBBLE
BOY, DID I WALK INTO THAT ONE
JIM DAVIS
4-6

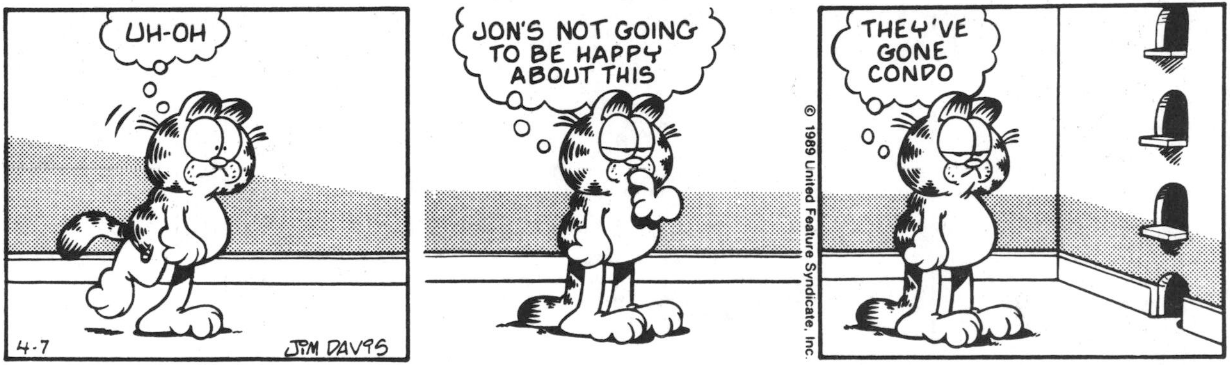
UH-OH
4-7
JIM DAVIS
JON'S NOT GOING TO BE HAPPY ABOUT THIS
© 1989 United Feature Syndicate, Inc.
THEY'VE GONE CONDO

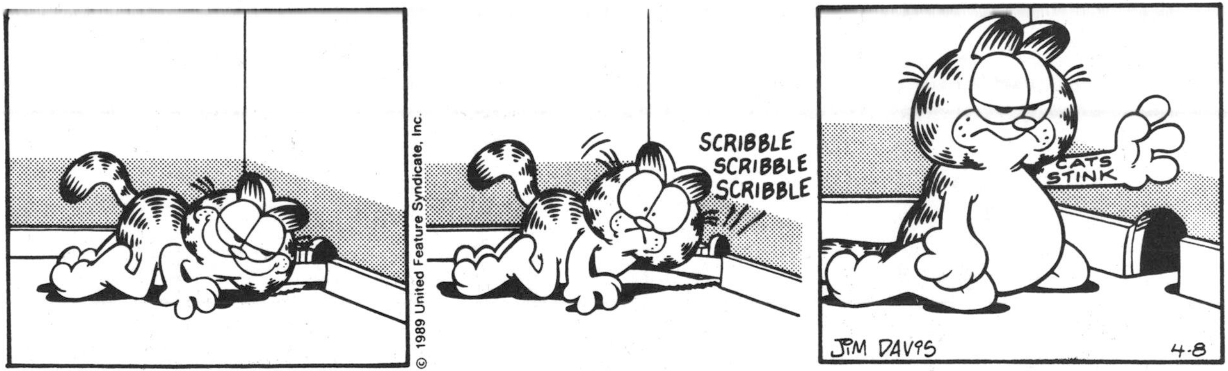
© 1989 United Feature Syndicate, Inc.
SCRIBBLE SCRIBBLE SCRIBBLE
CATS STINK
JIM DAVIS
4-8

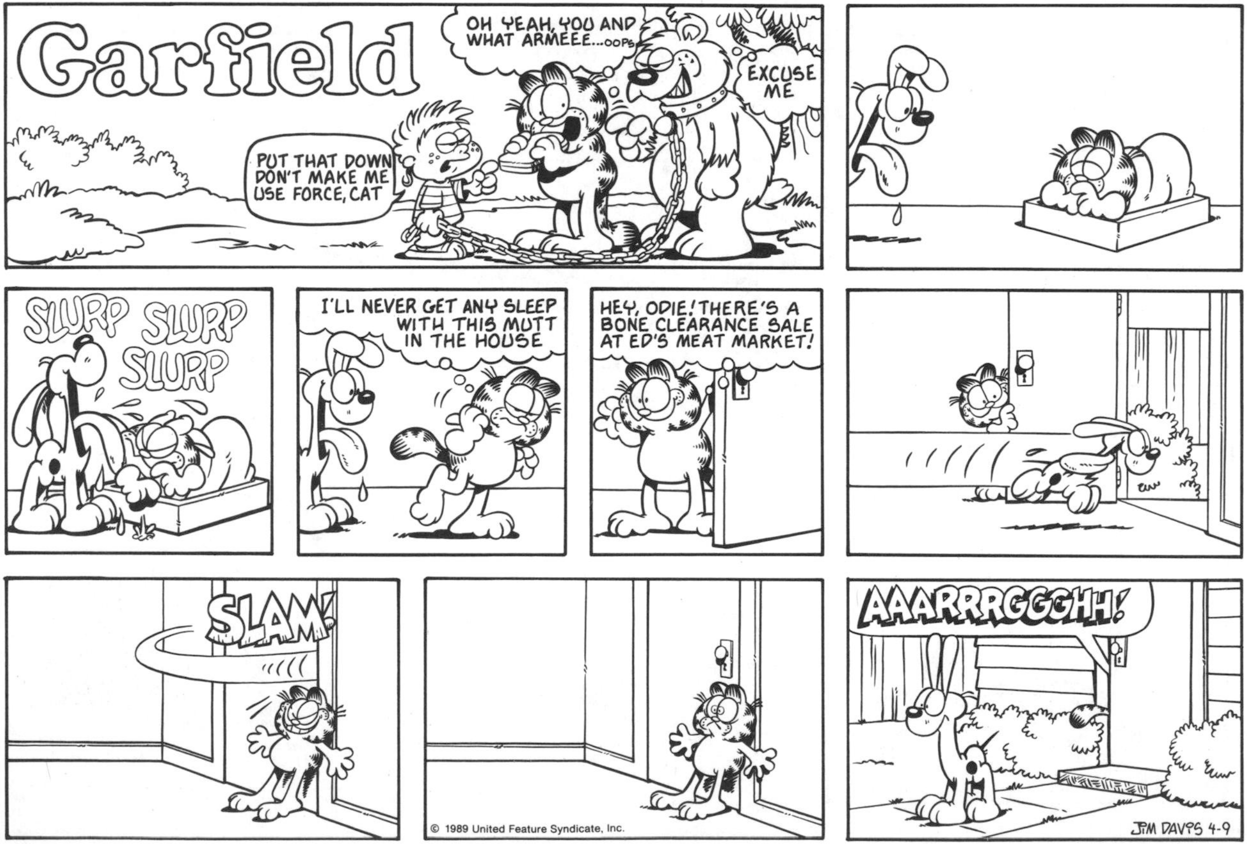Garfield
PUT THAT DOWN DON'T MAKE ME USE FORCE, CAT
OH YEAH, YOU AND WHAT ARMEEE...OOPS
EXCUSE ME
SLURP SLURP SLURP
I'LL NEVER GET ANY SLEEP WITH THIS MUTT IN THE HOUSE
HEY, ODIE! THERE'S A BONE CLEARANCE SALE AT ED'S MEAT MARKET!
SLAM!
© 1989 United Feature Syndicate, Inc.
AAARRRGGGHH!
JIM DAVIS 4-9

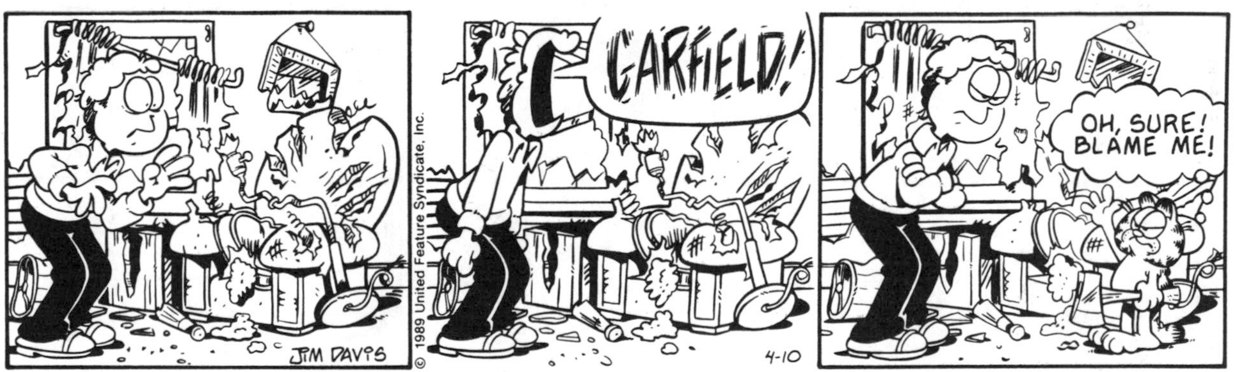
JIM DAVIS
© 1989 United Feature Syndicate, Inc.
GARFIELD!
4-10
OH, SURE! BLAME ME!

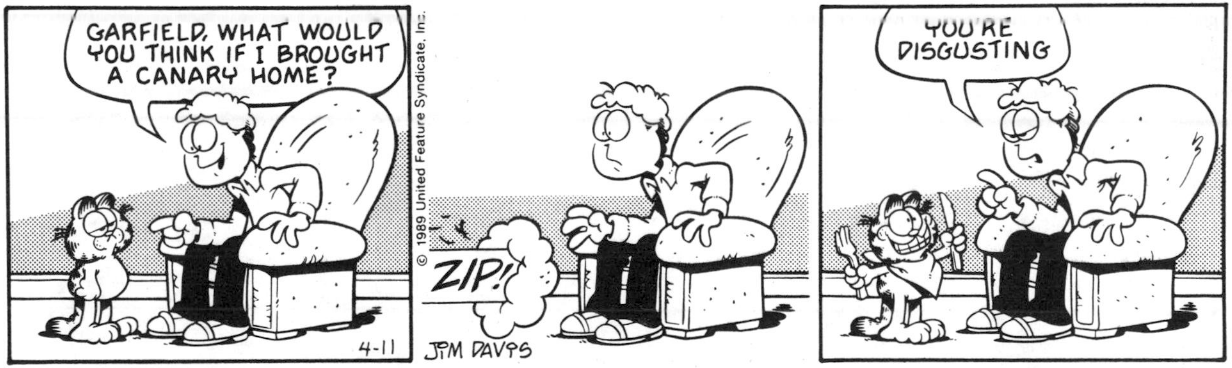
GARFIELD, WHAT WOULD YOU THINK IF I BROUGHT A CANARY HOME?
4-11
© 1989 United Feature Syndicate, Inc.
ZIP!
JIM DAVIS
YOU'RE DISGUSTING

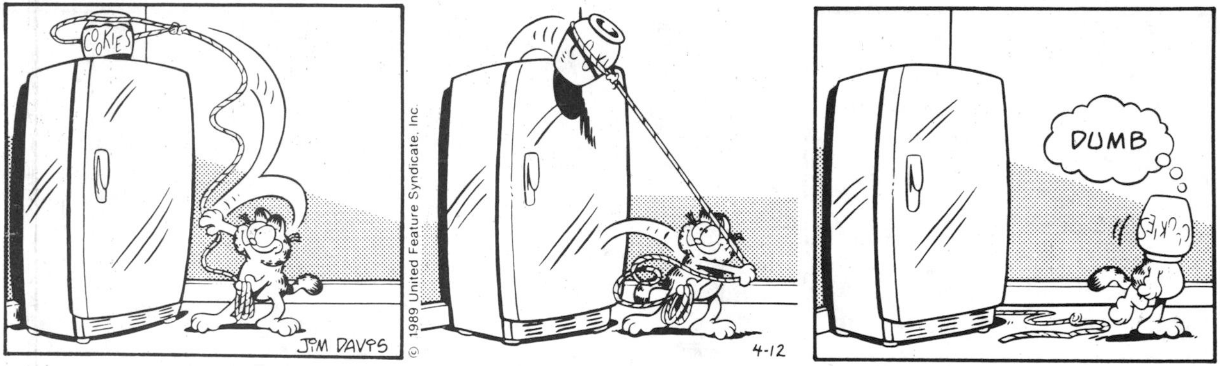
COOKIES
JIM DAVIS
© 1989 United Feature Syndicate, Inc.
4-12
DUMB

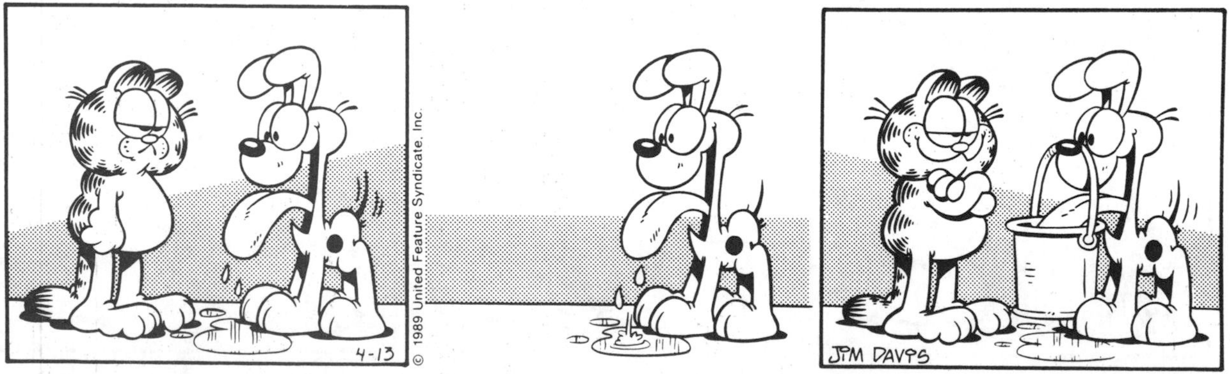
© 1989 United Feature Syndicate, Inc.
4-13
JIM DAVIS

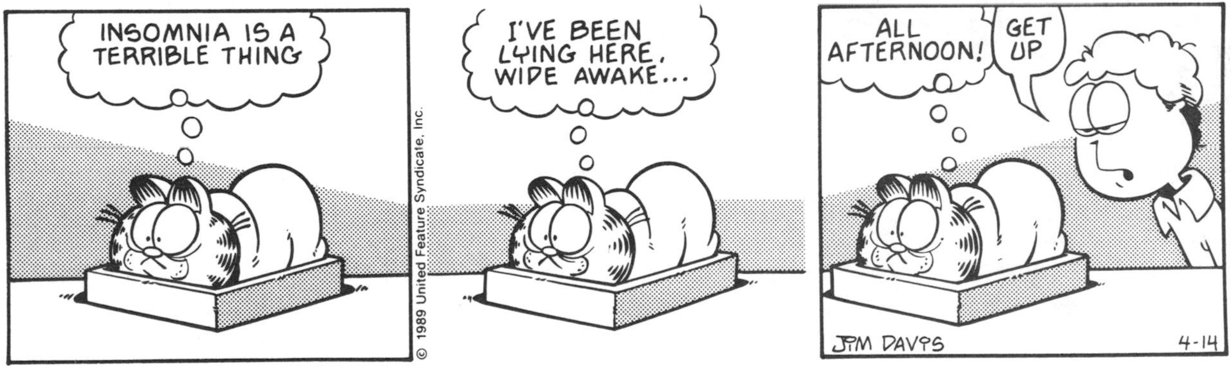
INSOMNIA IS A TERRIBLE THING
I'VE BEEN LYING HERE, WIDE AWAKE...
ALL AFTERNOON!
GET UP
JIM DAVIS 4-14
© 1989 United Feature Syndicate, Inc.

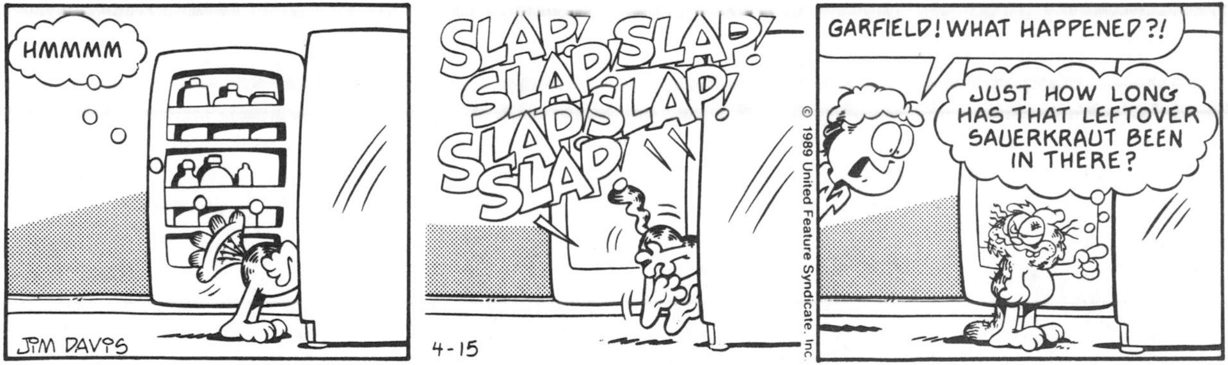
HMMMM
JIM DAVIS
SLAP! SLAP! SLAP! SLAP! SLAP! SLAP! SLAP! SLAP!
4-15
GARFIELD! WHAT HAPPENED?!
JUST HOW LONG HAS THAT LEFTOVER SAUERKRAUT BEEN IN THERE?
© 1989 United Feature Syndicate, Inc.

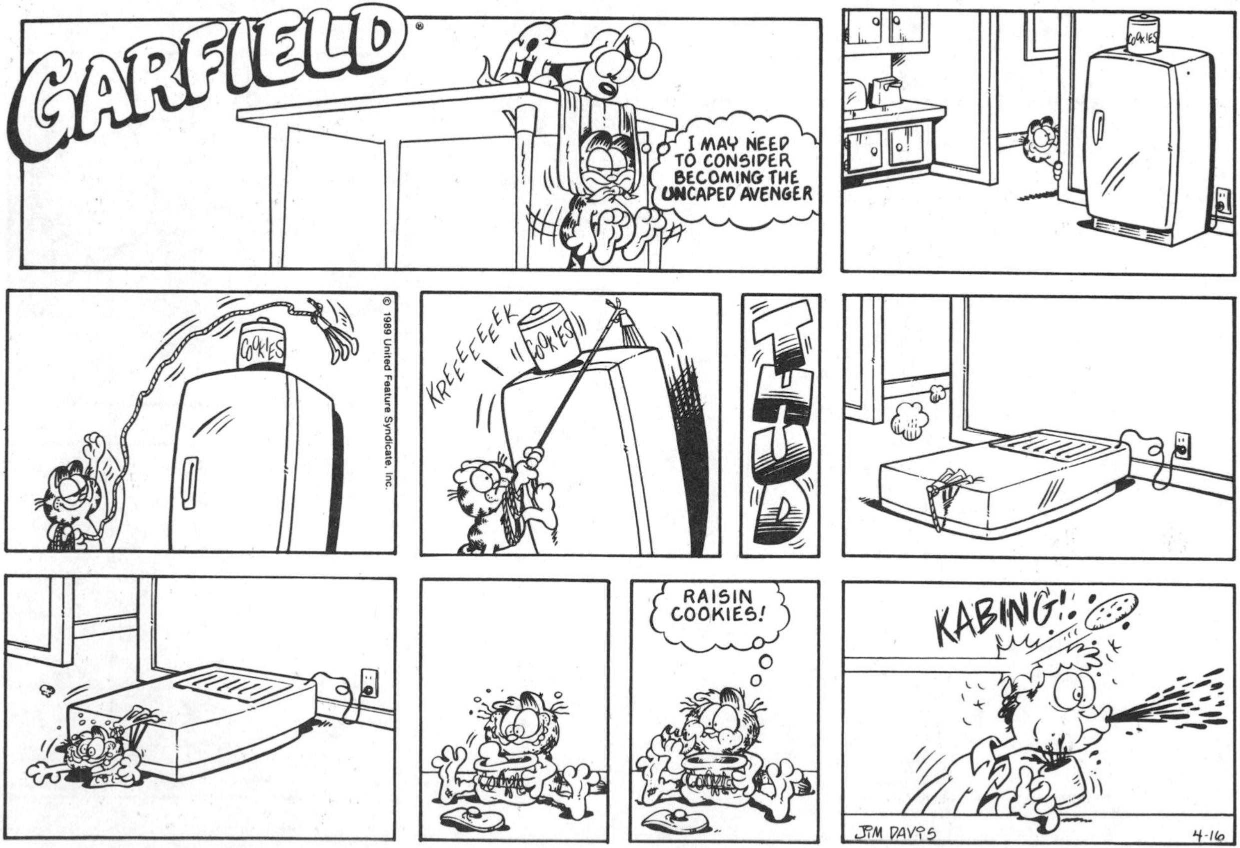
GARFIELD
I MAY NEED TO CONSIDER BECOMING THE UNCAPED AVENGER
COOKIES
© 1989 United Feature Syndicate, Inc.
KREEEEEEEEK
THUD
RAISIN COOKIES!
KABING!
JIM DAVIS
4-16

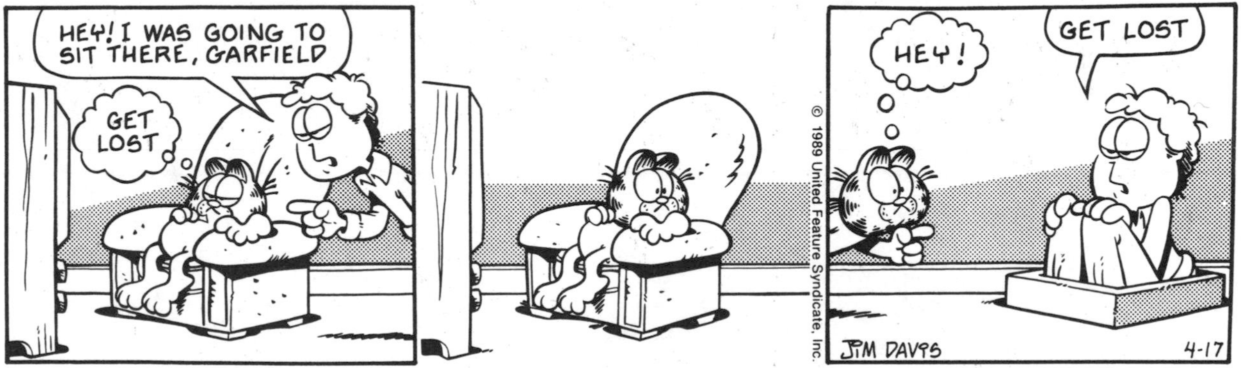
HEY! I WAS GOING TO SIT THERE, GARFIELD
GET LOST
HEY!
GET LOST
© 1989 United Feature Syndicate, Inc.
JIM DAVIS
4-17

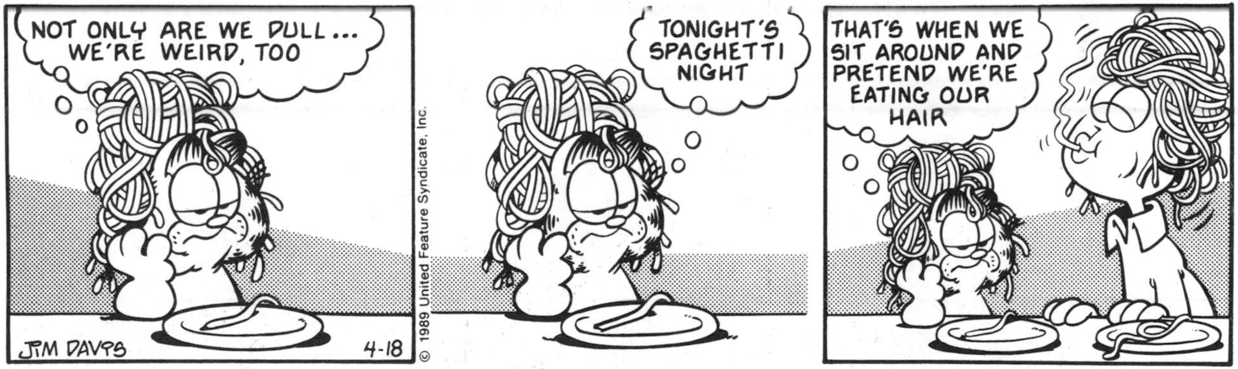
NOT ONLY ARE WE DULL... WE'RE WEIRD, TOO
JIM DAVIS
4-18
© 1989 United Feature Syndicate, Inc.
TONIGHT'S SPAGHETTI NIGHT
THAT'S WHEN WE SIT AROUND AND PRETEND WE'RE EATING OUR HAIR

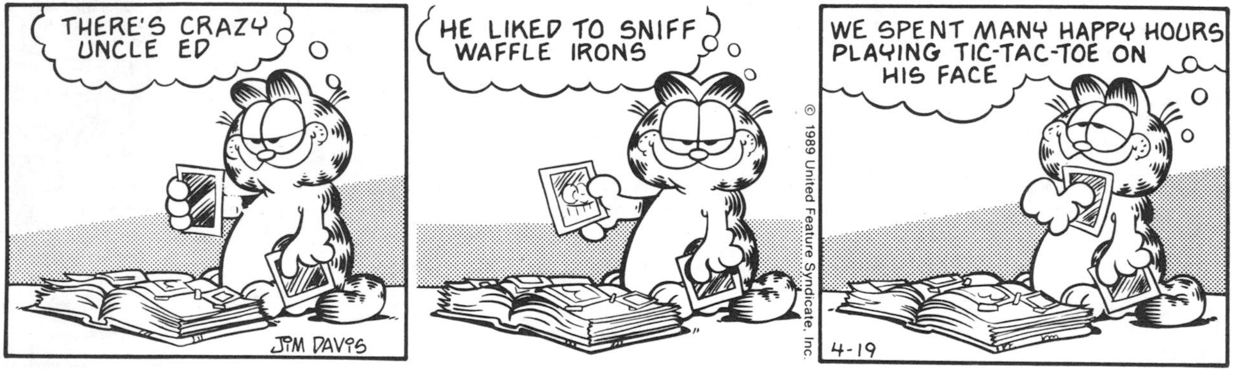
THERE'S CRAZY UNCLE ED
HE LIKED TO SNIFF WAFFLE IRONS
WE SPENT MANY HAPPY HOURS PLAYING TIC-TAC-TOE ON HIS FACE
JIM DAVIS
4-19
© 1989 United Feature Syndicate, Inc.

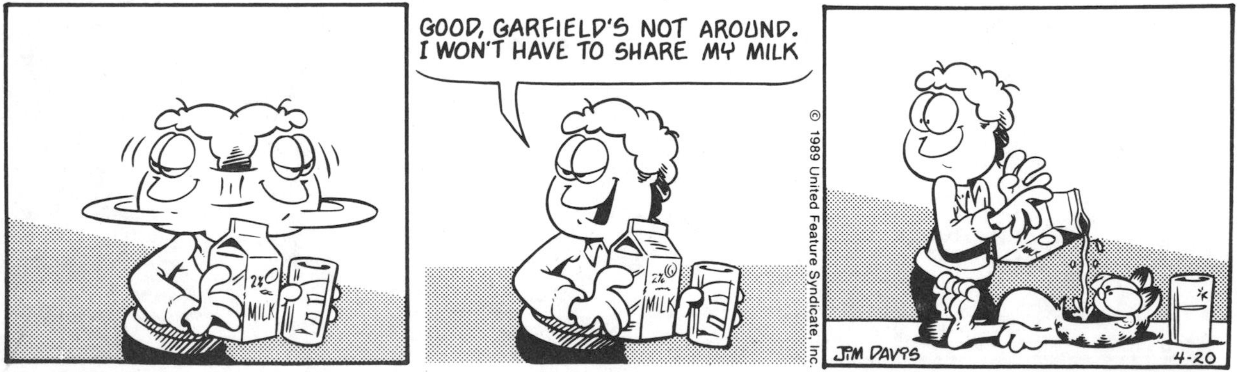
2%
MILK
GOOD, GARFIELD'S NOT AROUND. I WON'T HAVE TO SHARE MY MILK
JIM DAVIS
4-20
© 1989 United Feature Syndicate, Inc.

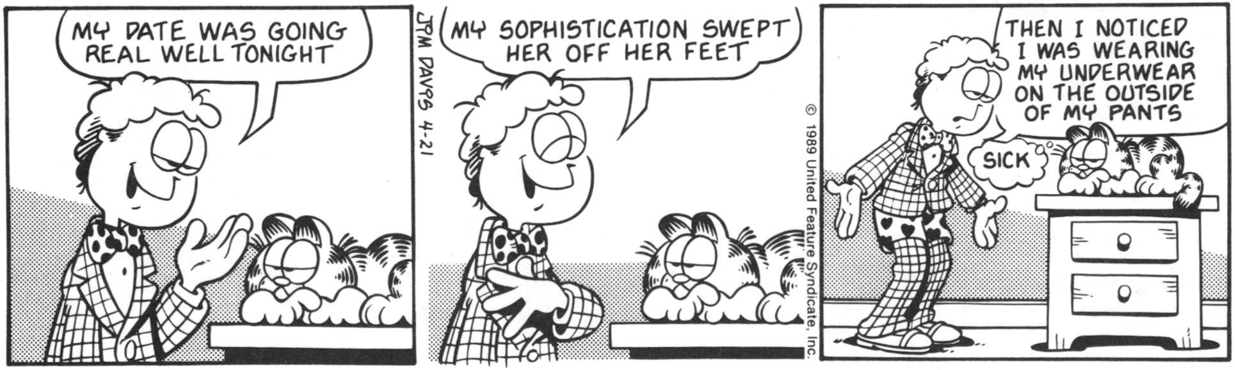
MY DATE WAS GOING REAL WELL TONIGHT
JIM DAVIS 4-21
MY SOPHISTICATION SWEPT HER OFF HER FEET
© 1989 United Feature Syndicate, Inc.
THEN I NOTICED I WAS WEARING MY UNDERWEAR ON THE OUTSIDE OF MY PANTS
SICK

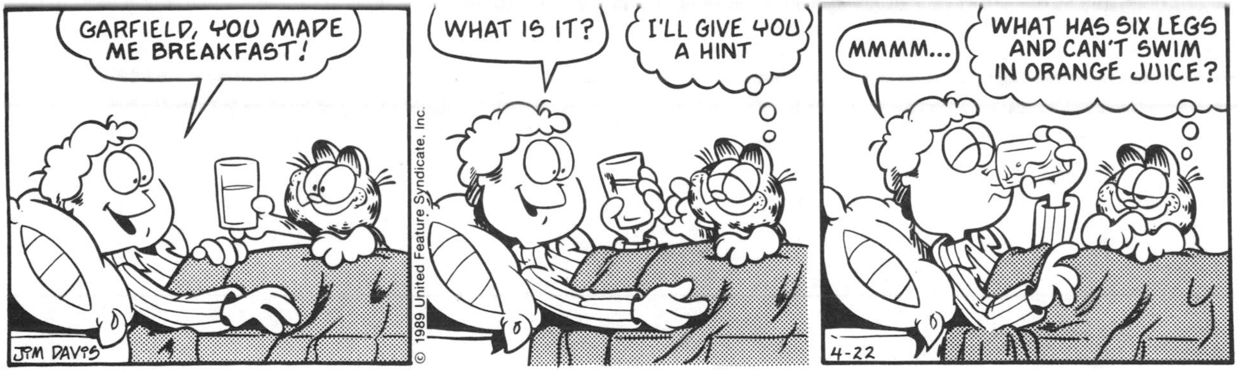
GARFIELD, YOU MADE ME BREAKFAST!
JIM DAVIS
© 1989 United Feature Syndicate, Inc.
WHAT IS IT?
I'LL GIVE YOU A HINT
MMMM...
WHAT HAS SIX LEGS AND CAN'T SWIM IN ORANGE JUICE?
4-22

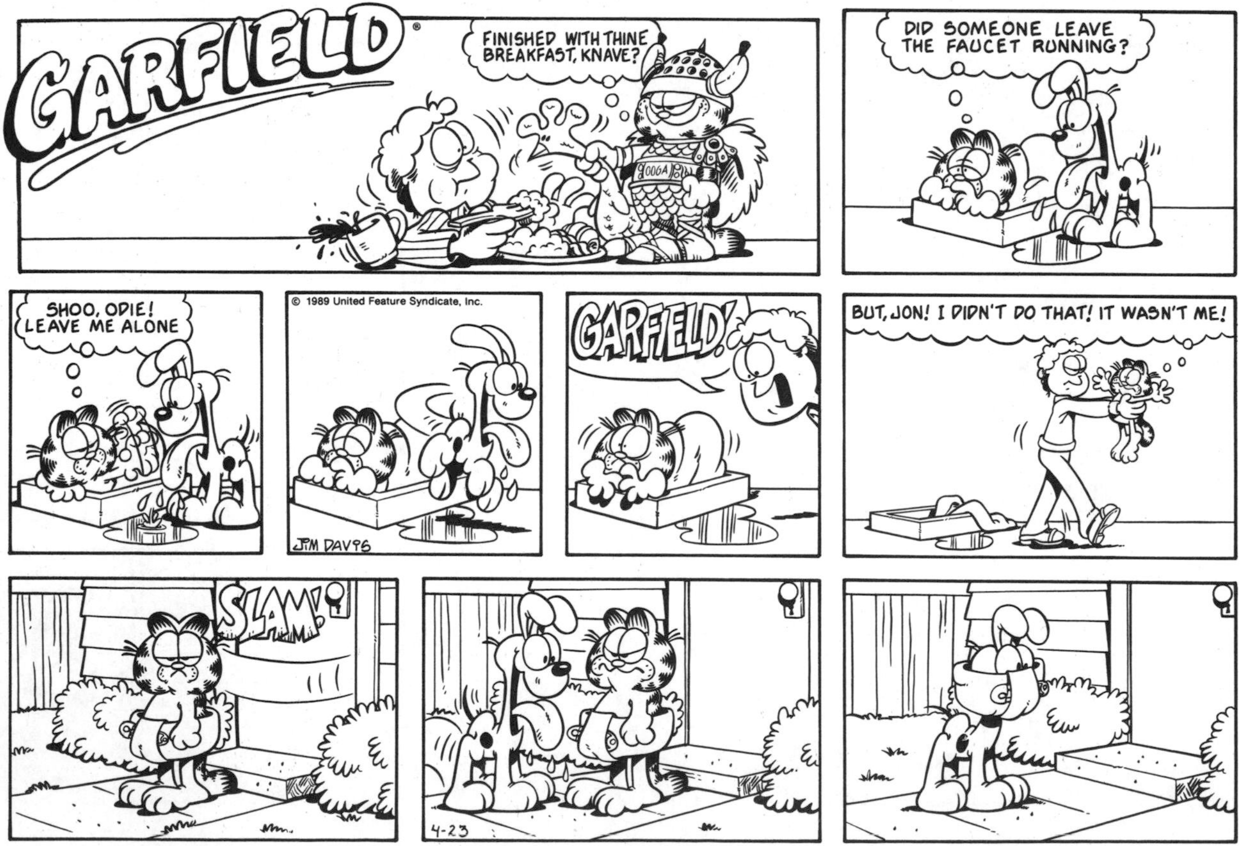
GARFIELD
FINISHED WITH THINE BREAKFAST, KNAVE?
OOGA
DID SOMEONE LEAVE THE FAUCET RUNNING?
SHOO, ODIE! LEAVE ME ALONE
© 1989 United Feature Syndicate, Inc.
JIM DAVIS
GARFIELD!
BUT, JON! I DIDN'T DO THAT! IT WASN'T ME!
SLAM!
4-23

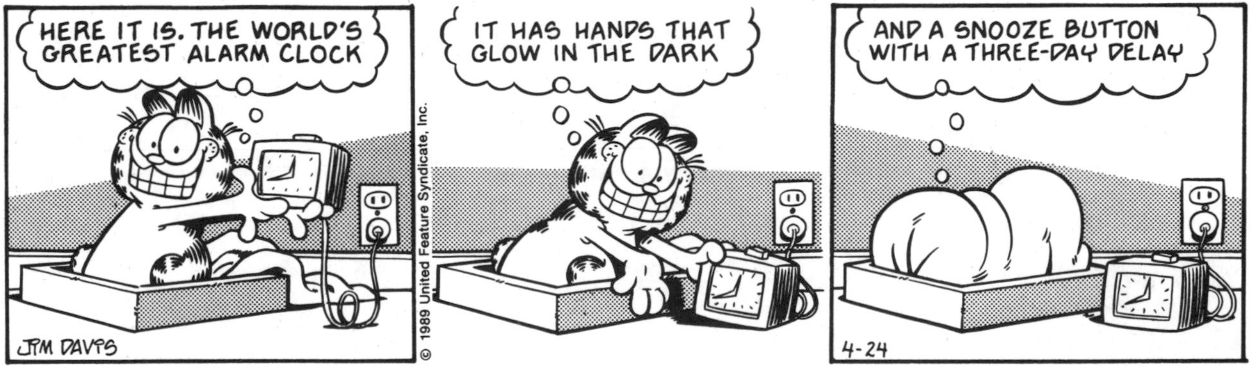
HERE IT IS. THE WORLD'S GREATEST ALARM CLOCK
JIM DAVIS
© 1989 United Feature Syndicate, Inc.
IT HAS HANDS THAT GLOW IN THE DARK
AND A SNOOZE BUTTON WITH A THREE-DAY DELAY
4-24

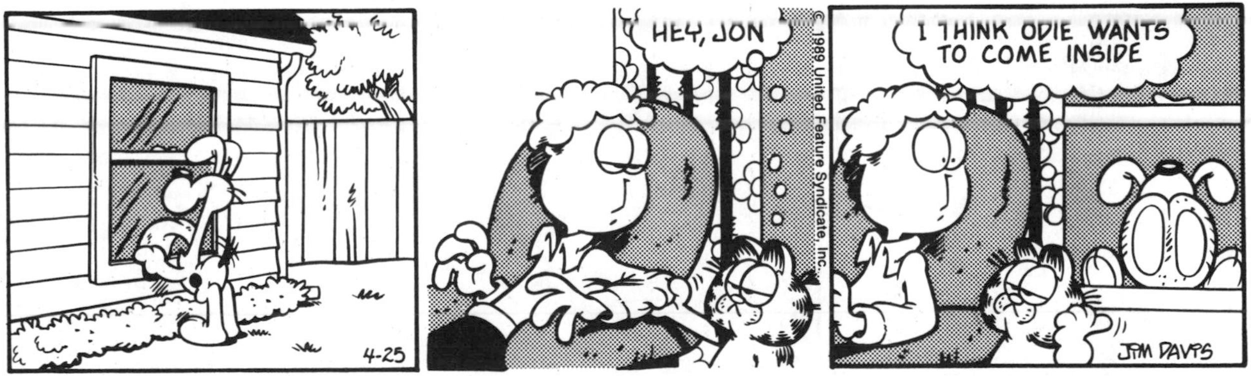
4-25
HEY, JON
© 1989 United Feature Syndicate, Inc.
I THINK ODIE WANTS TO COME INSIDE
JIM DAVIS

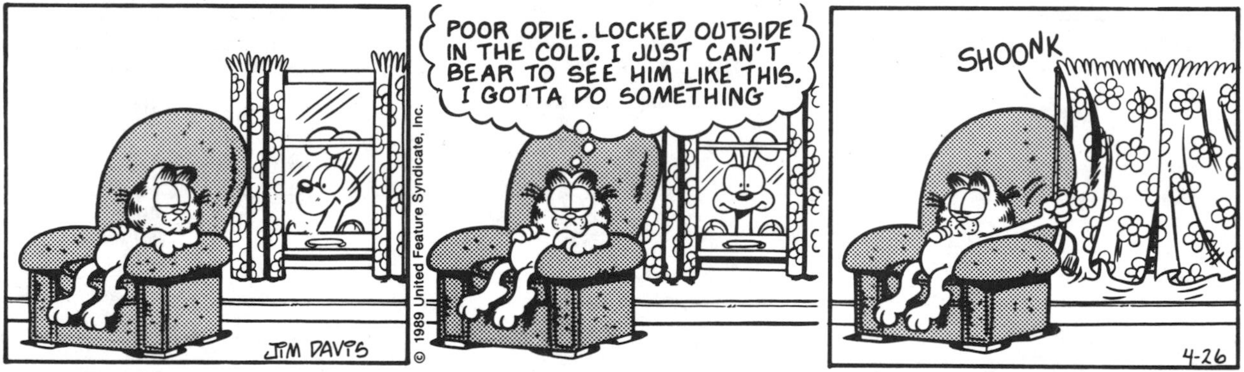
JIM DAVIS
© 1989 United Feature Syndicate, Inc.
POOR ODIE. LOCKED OUTSIDE IN THE COLD. I JUST CAN'T BEAR TO SEE HIM LIKE THIS. I GOTTA DO SOMETHING
SHOONK
4-26

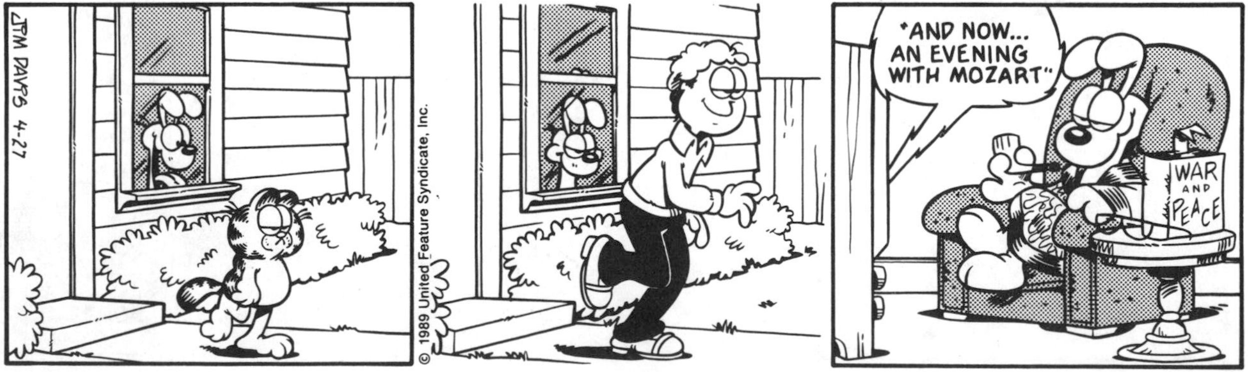
JIM DAVIS 4-27
© 1989 United Feature Syndicate, Inc.
"AND NOW... AN EVENING WITH MOZART"
WAR AND PEACE

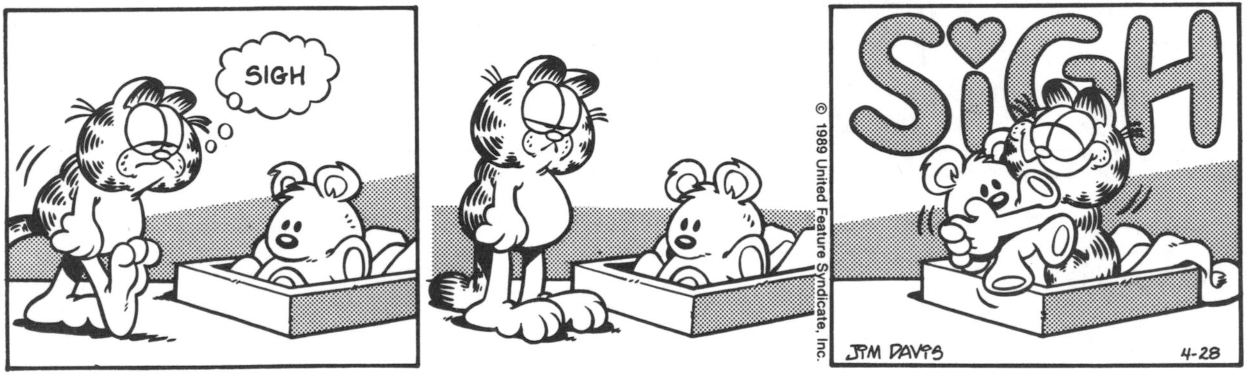
SIGH
SIGH
© 1989 United Feature Syndicate, Inc.
JIM DAVIS
4-28

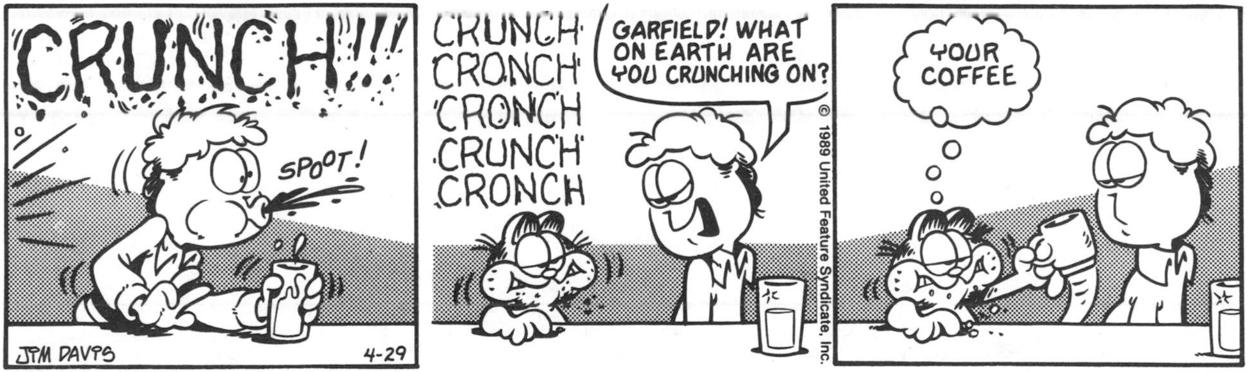
CRUNCH!!!
SPOOT!
JIM DAVIS
4-29
CRUNCH
CRONCH
CRONCH
CRUNCH
CRONCH
GARFIELD! WHAT ON EARTH ARE YOU CRUNCHING ON?
© 1989 United Feature Syndicate, Inc.
YOUR COFFEE

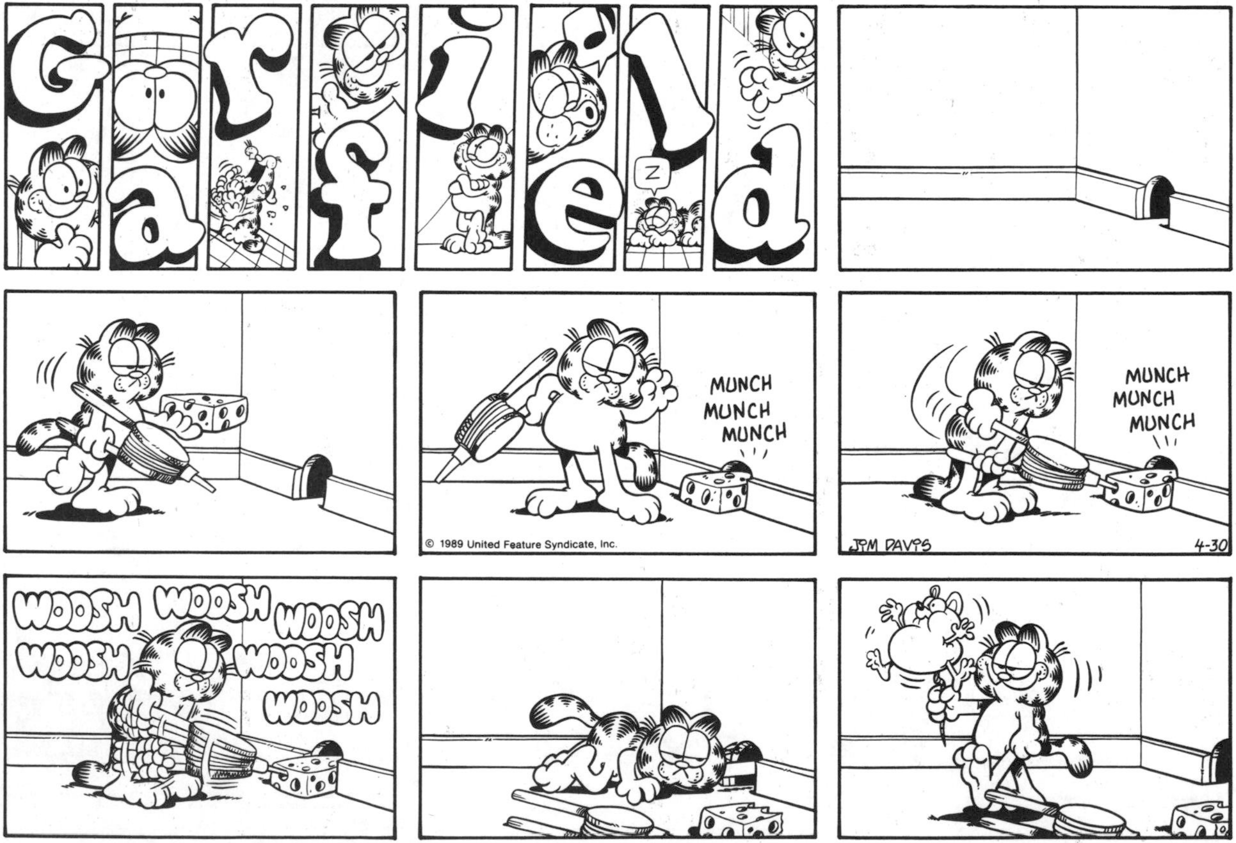
Garfield
MUNCH
MUNCH
MUNCH
© 1989 United Feature Syndicate, Inc.
MUNCH
MUNCH
MUNCH
JIM DAVIS
4-30
WOOSH WOOSH WOOSH
WOOSH WOOSH
WOOSH

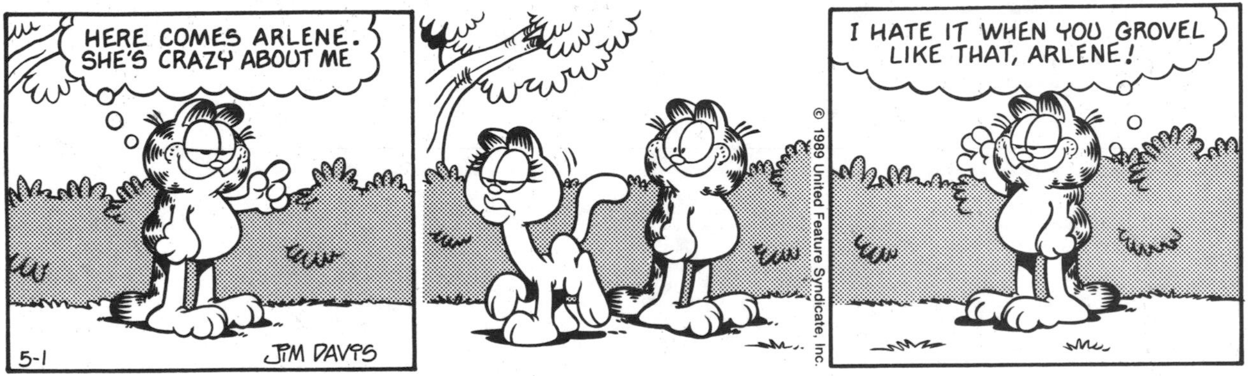
HERE COMES ARLENE. SHE'S CRAZY ABOUT ME
© 1989 United Feature Syndicate, Inc.
I HATE IT WHEN YOU GROVEL LIKE THAT, ARLENE!
5-1
JIM DAVIS

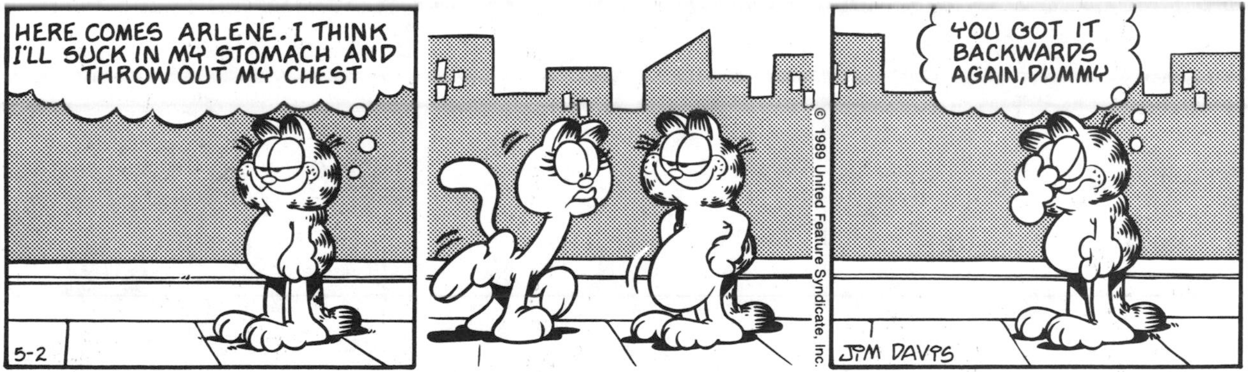
HERE COMES ARLENE. I THINK I'LL SUCK IN MY STOMACH AND THROW OUT MY CHEST
© 1989 United Feature Syndicate, Inc.
YOU GOT IT BACKWARDS AGAIN, DUMMY
5-2
JIM DAVIS

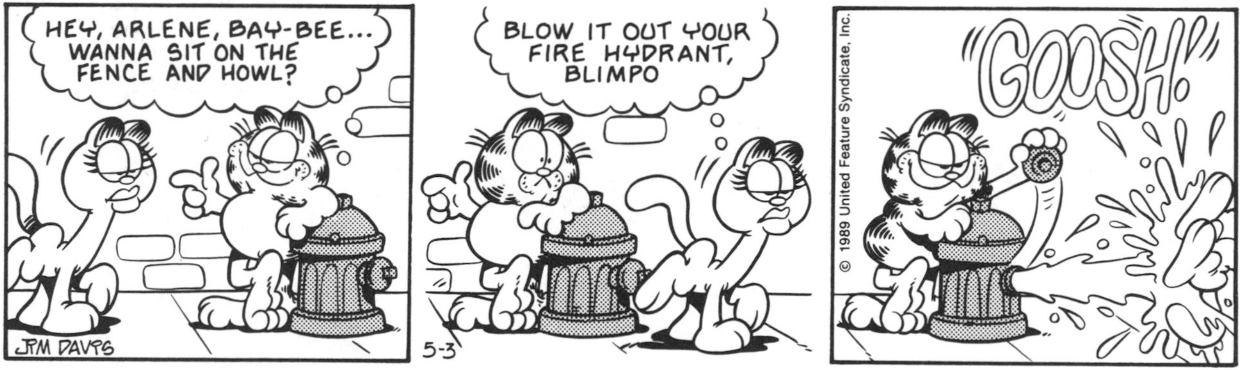
HEY, ARLENE, BAY-BEE... WANNA SIT ON THE FENCE AND HOWL?
JIM DAVIS
BLOW IT OUT YOUR FIRE HYDRANT, BLIMPO
5-3
© 1989 United Feature Syndicate, Inc.
GOOSH!

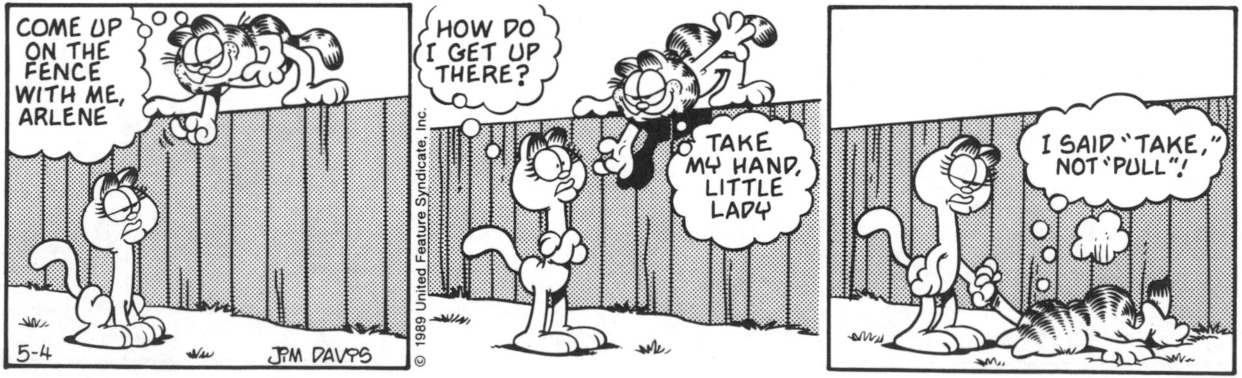
COME UP ON THE FENCE WITH ME, ARLENE
5-4
JIM DAVIS
© 1989 United Feature Syndicate, Inc.
HOW DO I GET UP THERE?
TAKE MY HAND, LITTLE LADY
I SAID "TAKE," NOT "PULL"!

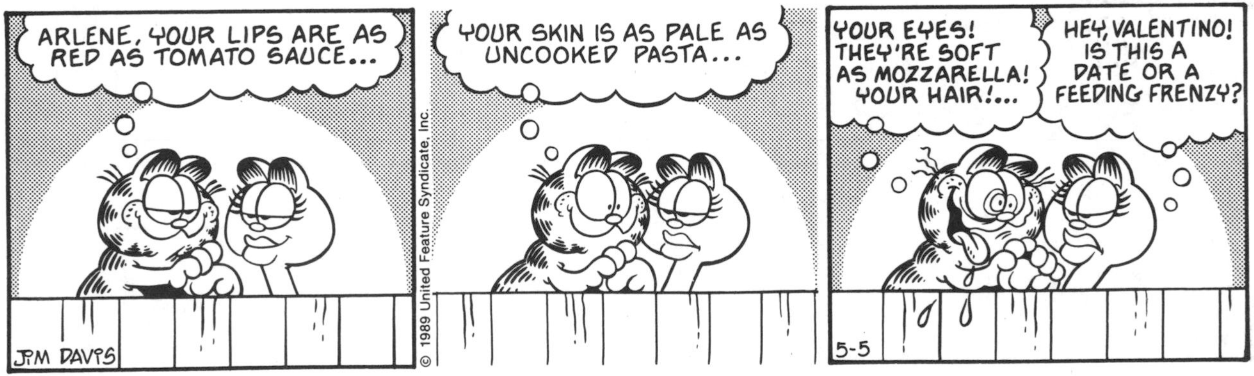
ARLENE, YOUR LIPS ARE AS RED AS TOMATO SAUCE...
JIM DAVIS
© 1989 United Feature Syndicate, Inc.
YOUR SKIN IS AS PALE AS UNCOOKED PASTA...
YOUR EYES! THEY'RE SOFT AS MOZZARELLA! YOUR HAIR!...
HEY, VALENTINO! IS THIS A DATE OR A FEEDING FRENZY?
5-5

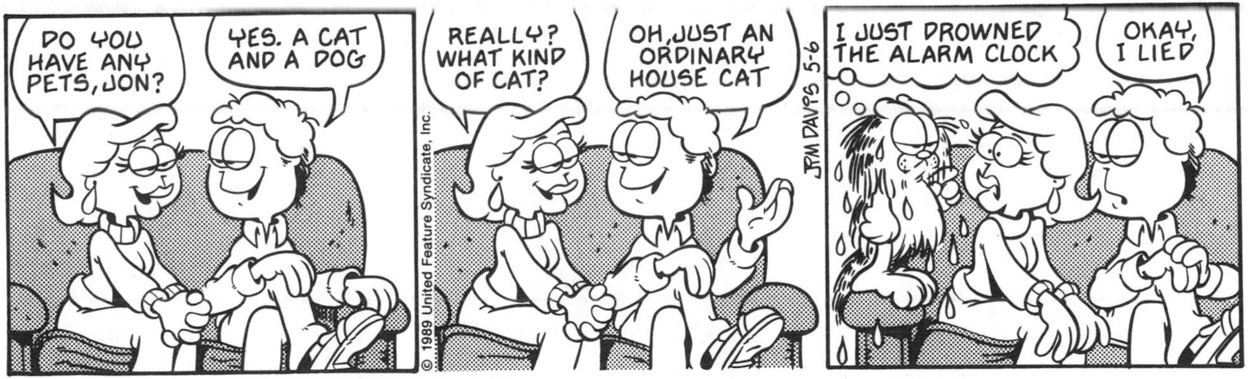
DO YOU HAVE ANY PETS, JON?
YES. A CAT AND A DOG
© 1989 United Feature Syndicate, Inc.
REALLY? WHAT KIND OF CAT?
OH, JUST AN ORDINARY HOUSE CAT
JIM DAVIS 5-6
I JUST DROWNED THE ALARM CLOCK
OKAY, I LIED

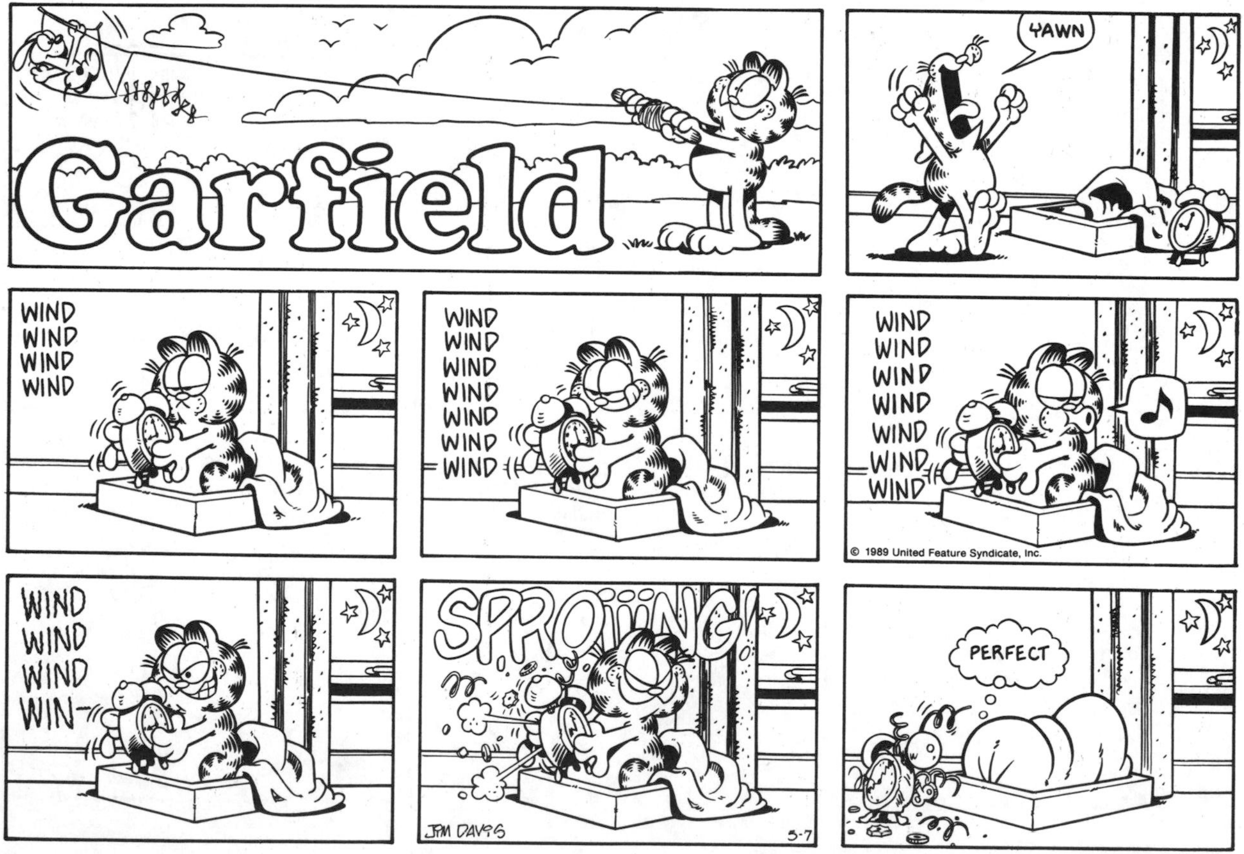

Garfield
YAWN
WIND
WIND
WIND
WIND
WIND
WIND
WIND
WIND
WIND
WIND
WIND
WIND
WIND
WIND
WIND
WIND
WIND
WIND
© 1989 United Feature Syndicate, Inc.
WIND
WIND
WIND
WIN—
SPROIIING!
JPM DAVIS
5-7
PERFECT

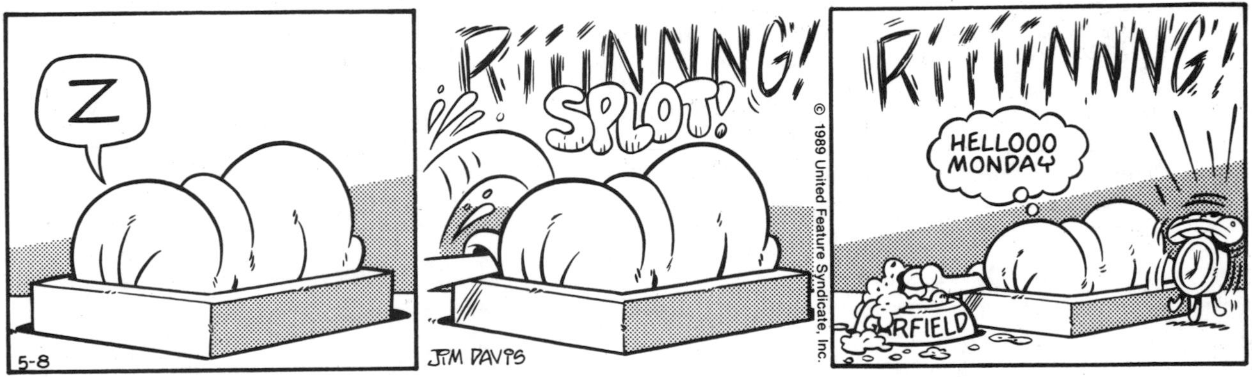
Z
RIIINNNG!
SPLOT!
JIM DAVIS
RIIIINNNG!
HELLOOO MONDAY
RFIELD
5-8
© 1989 United Feature Syndicate, Inc.

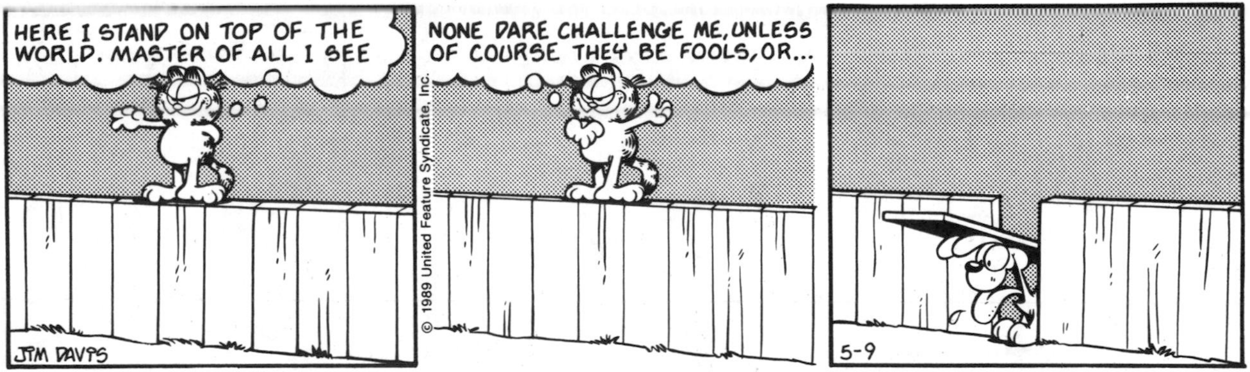
HERE I STAND ON TOP OF THE WORLD. MASTER OF ALL I SEE
JIM DAVIS
NONE DARE CHALLENGE ME, UNLESS OF COURSE THEY BE FOOLS, OR...
5-9
© 1989 United Feature Syndicate, Inc.

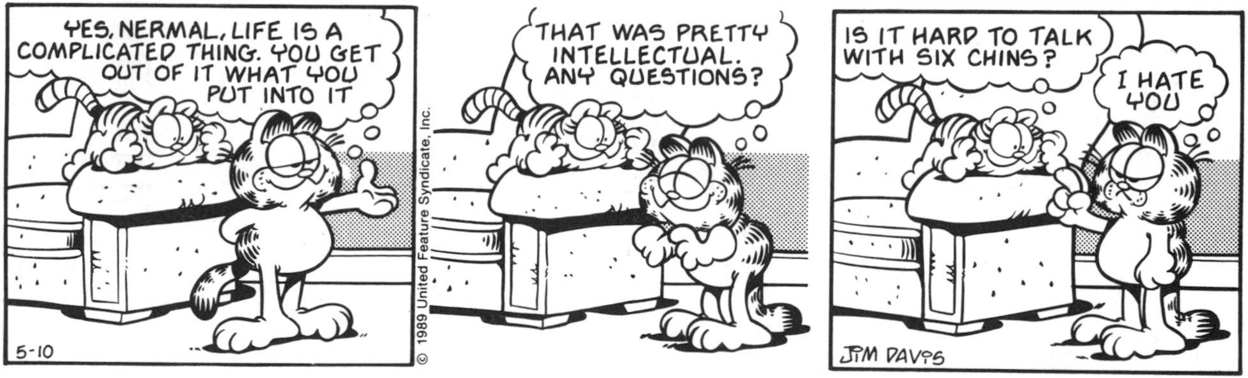
YES, NERMAL, LIFE IS A COMPLICATED THING. YOU GET OUT OF IT WHAT YOU PUT INTO IT
THAT WAS PRETTY INTELLECTUAL. ANY QUESTIONS?
IS IT HARD TO TALK WITH SIX CHINS?
I HATE YOU
5-10
© 1989 United Feature Syndicate, Inc.
JIM DAVIS

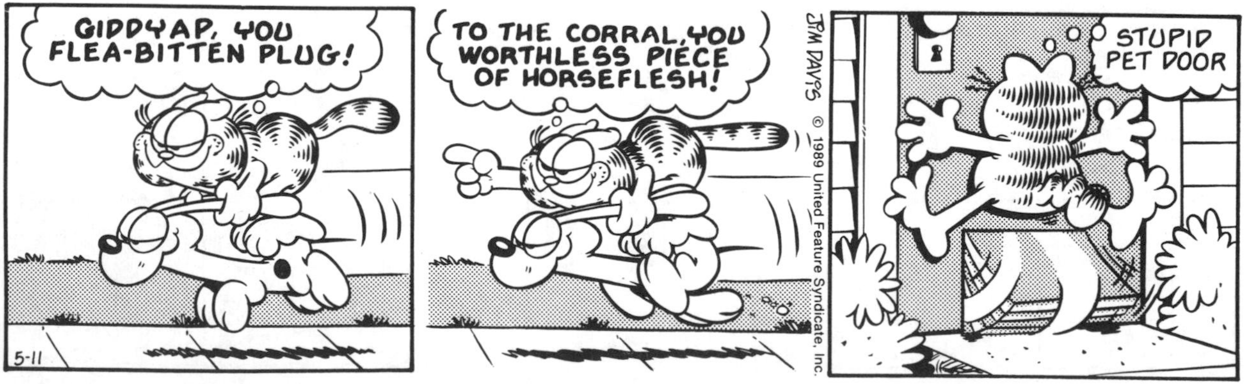
GIDDYAP, YOU FLEA-BITTEN PLUG!
TO THE CORRAL, YOU WORTHLESS PIECE OF HORSEFLESH!
STUPID PET DOOR
5-11
JIM DAVIS
© 1989 United Feature Syndicate, Inc.

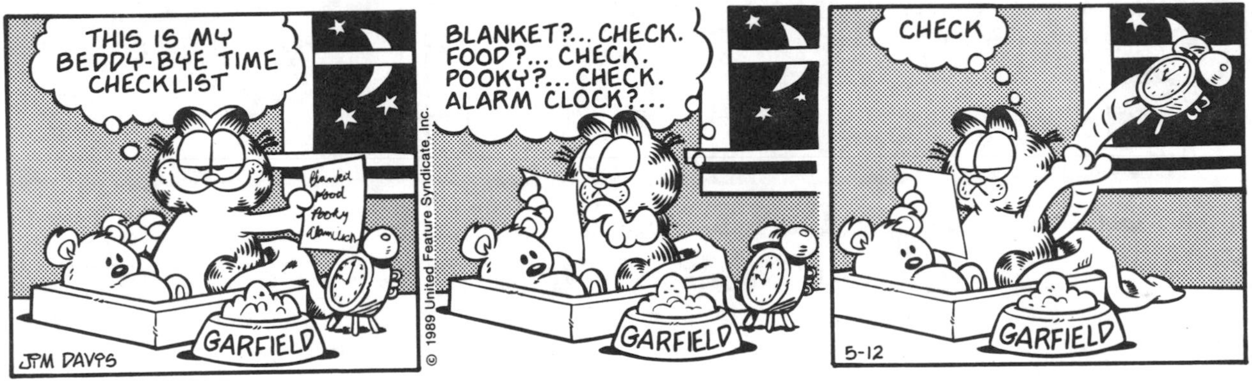
THIS IS MY BEDDY-BYE TIME CHECKLIST
JIM DAVIS
GARFIELD
BLANKET?... CHECK. FOOD?... CHECK. POOKY?... CHECK. ALARM CLOCK?...
GARFIELD
CHECK
GARFIELD
5-12

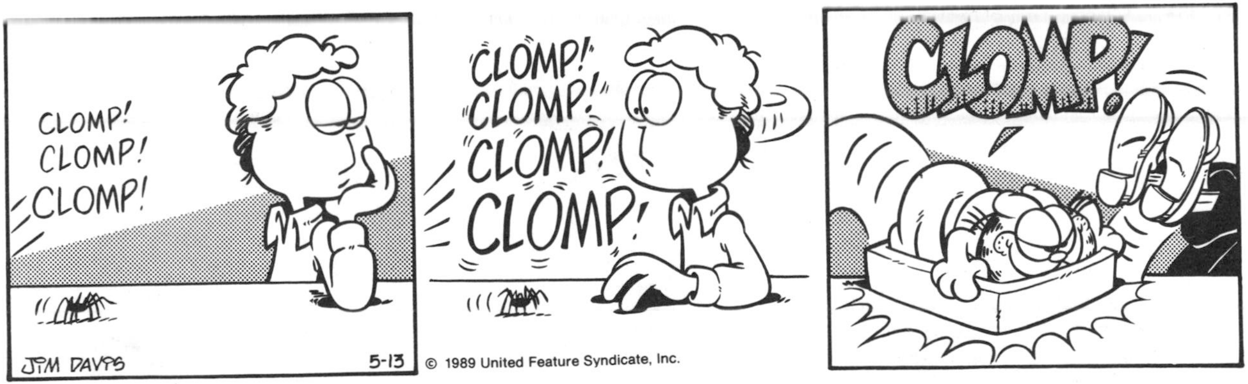
CLOMP!
CLOMP!
CLOMP!
JIM DAVIS
5-13
CLOMP!
CLOMP!
CLOMP!
CLOMP!
CLOMP!

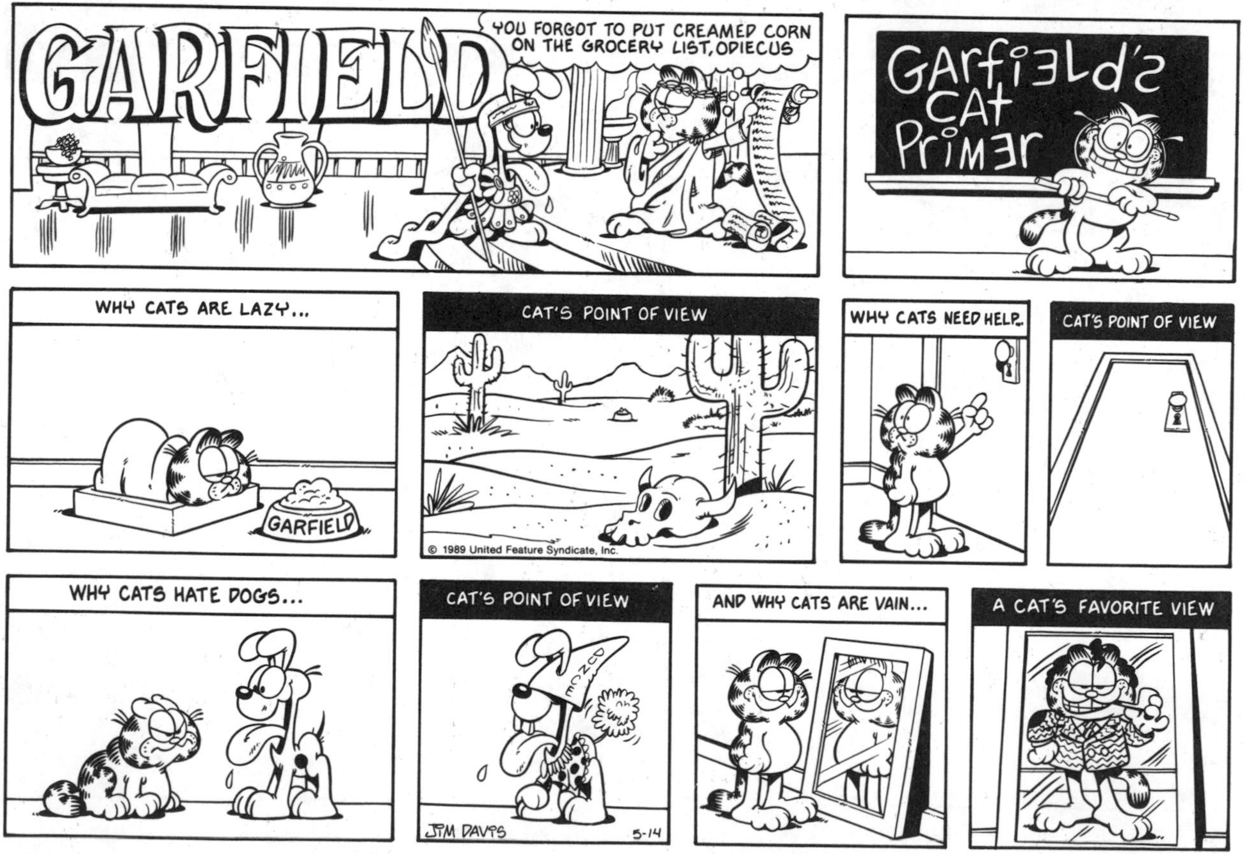
GARFIELD
YOU FORGOT TO PUT CREAMED CORN ON THE GROCERY LIST, ODIECUS
Garfield's Cat Primer
WHY CATS ARE LAZY...
GARFIELD
CAT'S POINT OF VIEW
© 1989 United Feature Syndicate, Inc.
WHY CATS NEED HELP...
CAT'S POINT OF VIEW
WHY CATS HATE DOGS...
CAT'S POINT OF VIEW
JIM DAVIS
5-14
AND WHY CATS ARE VAIN...
A CAT'S FAVORITE VIEW

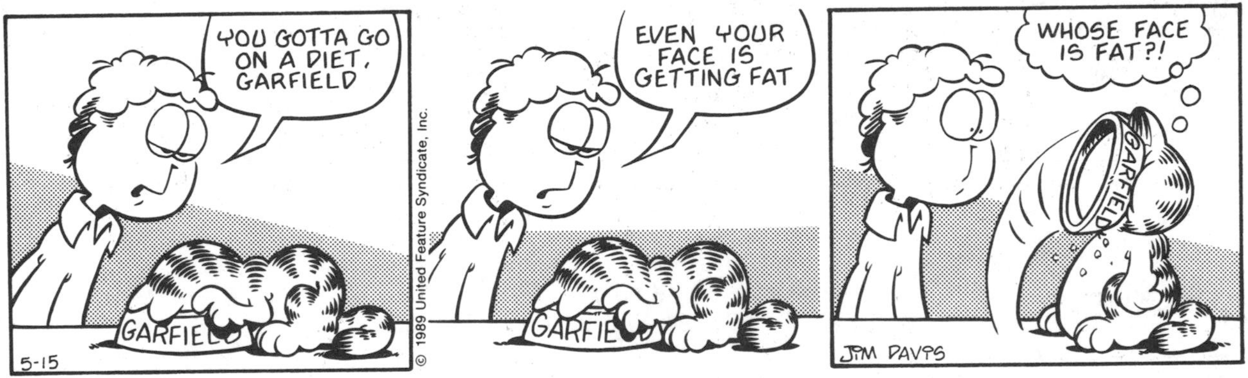
YOU GOTTA GO ON A DIET, GARFIELD
GARFIELD
5-15
EVEN YOUR FACE IS GETTING FAT
GARFIE
© 1989 United Feature Syndicate, Inc.
WHOSE FACE IS FAT?!
GARFIELD
JIM DAVIS

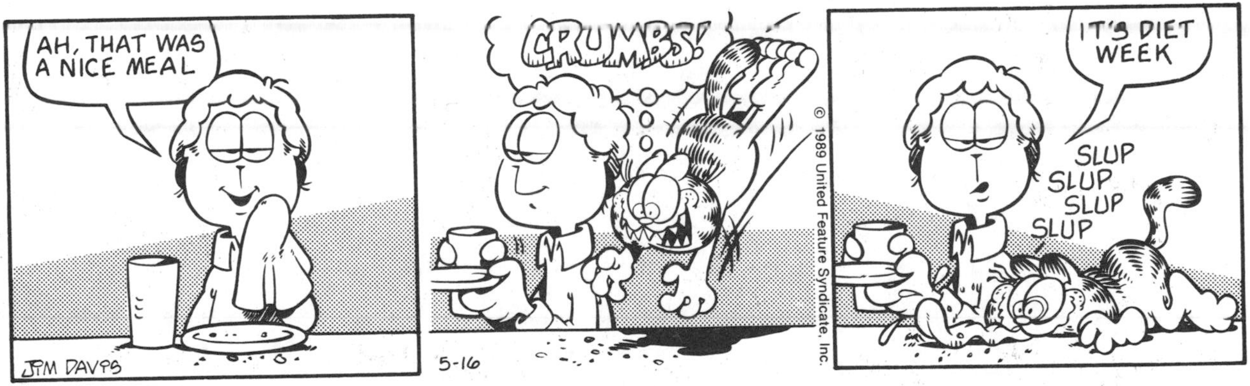
AH, THAT WAS A NICE MEAL
JIM DAVIS
CRUMBS!
5-16
© 1989 United Feature Syndicate, Inc.
IT'S DIET WEEK
SLUP
SLUP
SLUP
SLUP

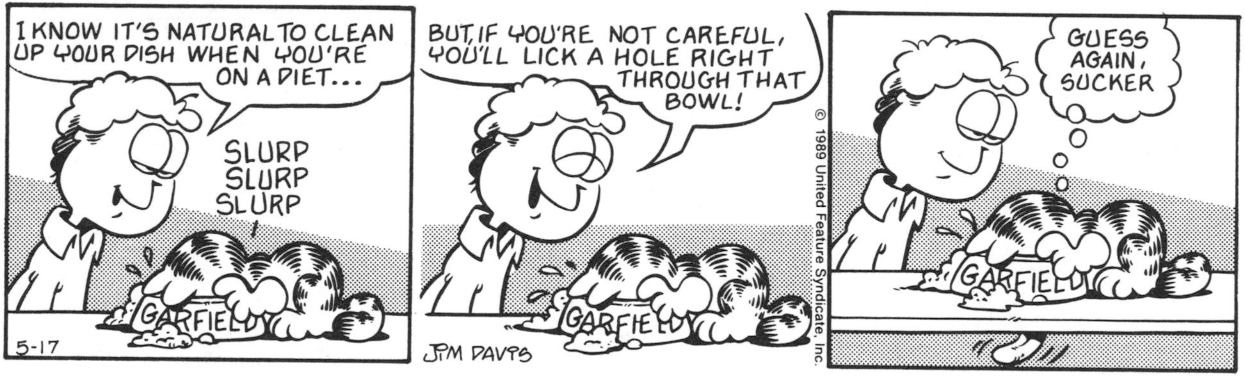
I KNOW IT'S NATURAL TO CLEAN UP YOUR DISH WHEN YOU'RE ON A DIET...
SLURP SLURP SLURP
5-17
BUT, IF YOU'RE NOT CAREFUL, YOU'LL LICK A HOLE RIGHT THROUGH THAT BOWL!
GARFIELD
JIM DAVIS
© 1989 United Feature Syndicate, Inc.
GUESS AGAIN, SUCKER

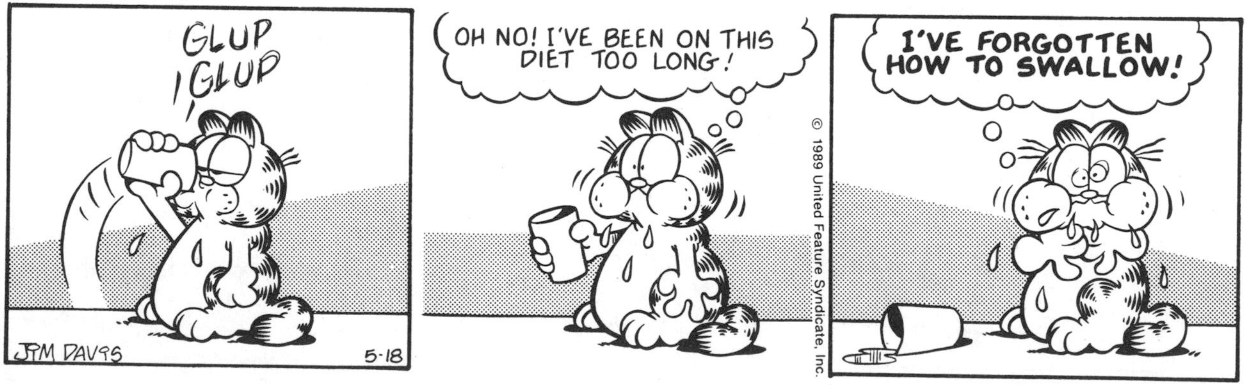
GLUP GLUP
JIM DAVIS
5-18
OH NO! I'VE BEEN ON THIS DIET TOO LONG!
© 1989 United Feature Syndicate, Inc.
I'VE FORGOTTEN HOW TO SWALLOW!

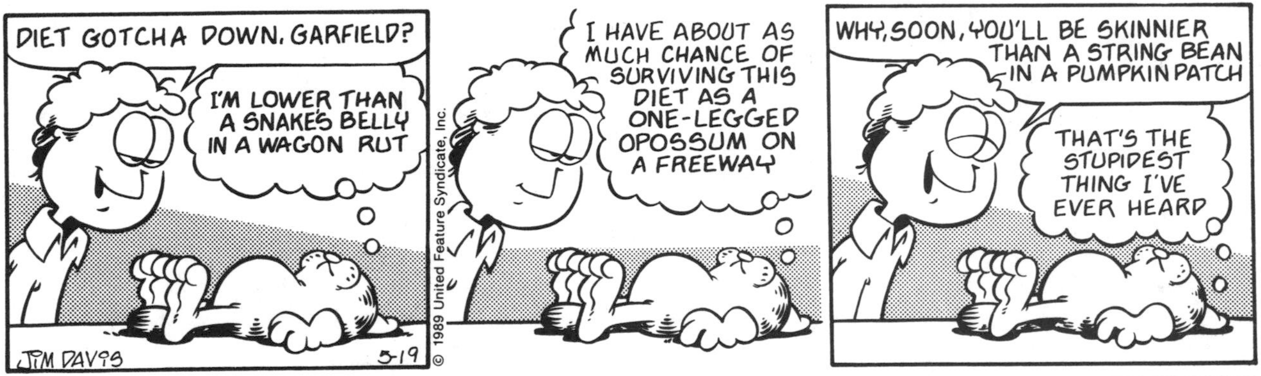
DIET GOTCHA DOWN, GARFIELD?
I'M LOWER THAN A SNAKE'S BELLY IN A WAGON RUT
I HAVE ABOUT AS MUCH CHANCE OF SURVIVING THIS DIET AS A ONE-LEGGED OPOSSUM ON A FREEWAY
WHY, SOON, YOU'LL BE SKINNIER THAN A STRING BEAN IN A PUMPKIN PATCH
THAT'S THE STUPIDEST THING I'VE EVER HEARD
JIM DAVIS
5-19
© 1989 United Feature Syndicate, Inc.

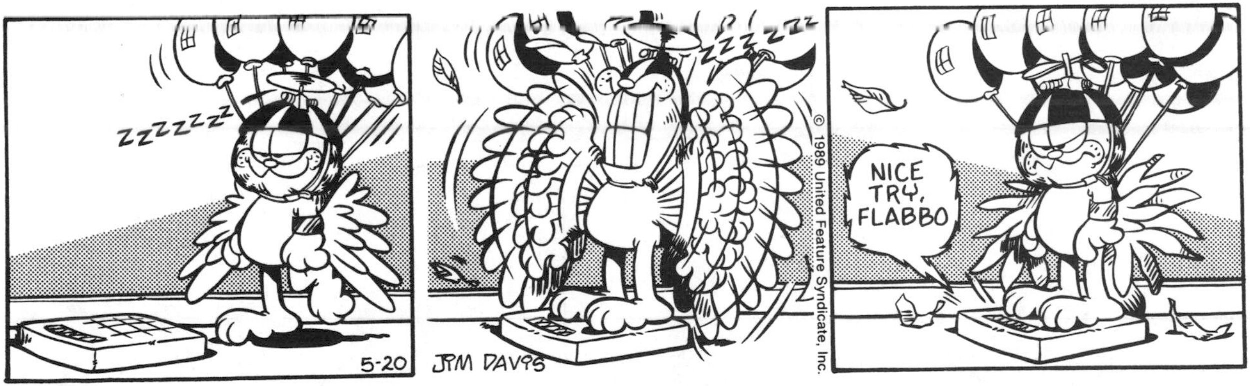
ZZZZZZZ
5-20
ZZZZZZZ
JIM DAVIS
NICE TRY, FLABBO
© 1989 United Feature Syndicate, Inc.

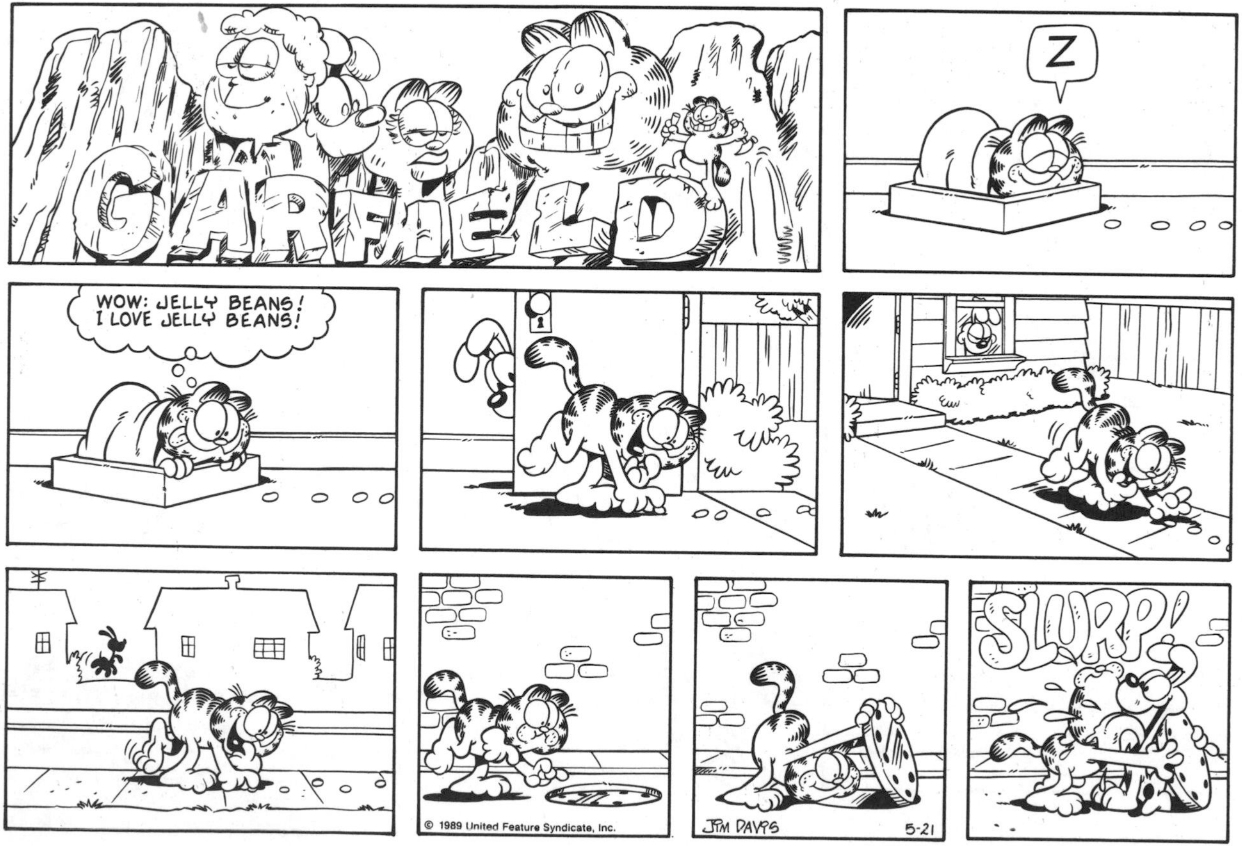
GARFIELD
Z
WOW: JELLY BEANS!
I LOVE JELLY BEANS!
© 1989 United Feature Syndicate, Inc.
JIM DAVIS
5-21
SLURP!

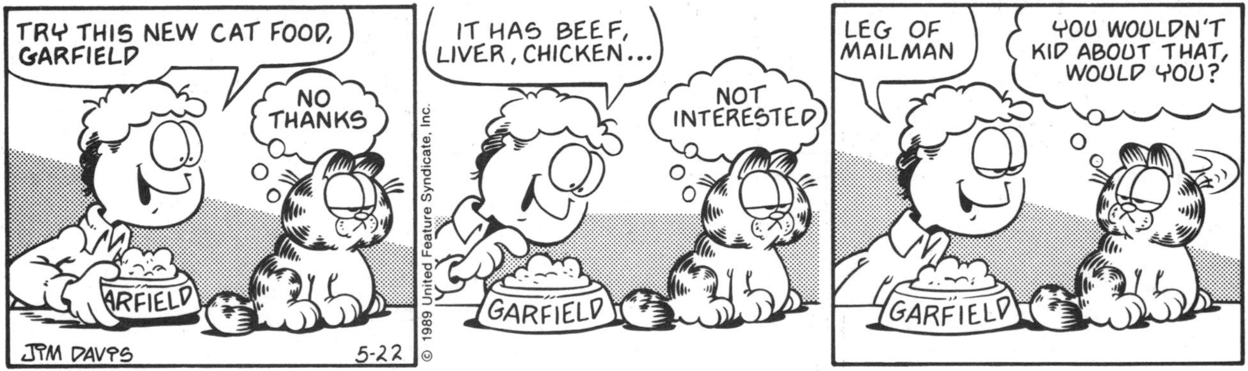
TRY THIS NEW CAT FOOD, GARFIELD
NO THANKS
GARFIELD
JIM DAVIS
5-22
© 1989 United Feature Syndicate, Inc.
IT HAS BEEF, LIVER, CHICKEN...
NOT INTERESTED
GARFIELD
LEG OF MAILMAN
YOU WOULDN'T KID ABOUT THAT, WOULD YOU?
GARFIELD

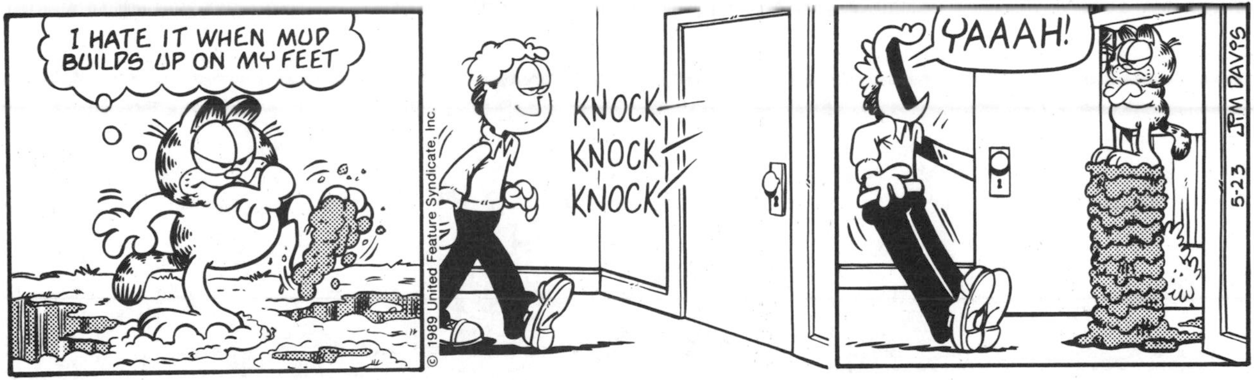
I HATE IT WHEN MUD BUILDS UP ON MY FEET
© 1989 United Feature Syndicate, Inc.
KNOCK
KNOCK
KNOCK
YAAAH!
JIM DAVIS
5-23

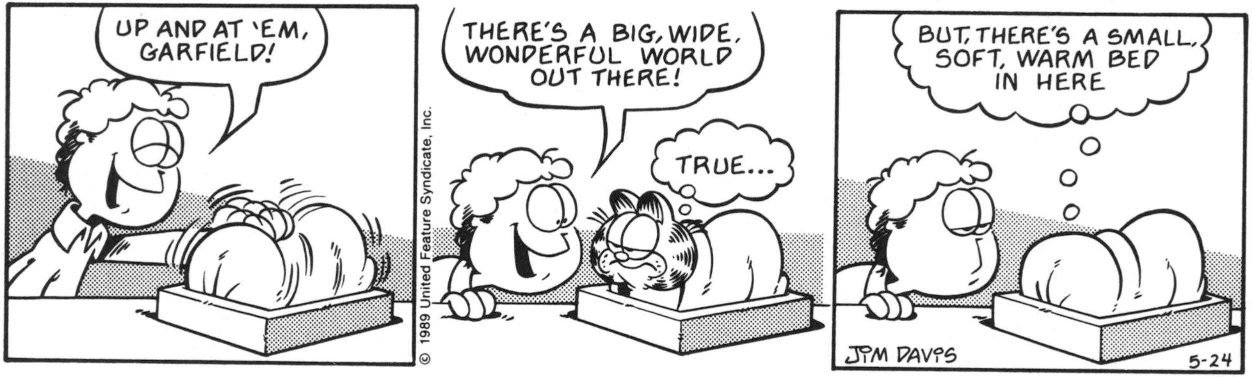
UP AND AT 'EM, GARFIELD!
THERE'S A BIG, WIDE, WONDERFUL WORLD OUT THERE!
TRUE...
BUT, THERE'S A SMALL, SOFT, WARM BED IN HERE
JIM DAVIS
5-24

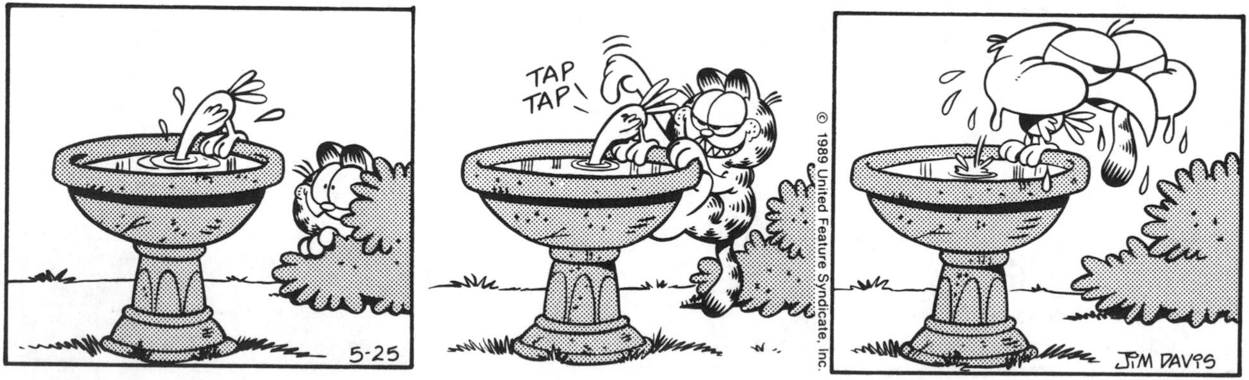
5-25
TAP TAP
JIM DAVIS

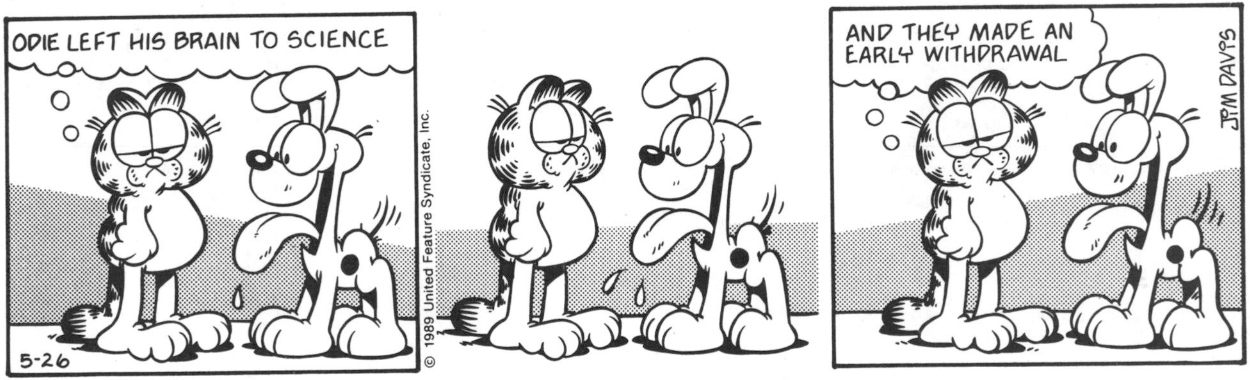
ODIE LEFT HIS BRAIN TO SCIENCE
5-26
© 1989 United Feature Syndicate, Inc.
AND THEY MADE AN EARLY WITHDRAWAL
JIM DAVIS

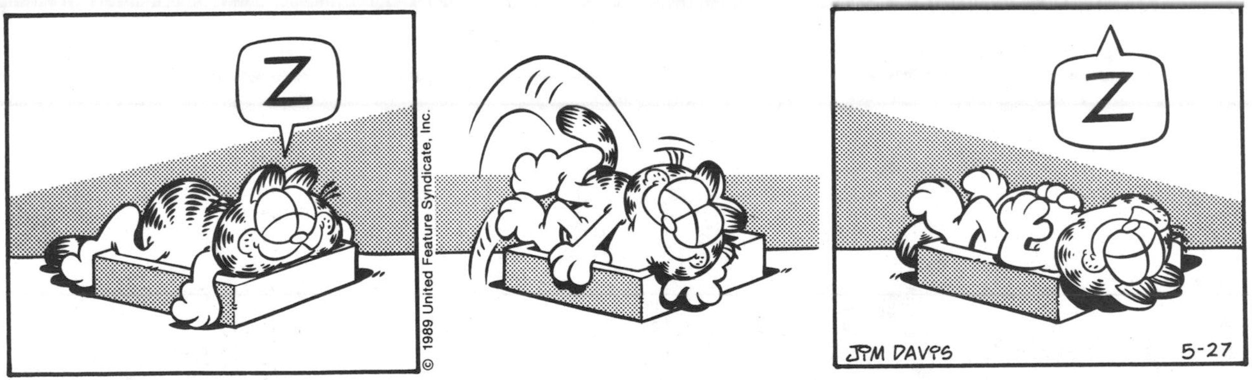
Z
© 1989 United Feature Syndicate, Inc.
Z
JIM DAVIS
5-27

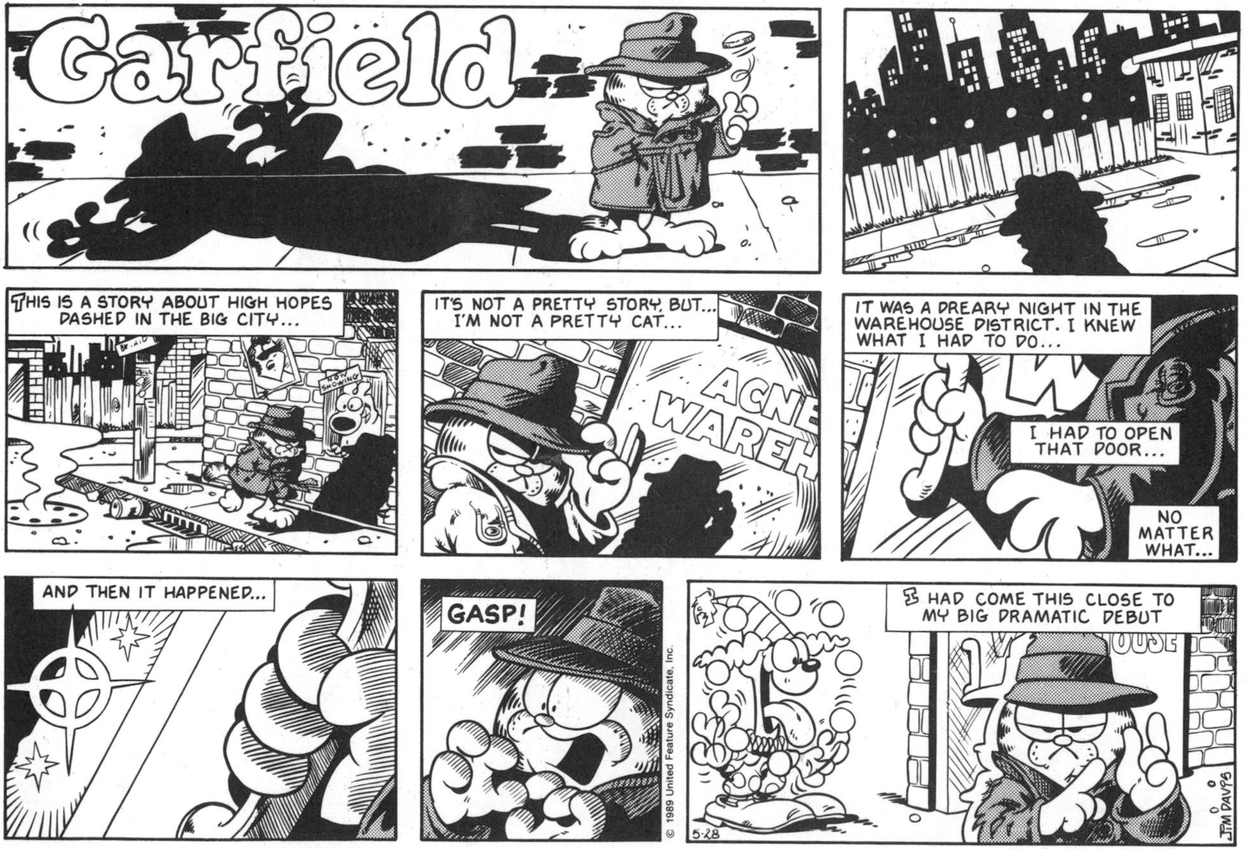
Garfield
THIS IS A STORY ABOUT HIGH HOPES DASHED IN THE BIG CITY...
NOW SHOWING
IT'S NOT A PRETTY STORY, BUT... I'M NOT A PRETTY CAT...
ACNE WAREH
IT WAS A DREARY NIGHT IN THE WAREHOUSE DISTRICT. I KNEW WHAT I HAD TO DO...
I HAD TO OPEN THAT DOOR...
NO MATTER WHAT...
AND THEN IT HAPPENED...
GASP!
I HAD COME THIS CLOSE TO MY BIG DRAMATIC DEBUT
OUSE
JIM DAVIS
5-28

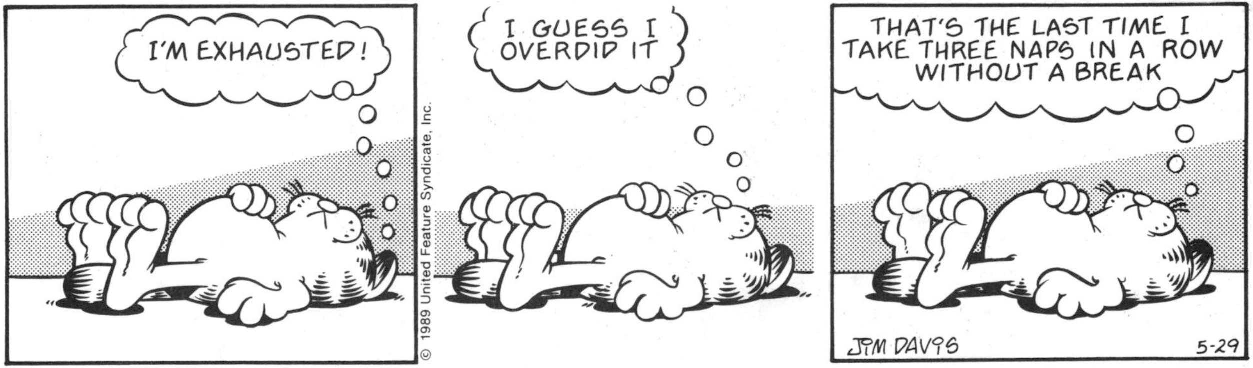
I'M EXHAUSTED!
I GUESS I OVERDID IT
THAT'S THE LAST TIME I TAKE THREE NAPS IN A ROW WITHOUT A BREAK
© 1989 United Feature Syndicate, Inc.
JIM DAVIS
5-29

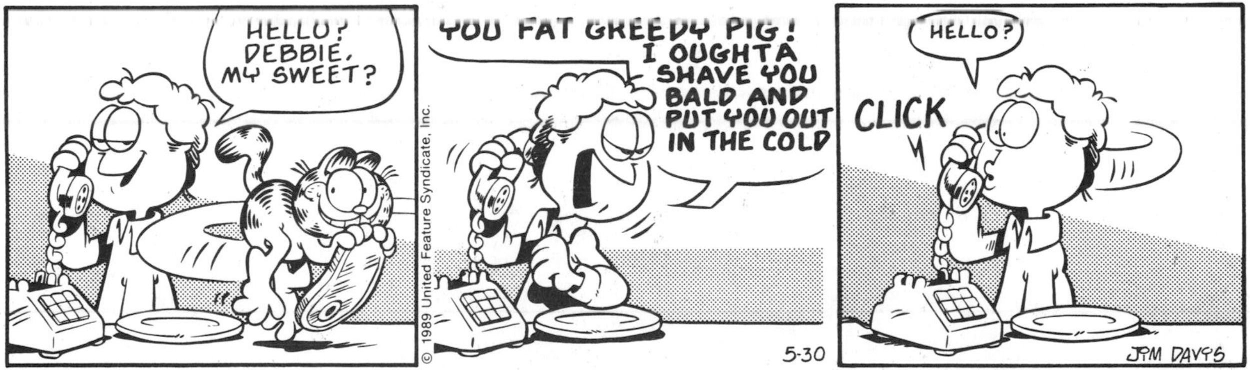
HELLO? DEBBIE, MY SWEET?
YOU FAT GREEDY PIG! I OUGHTA SHAVE YOU BALD AND PUT YOU OUT IN THE COLD
CLICK
HELLO?
© 1989 United Feature Syndicate, Inc.
5-30
JIM DAVIS

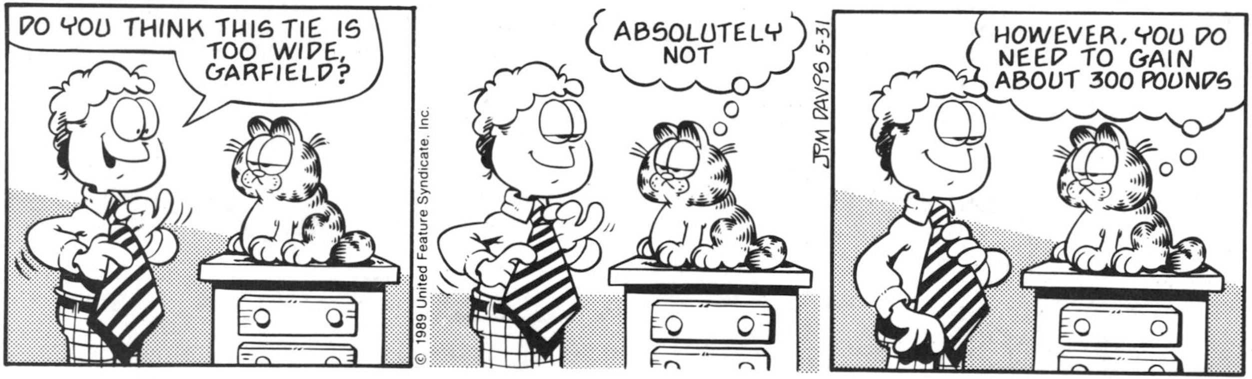
DO YOU THINK THIS TIE IS TOO WIDE, GARFIELD?
© 1989 United Feature Syndicate, Inc.
ABSOLUTELY NOT
JIM DAVIS 5-31
HOWEVER, YOU DO NEED TO GAIN ABOUT 300 POUNDS

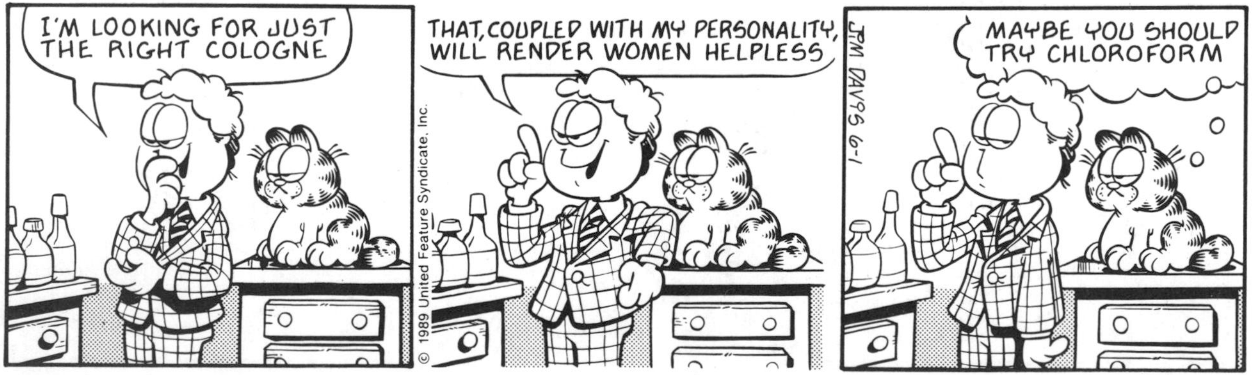
I'M LOOKING FOR JUST THE RIGHT COLOGNE
© 1989 United Feature Syndicate, Inc.
THAT, COUPLED WITH MY PERSONALITY, WILL RENDER WOMEN HELPLESS
JIM DAVIS 6-1
MAYBE YOU SHOULD TRY CHLOROFORM

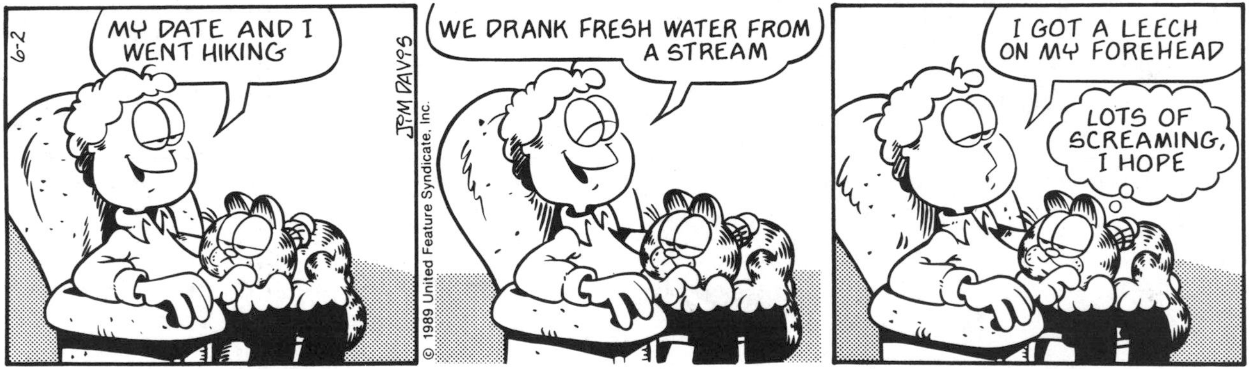
6-2
MY DATE AND I WENT HIKING
JIM DAVIS
© 1989 United Feature Syndicate, Inc.
WE DRANK FRESH WATER FROM A STREAM
I GOT A LEECH ON MY FOREHEAD
LOTS OF SCREAMING, I HOPE

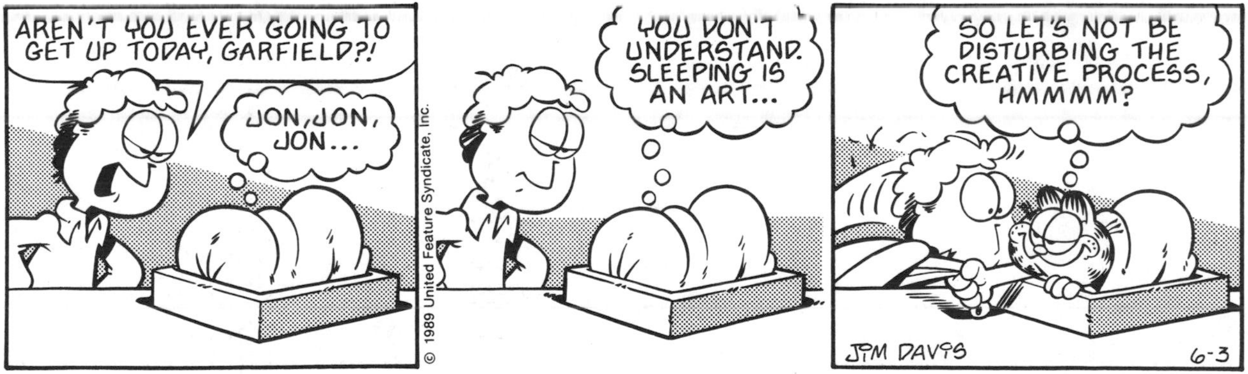
AREN'T YOU EVER GOING TO GET UP TODAY, GARFIELD?!
JON, JON, JON...
© 1989 United Feature Syndicate, Inc.
YOU DON'T UNDERSTAND. SLEEPING IS AN ART...
SO LET'S NOT BE DISTURBING THE CREATIVE PROCESS, HMMMM?
JIM DAVIS
6-3

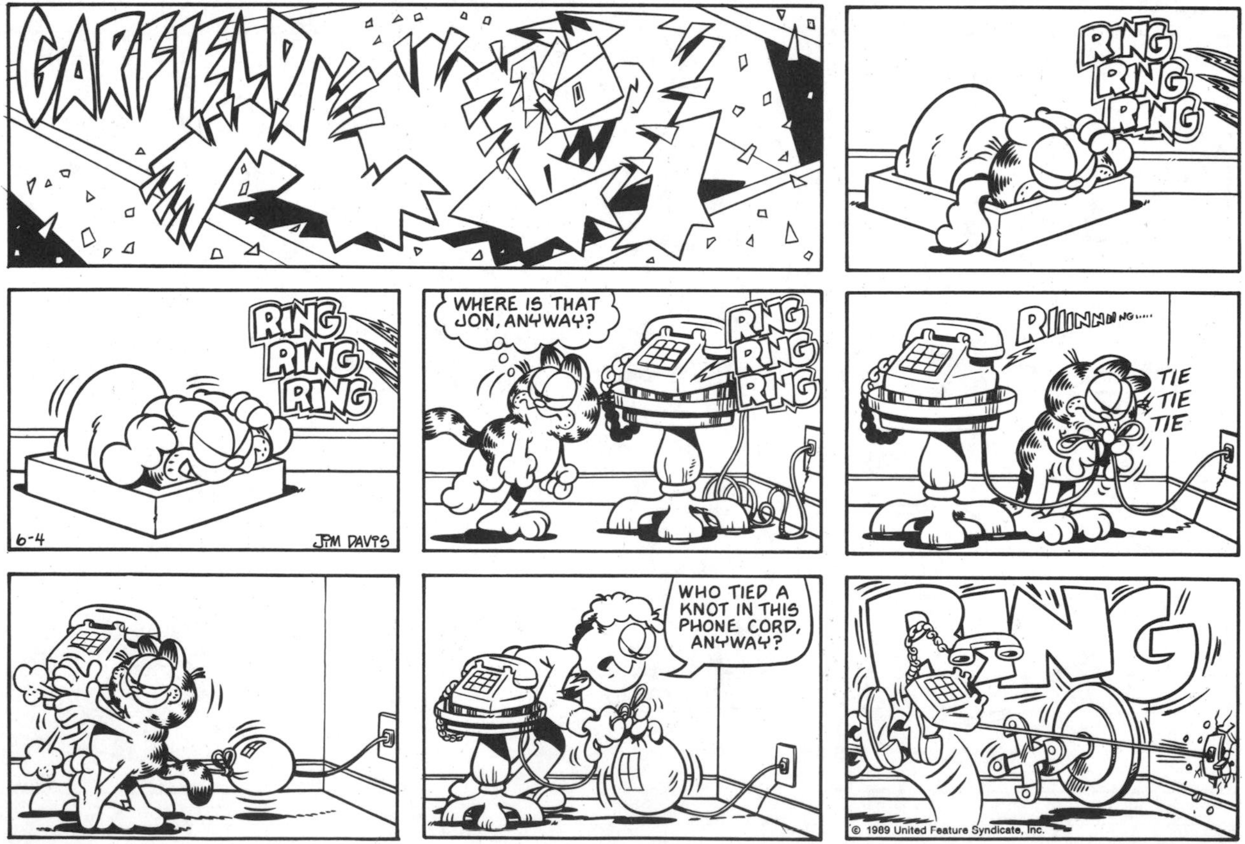
GARFIELD
RING
RING
RING
RING
RING
RING
6-4
JIM DAVIS
WHERE IS THAT JON, ANYWAY?
RING
RING
RING
RIIINNNNNG.....
TIE
TIE
TIE
WHO TIED A KNOT IN THIS PHONE CORD, ANYWAY?
RING
© 1989 United Feature Syndicate, Inc.

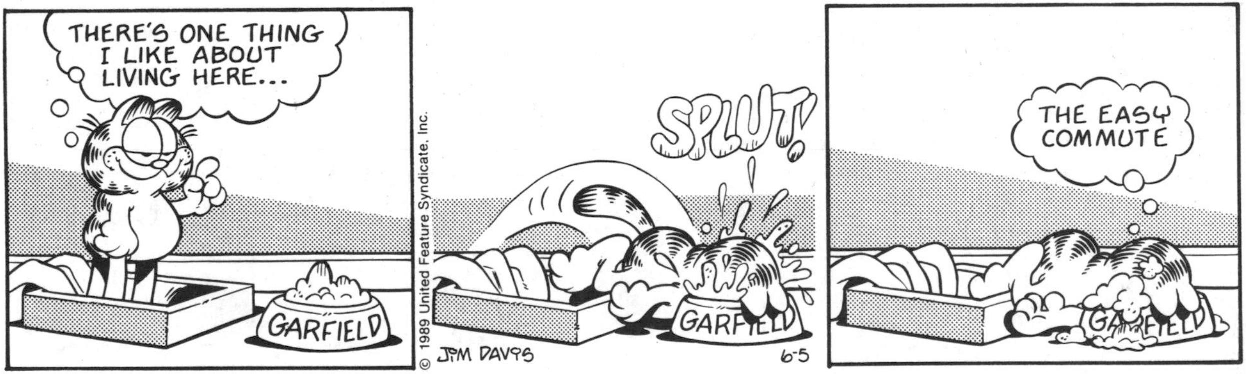
THERE'S ONE THING I LIKE ABOUT LIVING HERE...
SPLUT!
THE EASY COMMUTE
GARFIELD
© 1989 United Feature Syndicate, Inc.
JIM DAVIS
6-5

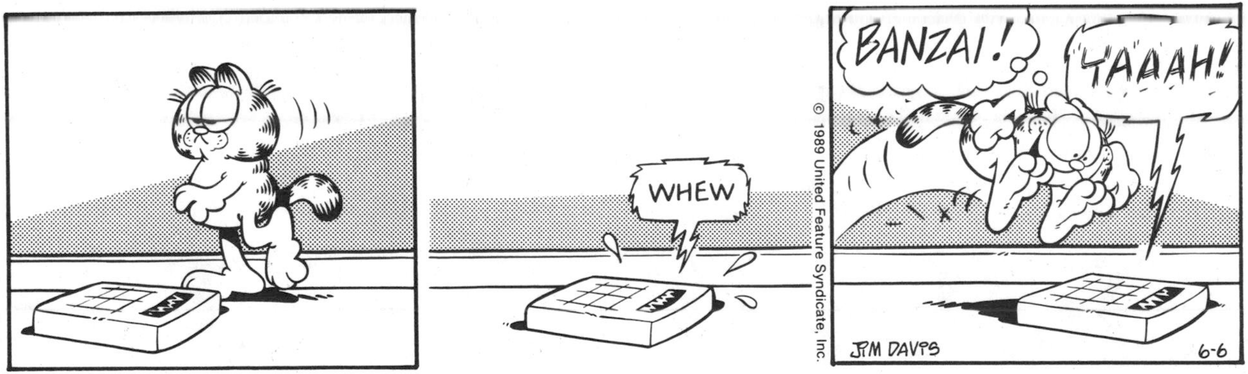
WHEW
BANZAI!
YAAAH!
© 1989 United Feature Syndicate, Inc.
JIM DAVIS
6-6

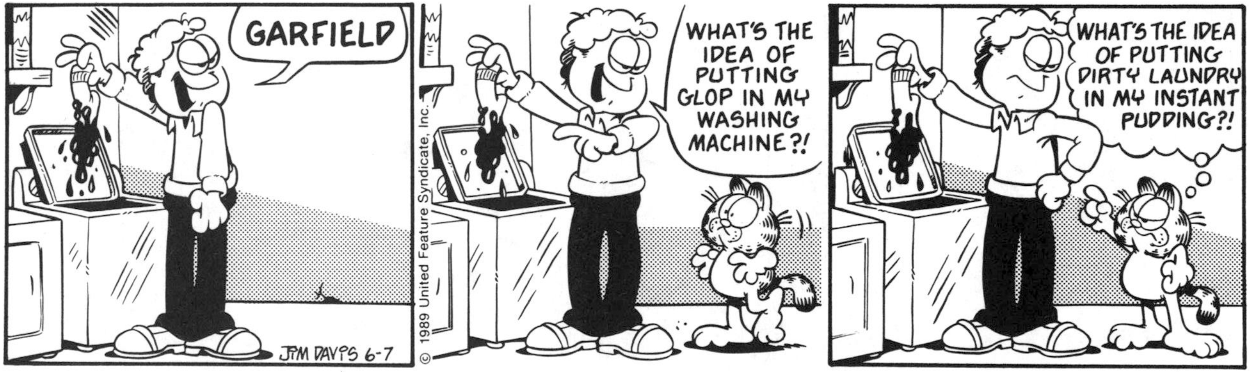
GARFIELD
WHAT'S THE IDEA OF PUTTING GLOP IN MY WASHING MACHINE?!
WHAT'S THE IDEA OF PUTTING DIRTY LAUNDRY IN MY INSTANT PUDDING?!
JIM DAVIS 6-7
© 1989 United Feature Syndicate, Inc.

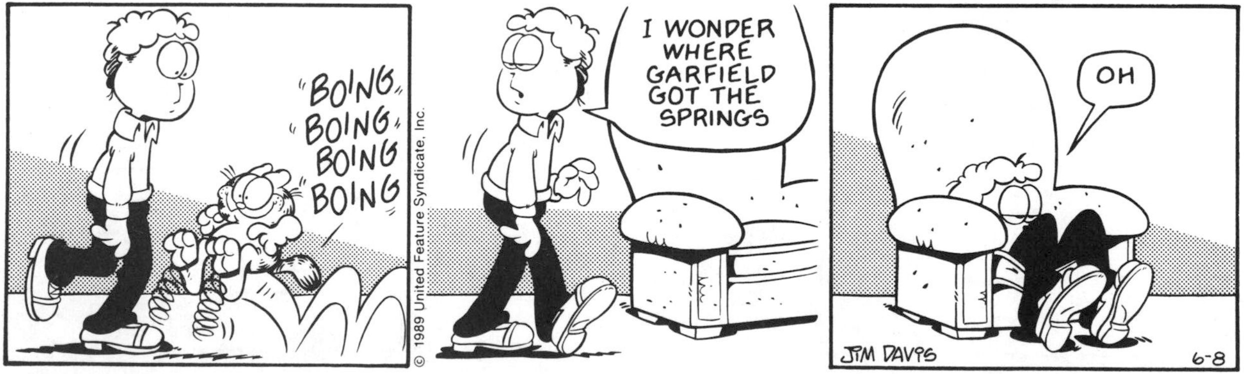
"BOING" "BOING" BOING "BOING
I WONDER WHERE GARFIELD GOT THE SPRINGS
OH
JIM DAVIS 6-8
© 1989 United Feature Syndicate, Inc.

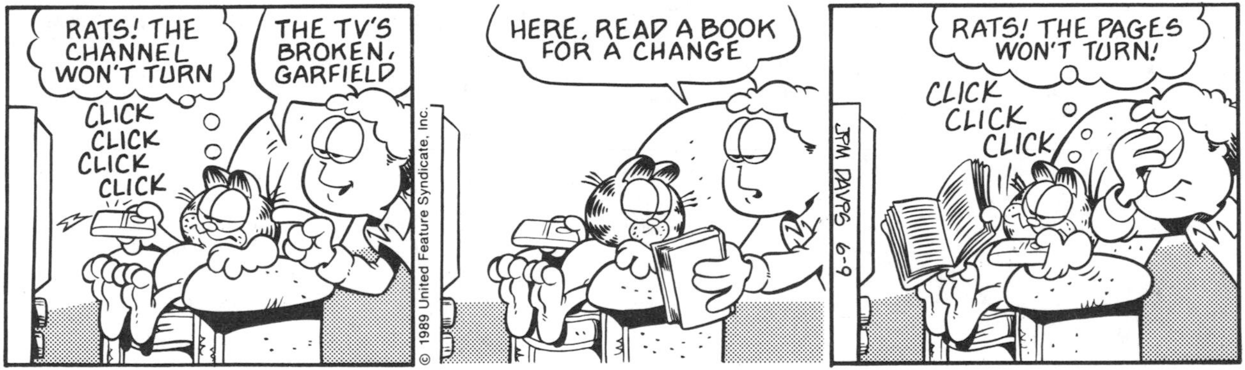
RATS! THE CHANNEL WON'T TURN
THE TV'S BROKEN, GARFIELD
CLICK CLICK CLICK CLICK
© 1989 United Feature Syndicate, Inc.
HERE, READ A BOOK FOR A CHANGE
JIM DAVIS 6-9
RATS! THE PAGES WON'T TURN!
CLICK CLICK CLICK

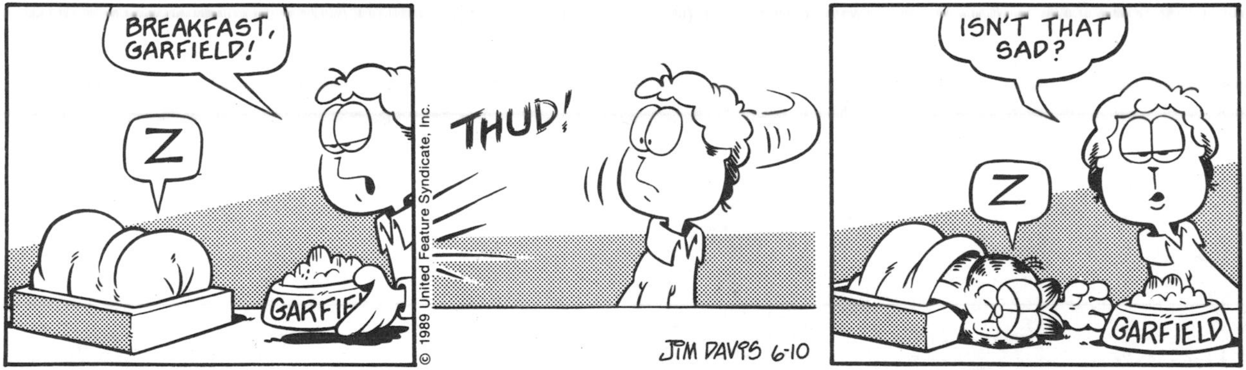
BREAKFAST, GARFIELD!
Z
GARFIE
© 1989 United Feature Syndicate, Inc.
THUD!
JIM DAVIS 6-10
ISN'T THAT SAD?
Z
GARFIELD

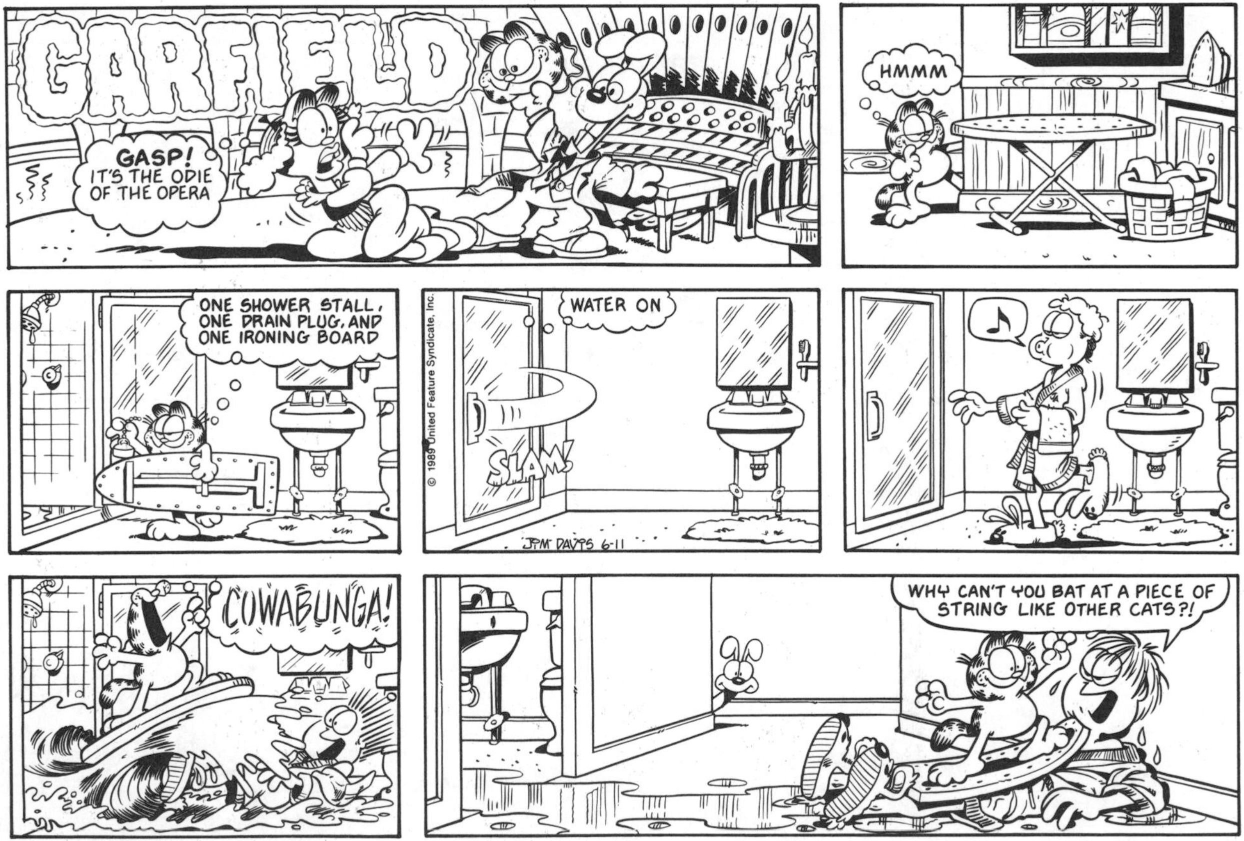
GARFIELD
GASP! IT'S THE ODIE OF THE OPERA
HMMM
ONE SHOWER STALL, ONE DRAIN PLUG, AND ONE IRONING BOARD
© 1989 United Feature Syndicate, Inc.
WATER ON
SLAM!
JIM DAVIS 6-11
COWABUNGA!
WHY CAN'T YOU BAT AT A PIECE OF STRING LIKE OTHER CATS?!

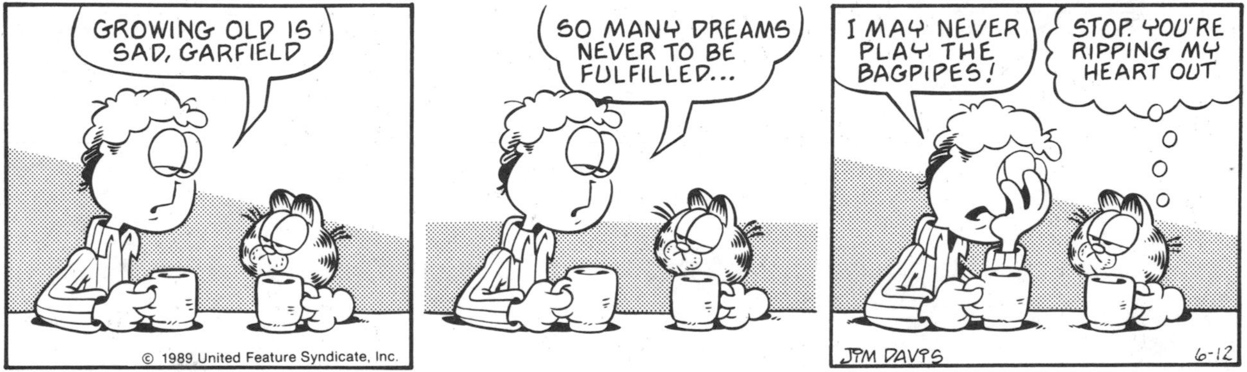
GROWING OLD IS SAD, GARFIELD
© 1989 United Feature Syndicate, Inc.
SO MANY DREAMS NEVER TO BE FULFILLED...
I MAY NEVER PLAY THE BAGPIPES!
STOP. YOU'RE RIPPING MY HEART OUT
JIM DAVIS
6-12

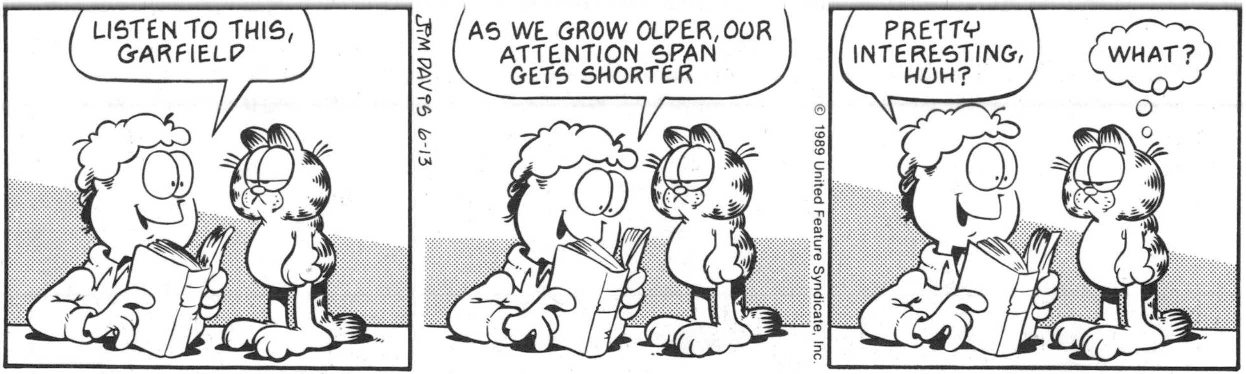
LISTEN TO THIS, GARFIELD
JIM DAVIS 6-13
AS WE GROW OLDER, OUR ATTENTION SPAN GETS SHORTER
© 1989 United Feature Syndicate, Inc.
PRETTY INTERESTING, HUH?
WHAT?

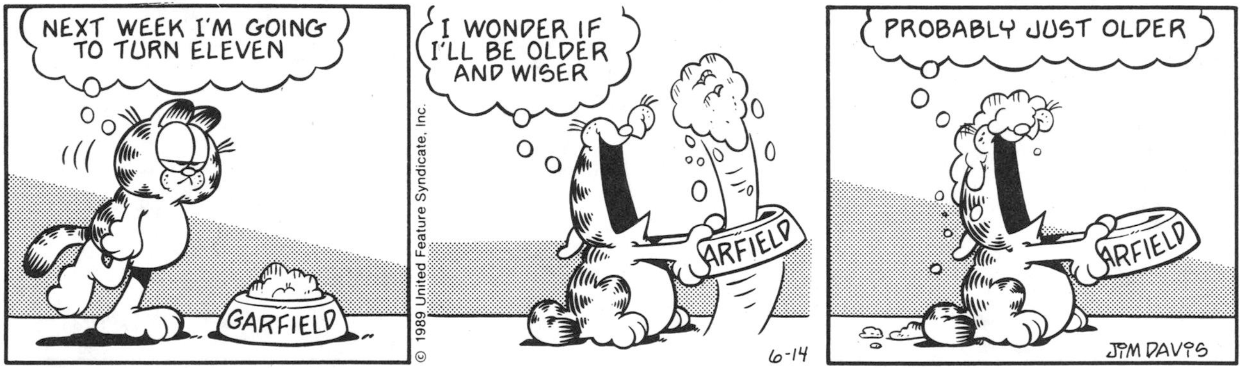
NEXT WEEK I'M GOING TO TURN ELEVEN
GARFIELD
© 1989 United Feature Syndicate, Inc.
I WONDER IF I'LL BE OLDER AND WISER
ARFIELD
6-14
PROBABLY JUST OLDER
ARFIELD
JIM DAVIS

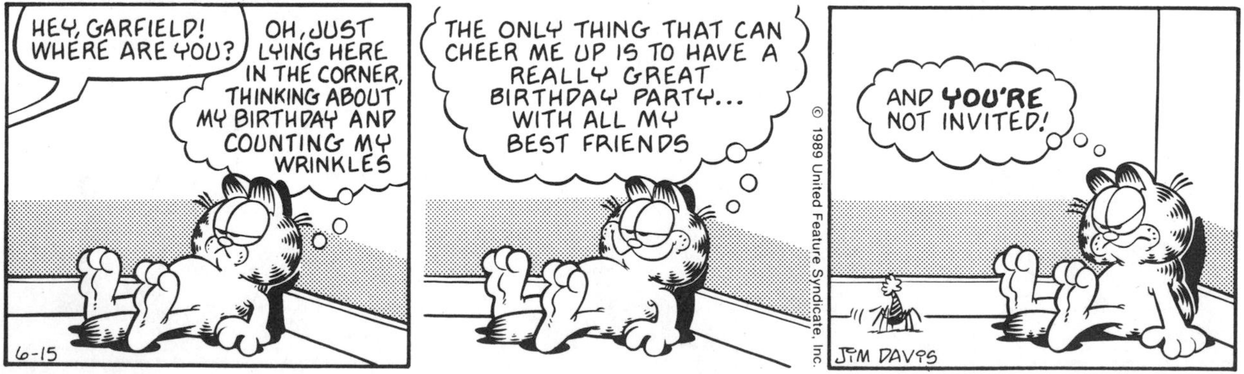
HEY, GARFIELD! WHERE ARE YOU?
OH, JUST LYING HERE IN THE CORNER, THINKING ABOUT MY BIRTHDAY AND COUNTING MY WRINKLES
6-15
THE ONLY THING THAT CAN CHEER ME UP IS TO HAVE A REALLY GREAT BIRTHDAY PARTY... WITH ALL MY BEST FRIENDS
© 1989 United Feature Syndicate, Inc.
AND **YOU'RE** NOT INVITED!
JIM DAVIS

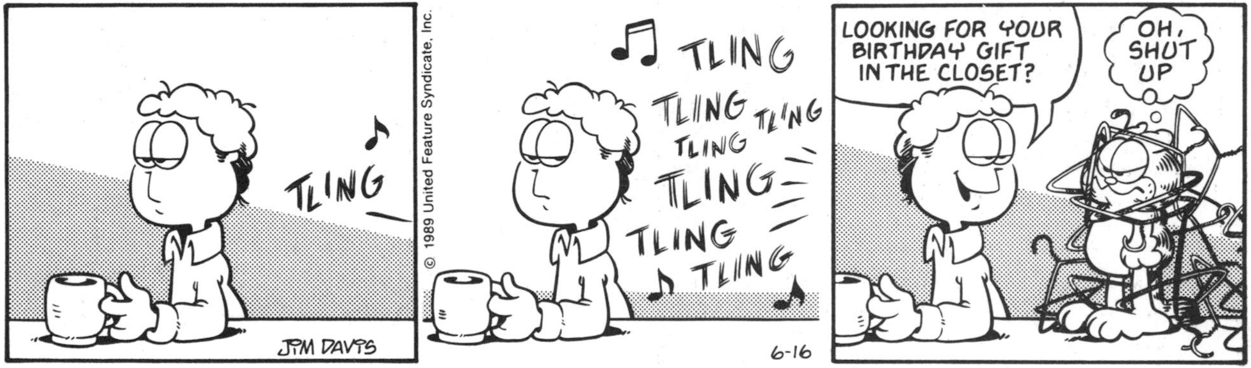
TLING
JIM DAVIS
© 1989 United Feature Syndicate, Inc.
TLING TLING TLING TLING TLING TLING TLING TLING
6-16
LOOKING FOR YOUR BIRTHDAY GIFT IN THE CLOSET?
OH, SHUT UP

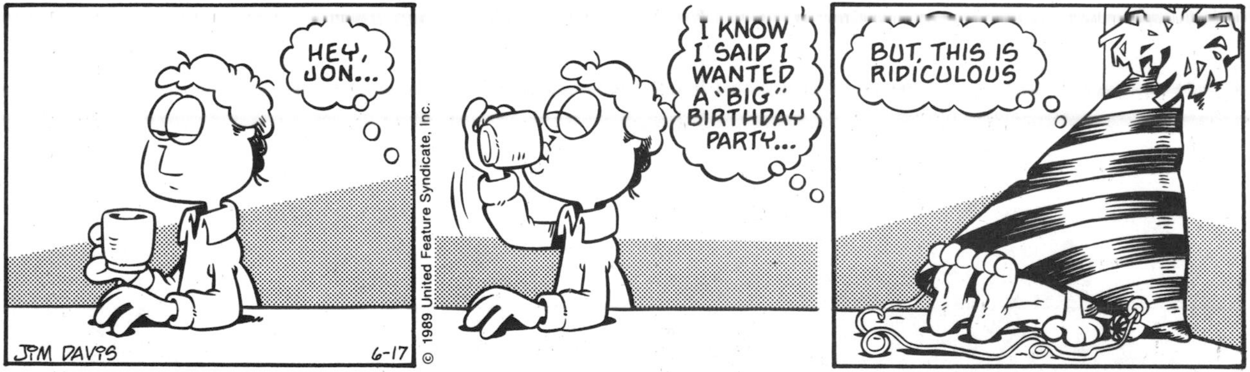
HEY, JON...
JIM DAVIS
6-17
© 1989 United Feature Syndicate, Inc.
I KNOW I SAID I WANTED A "BIG" BIRTHDAY PARTY...
BUT, THIS IS RIDICULOUS

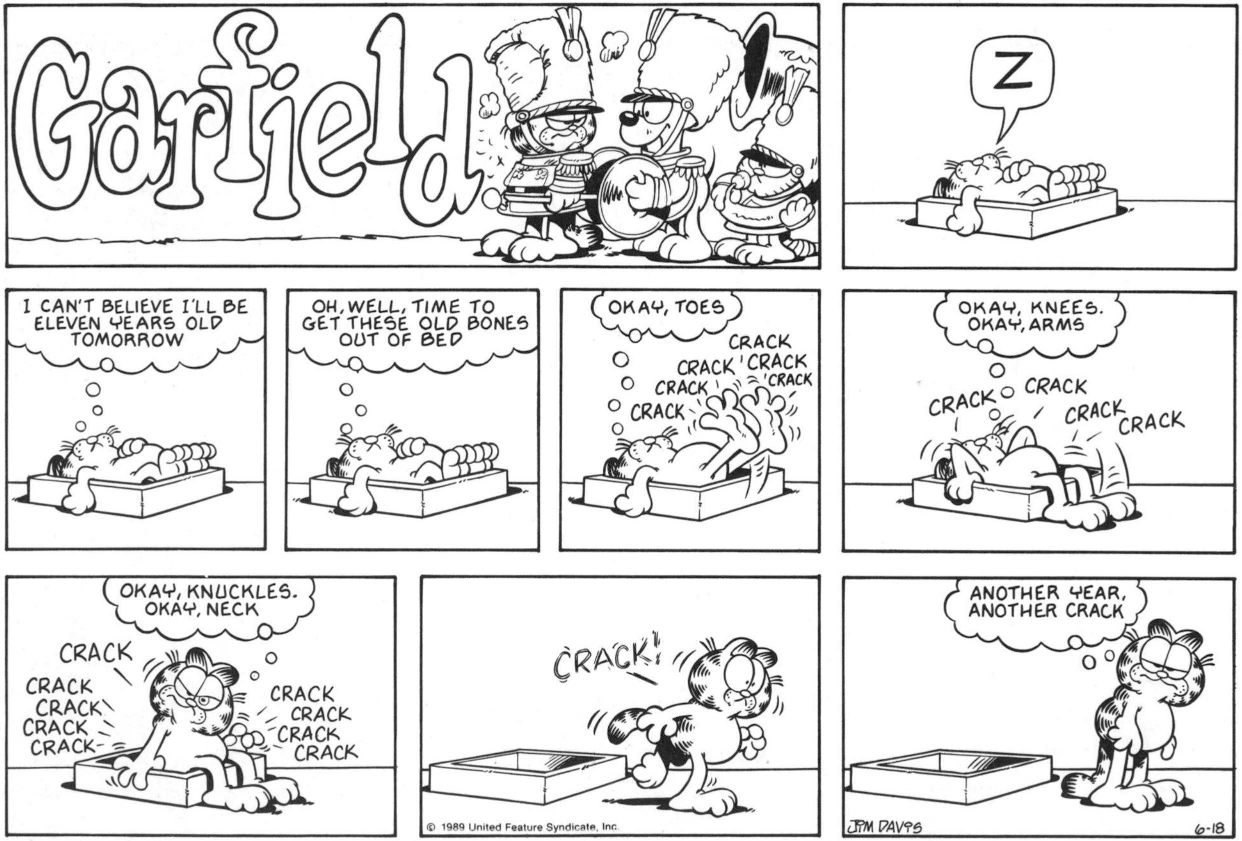
Garfield
Z
I CAN'T BELIEVE I'LL BE ELEVEN YEARS OLD TOMORROW
OH, WELL, TIME TO GET THESE OLD BONES OUT OF BED
OKAY, TOES
CRACK CRACK CRACK CRACK CRACK CRACK
OKAY, KNEES. OKAY, ARMS
CRACK CRACK CRACK CRACK
OKAY, KNUCKLES. OKAY, NECK
CRACK CRACK CRACK CRACK CRACK CRACK CRACK CRACK CRACK
CRACK!
© 1989 United Feature Syndicate, Inc.
ANOTHER YEAR, ANOTHER CRACK
JIM DAVIS
6-18

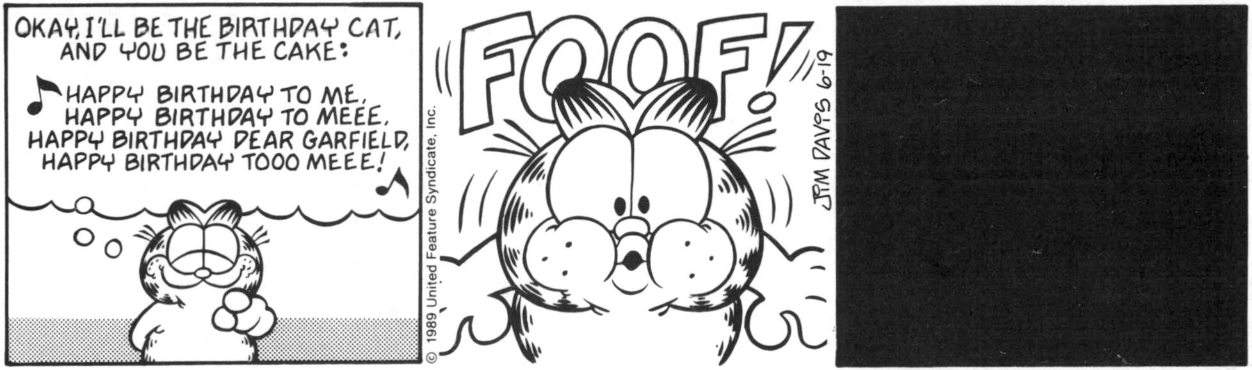
OKAY, I'LL BE THE BIRTHDAY CAT, AND YOU BE THE CAKE:
HAPPY BIRTHDAY TO ME, HAPPY BIRTHDAY TO MEEE, HAPPY BIRTHDAY DEAR GARFIELD, HAPPY BIRTHDAY TOOO MEEE!
FOOF!
© 1989 United Feature Syndicate, Inc.
JIM DAVIS 6-19

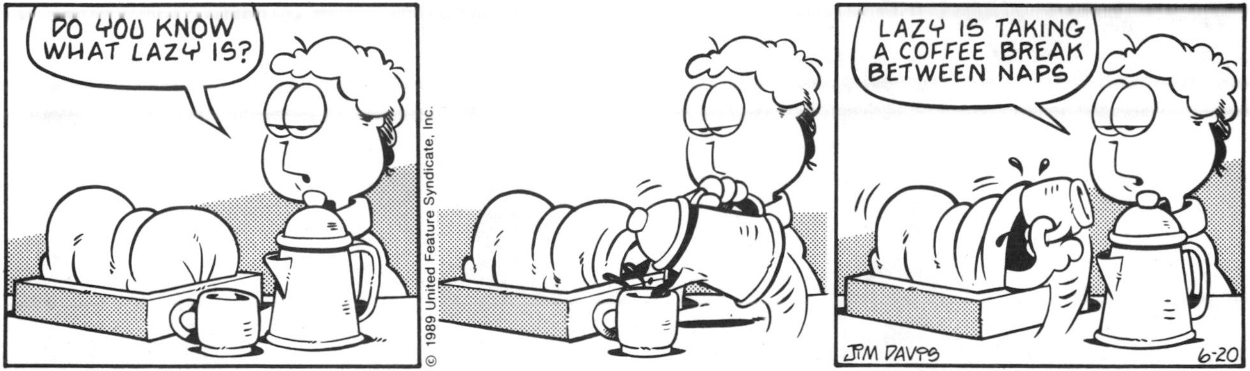
DO YOU KNOW WHAT LAZY IS?
© 1989 United Feature Syndicate, Inc.
LAZY IS TAKING A COFFEE BREAK BETWEEN NAPS
JIM DAVIS
6-20

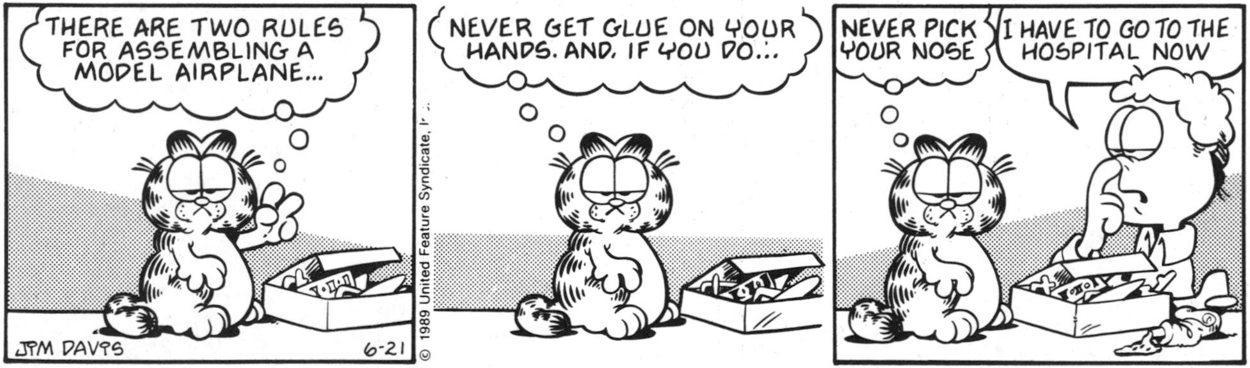
THERE ARE TWO RULES FOR ASSEMBLING A MODEL AIRPLANE...
JIM DAVIS
6-21
© 1989 United Feature Syndicate, Inc.
NEVER GET GLUE ON YOUR HANDS. AND, IF YOU DO...
NEVER PICK YOUR NOSE
I HAVE TO GO TO THE HOSPITAL NOW

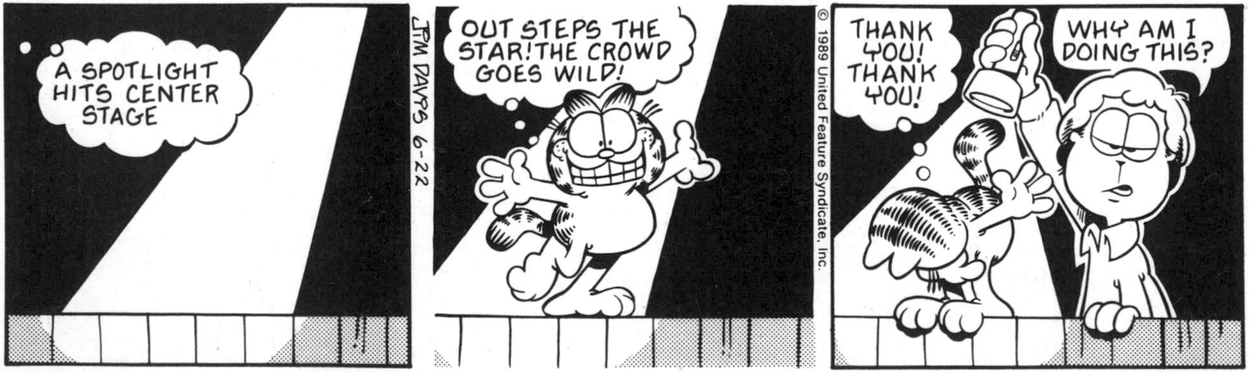
A SPOTLIGHT HITS CENTER STAGE
JIM DAVIS 6-22
OUT STEPS THE STAR! THE CROWD GOES WILD!
© 1989 United Feature Syndicate, Inc.
THANK YOU! THANK YOU!
WHY AM I DOING THIS?

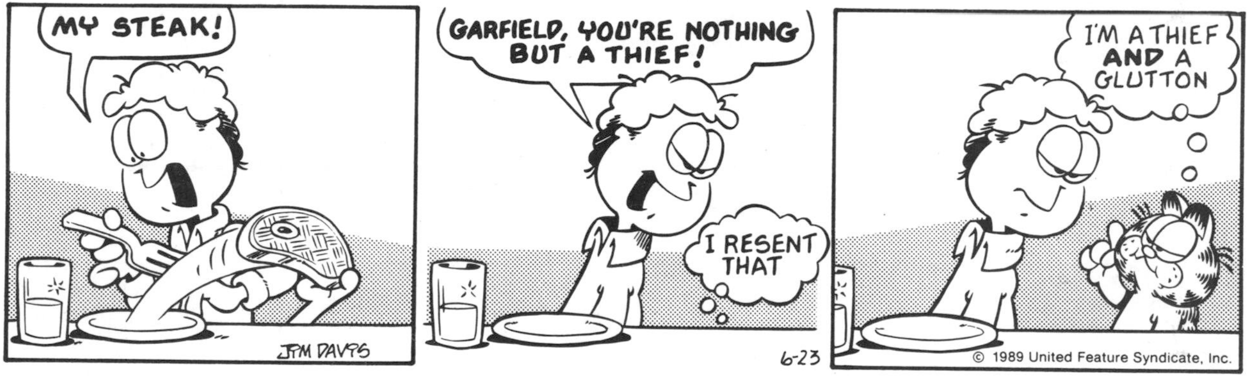
MY STEAK!
GARFIELD, YOU'RE NOTHING BUT A THIEF!
I RESENT THAT
I'M A THIEF AND A GLUTTON
JIM DAVIS
6-23
© 1989 United Feature Syndicate, Inc.

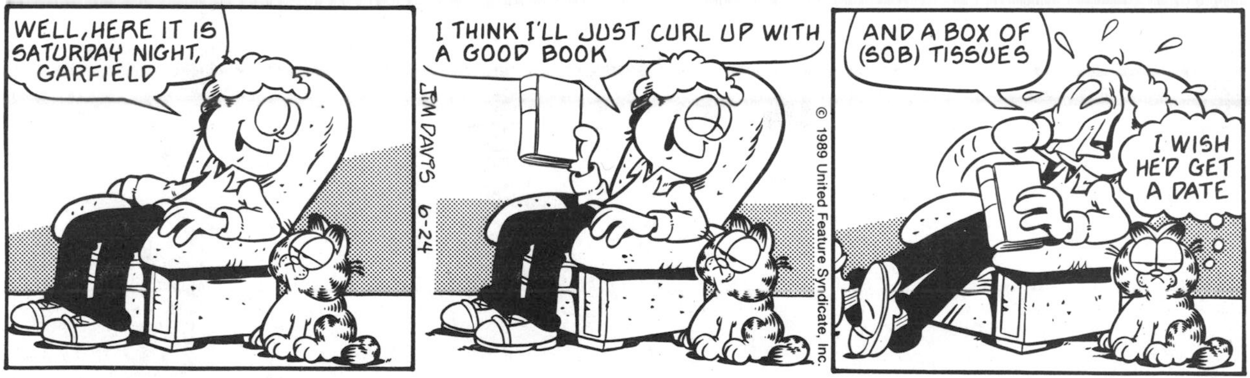
WELL, HERE IT IS SATURDAY NIGHT, GARFIELD
JIM DAVIS
6-24
I THINK I'LL JUST CURL UP WITH A GOOD BOOK
© 1989 United Feature Syndicate, Inc.
AND A BOX OF (SOB) TISSUES
I WISH HE'D GET A DATE

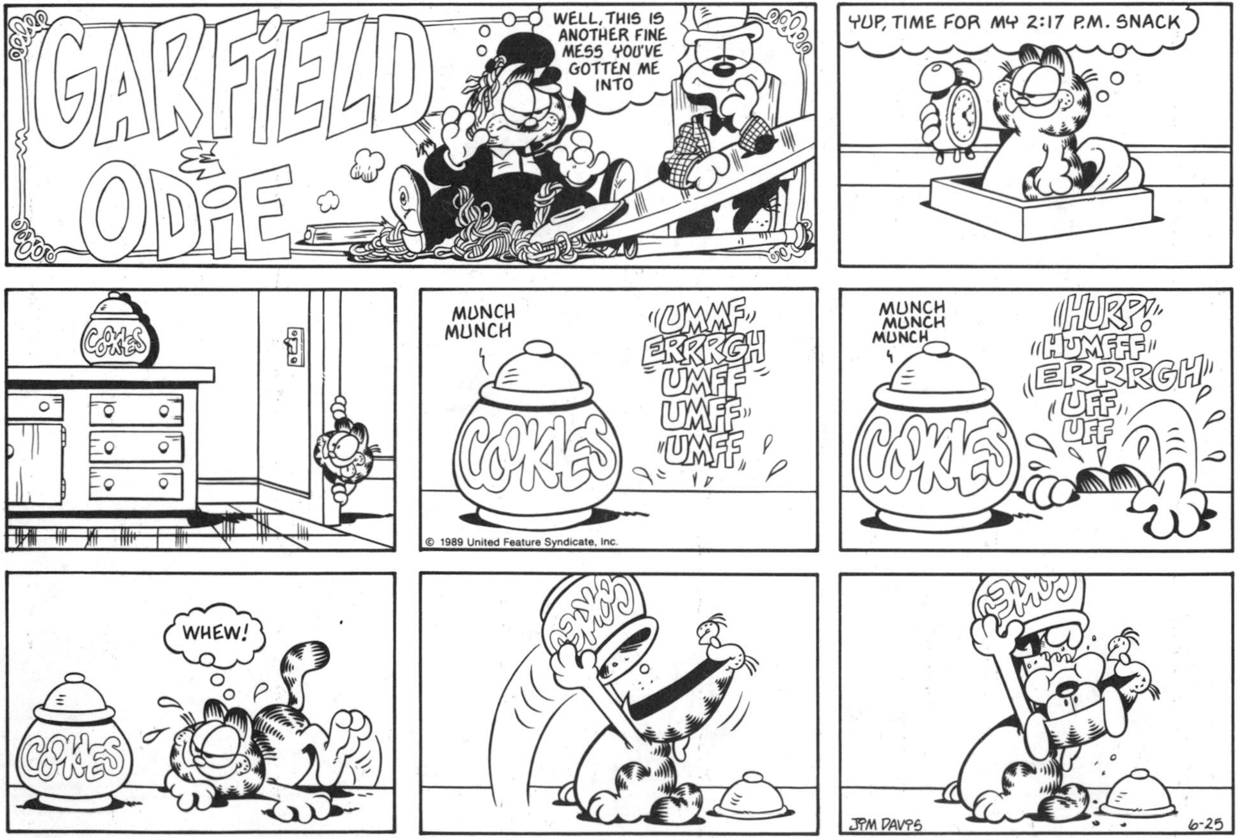
GARFIELD & ODIE
WELL, THIS IS ANOTHER FINE MESS YOU'VE GOTTEN ME INTO
YUP, TIME FOR MY 2:17 P.M. SNACK
COOKIES
MUNCH MUNCH
UMMF ERRRGH UMFF UMFF UMFF
MUNCH MUNCH MUNCH
HURP! HUMFFF ERRRGH UFF UFF
WHEW!
JIM DAVIS
6-25

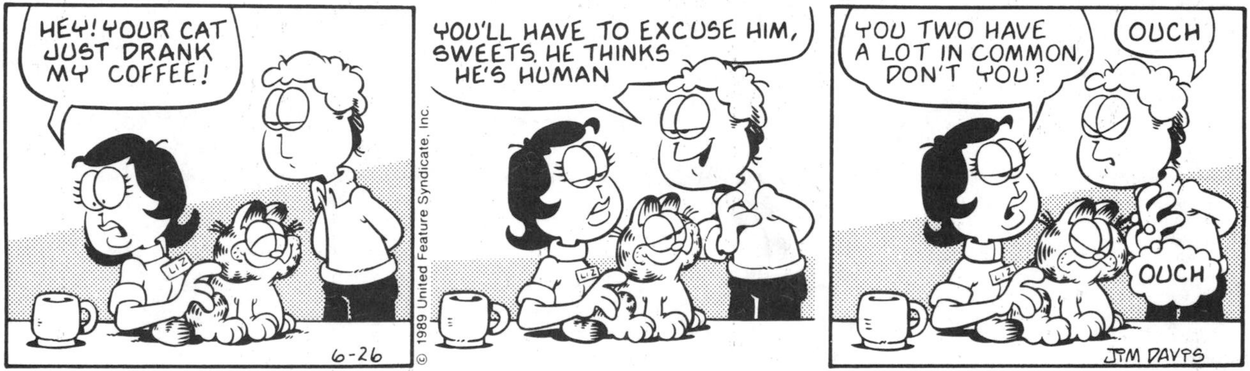
HEY! YOUR CAT JUST DRANK MY COFFEE!
6-26
© 1989 United Feature Syndicate, Inc.
YOU'LL HAVE TO EXCUSE HIM, SWEETS. HE THINKS HE'S HUMAN
YOU TWO HAVE A LOT IN COMMON, DON'T YOU?
OUCH
OUCH
JIM DAVIS

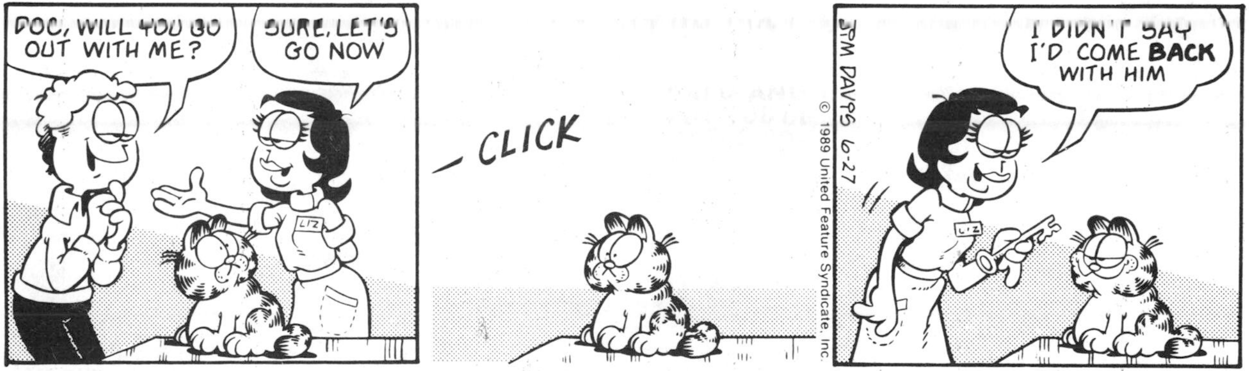
DOC, WILL YOU GO OUT WITH ME?
SURE, LET'S GO NOW
— CLICK
JIM DAVIS 6-27
© 1989 United Feature Syndicate, Inc.
I DIDN'T SAY I'D COME **BACK** WITH HIM

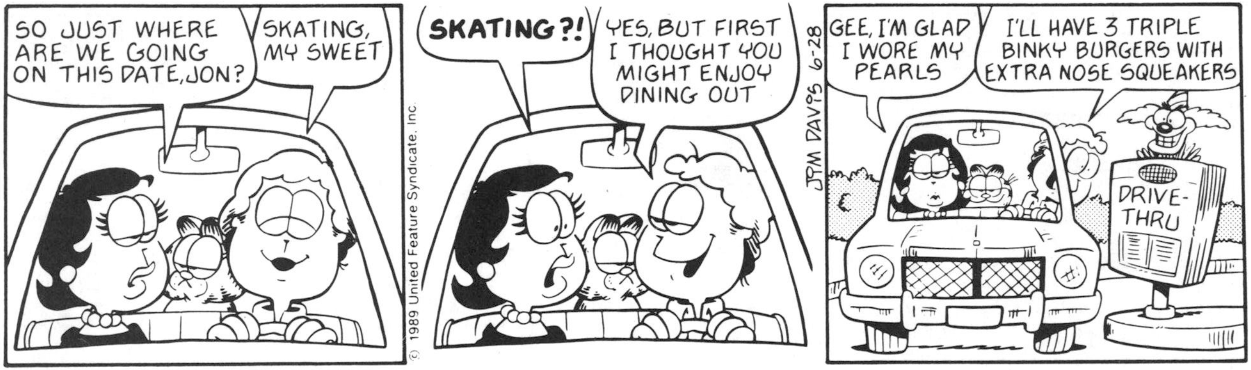
SO JUST WHERE ARE WE GOING ON THIS DATE, JON?
SKATING, MY SWEET
SKATING?!
YES, BUT FIRST I THOUGHT YOU MIGHT ENJOY DINING OUT
GEE, I'M GLAD I WORE MY PEARLS
I'LL HAVE 3 TRIPLE BINKY BURGERS WITH EXTRA NOSE SQUEAKERS
DRIVE-THRU
JIM DAVIS 6-28
© 1989 United Feature Syndicate, Inc.

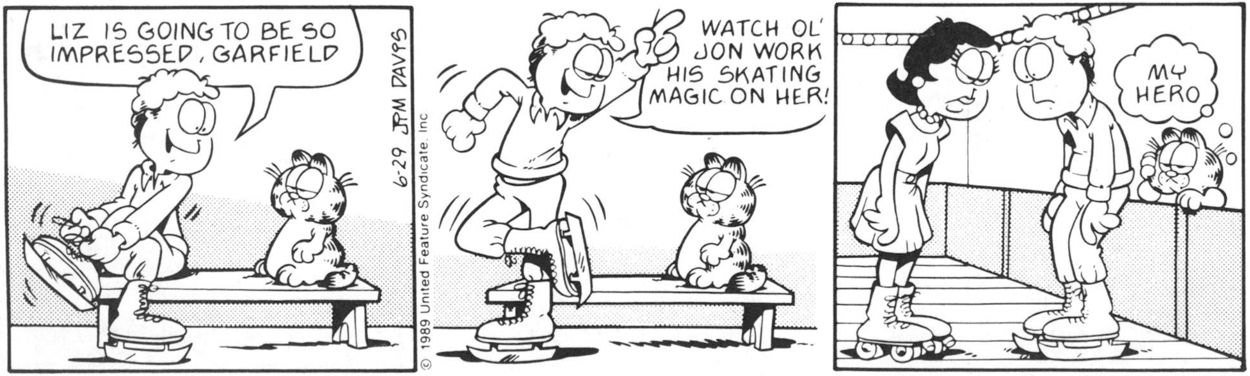
LIZ IS GOING TO BE SO IMPRESSED, GARFIELD
6-29 JIM DAVIS
WATCH OL' JON WORK HIS SKATING MAGIC ON HER!
MY HERO
© 1989 United Feature Syndicate, Inc

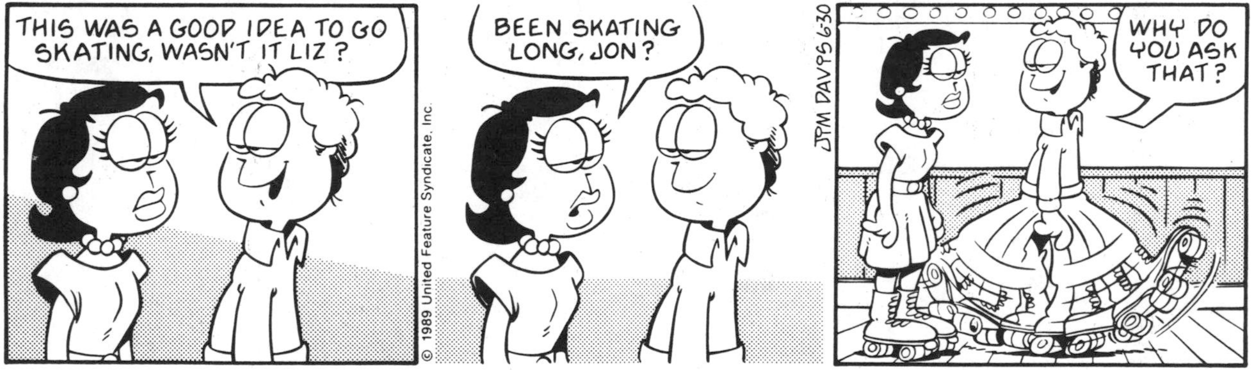
THIS WAS A GOOD IDEA TO GO SKATING, WASN'T IT LIZ?
BEEN SKATING LONG, JON?
WHY DO YOU ASK THAT?
JIM DAVIS 6-30
© 1989 United Feature Syndicate, Inc.

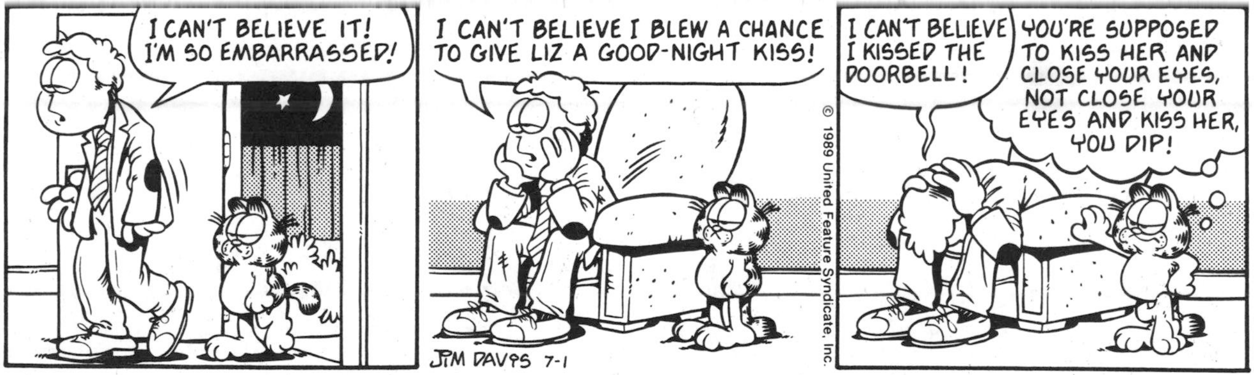
I CAN'T BELIEVE IT! I'M SO EMBARRASSED!
I CAN'T BELIEVE I BLEW A CHANCE TO GIVE LIZ A GOOD-NIGHT KISS!
I CAN'T BELIEVE I KISSED THE DOORBELL!
YOU'RE SUPPOSED TO KISS HER AND CLOSE YOUR EYES, NOT CLOSE YOUR EYES AND KISS HER, YOU DIP!
JIM DAVIS 7-1
© 1989 United Feature Syndicate, Inc.

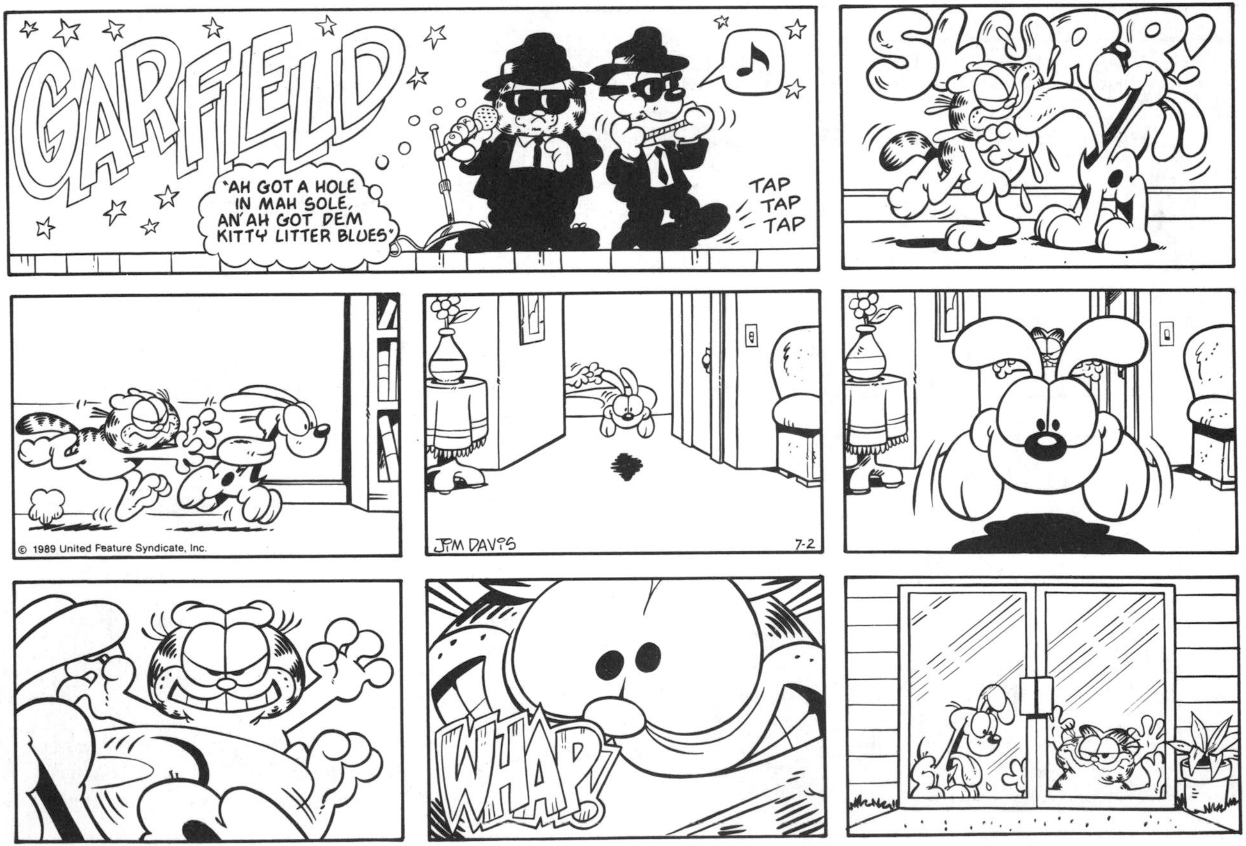
GARFIELD
"AH GOT A HOLE IN MAH SOLE, AN' AH GOT DEM KITTY LITTER BLUES"
TAP TAP TAP
SLURP!
© 1989 United Feature Syndicate, Inc.
JIM DAVIS
7-2
WHAP!

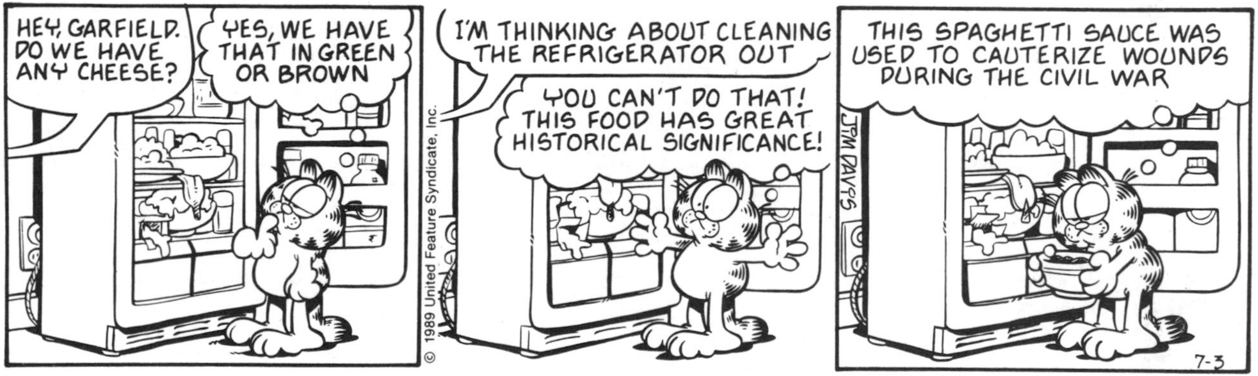
HEY, GARFIELD. DO WE HAVE ANY CHEESE?
YES, WE HAVE THAT IN GREEN OR BROWN
I'M THINKING ABOUT CLEANING THE REFRIGERATOR OUT
YOU CAN'T DO THAT! THIS FOOD HAS GREAT HISTORICAL SIGNIFICANCE!
THIS SPAGHETTI SAUCE WAS USED TO CAUTERIZE WOUNDS DURING THE CIVIL WAR
JIM DAVIS
7-3

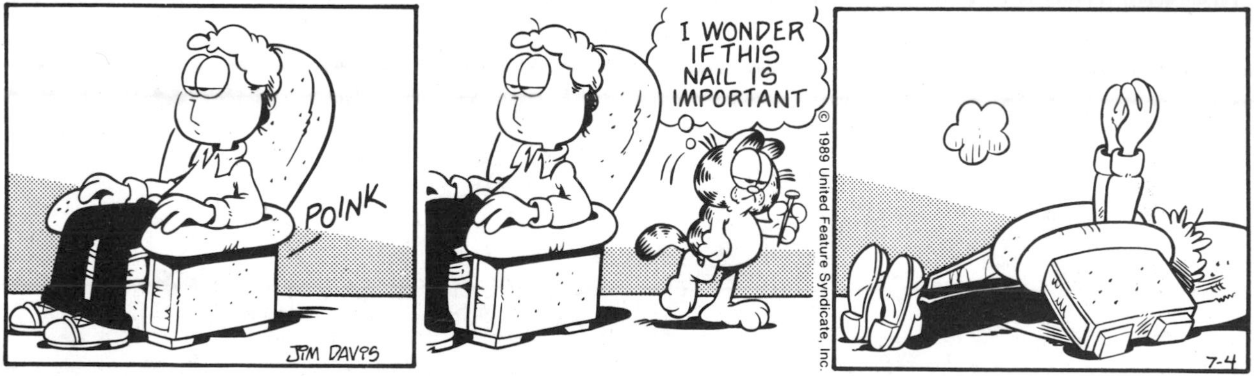
POINK
JIM DAVIS
I WONDER IF THIS NAIL IS IMPORTANT
7-4

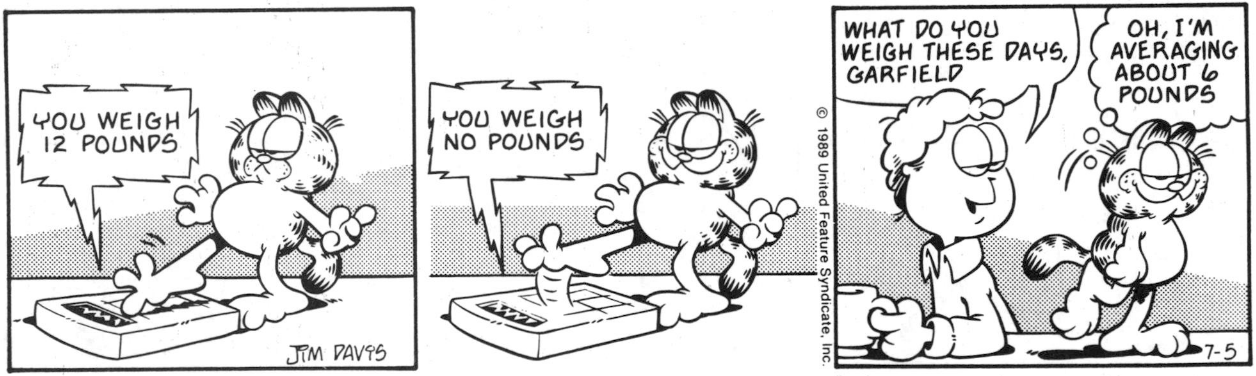
YOU WEIGH 12 POUNDS
JIM DAVIS
YOU WEIGH NO POUNDS
© 1989 United Feature Syndicate, Inc.
WHAT DO YOU WEIGH THESE DAYS, GARFIELD
OH, I'M AVERAGING ABOUT 6 POUNDS
7-5

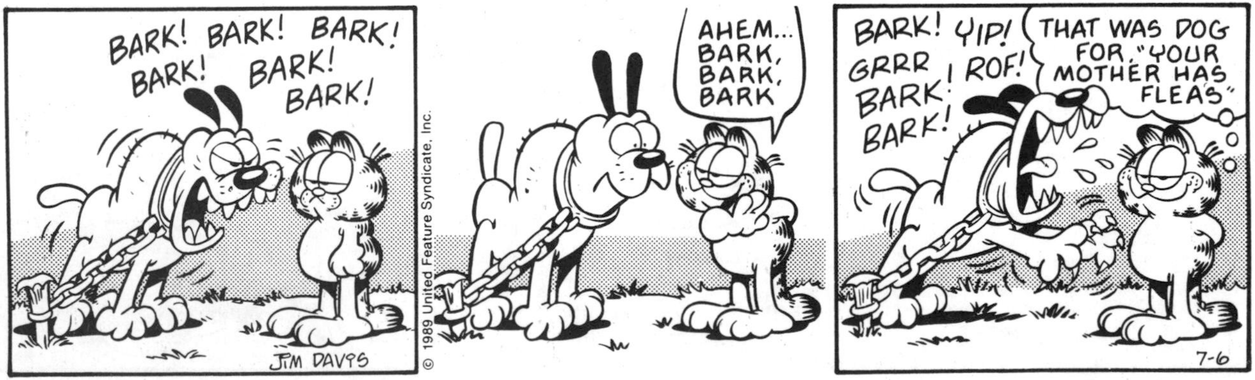
BARK! BARK! BARK! BARK! BARK! BARK!
JIM DAVIS
© 1989 United Feature Syndicate, Inc.
AHEM... BARK, BARK, BARK
BARK! GRRR BARK! BARK!
YIP! ROF!
THAT WAS DOG FOR "YOUR MOTHER HAS FLEAS"
7-6

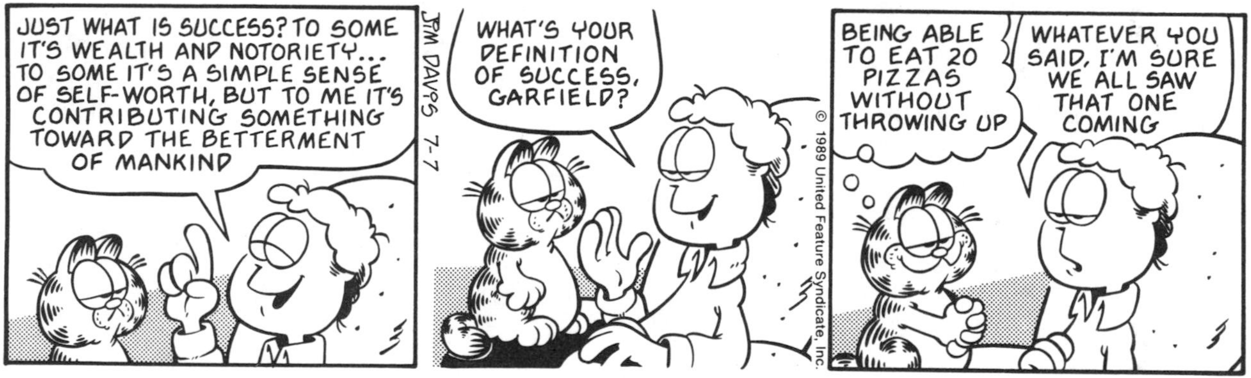
JUST WHAT IS SUCCESS? TO SOME IT'S WEALTH AND NOTORIETY... TO SOME IT'S A SIMPLE SENSE OF SELF-WORTH, BUT TO ME IT'S CONTRIBUTING SOMETHING TOWARD THE BETTERMENT OF MANKIND
JIM DAVIS 7-7
WHAT'S YOUR DEFINITION OF SUCCESS, GARFIELD?
© 1989 United Feature Syndicate, Inc.
BEING ABLE TO EAT 20 PIZZAS WITHOUT THROWING UP
WHATEVER YOU SAID, I'M SURE WE ALL SAW THAT ONE COMING

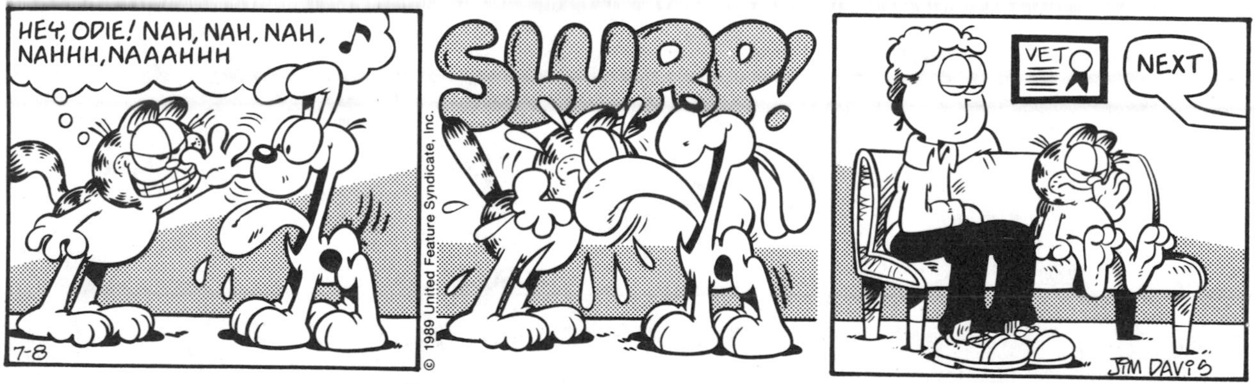
HEY, ODIE! NAH, NAH, NAH, NAHHH, NAAAHHH
7-8
© 1989 United Feature Syndicate, Inc.
SLURP!
VET
NEXT
JIM DAVIS

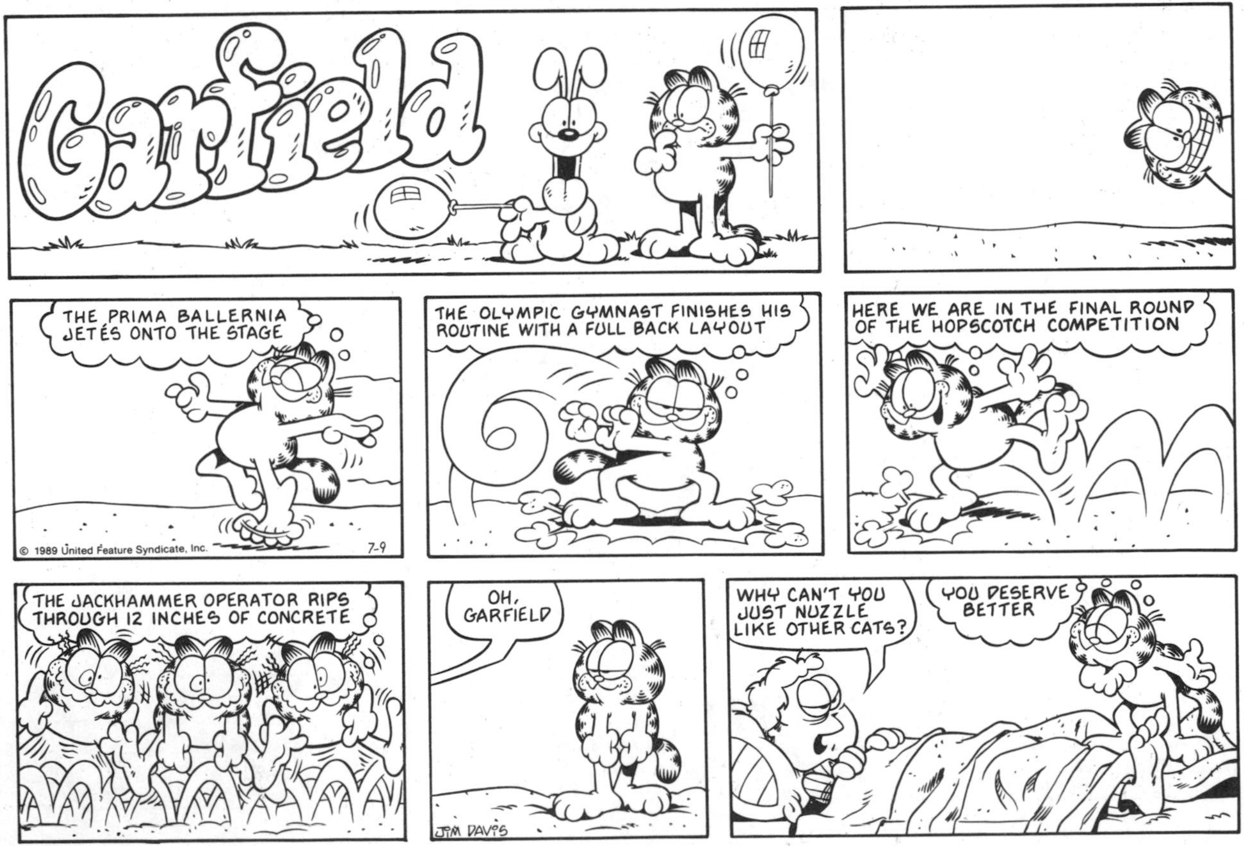
Garfield
THE PRIMA BALLERNIA JETÉS ONTO THE STAGE
© 1989 United Feature Syndicate, Inc.
7-9
THE OLYMPIC GYMNAST FINISHES HIS ROUTINE WITH A FULL BACK LAYOUT
HERE WE ARE IN THE FINAL ROUND OF THE HOPSCOTCH COMPETITION
THE JACKHAMMER OPERATOR RIPS THROUGH 12 INCHES OF CONCRETE
OH, GARFIELD
JIM DAVIS
WHY CAN'T YOU JUST NUZZLE LIKE OTHER CATS?
YOU DESERVE BETTER

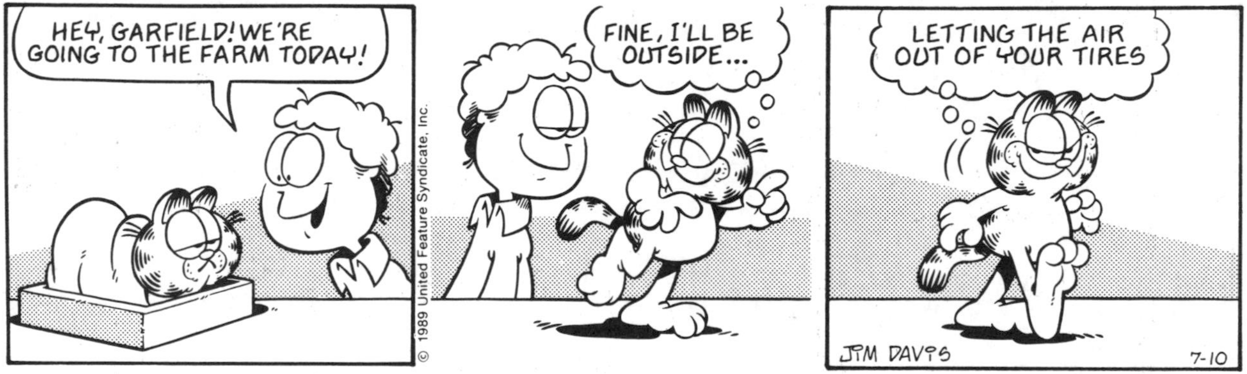
HEY, GARFIELD! WE'RE GOING TO THE FARM TODAY!
FINE, I'LL BE OUTSIDE...
LETTING THE AIR OUT OF YOUR TIRES
JIM DAVIS
7-10

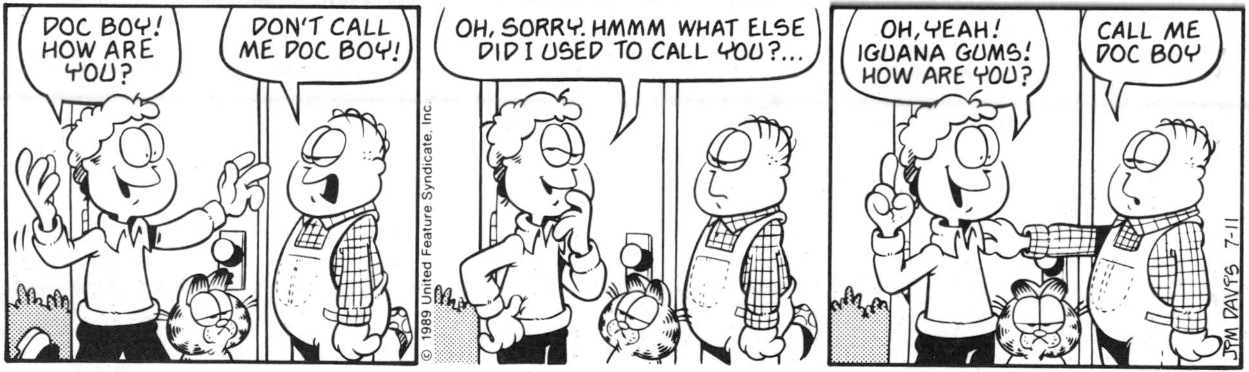
DOC BOY! HOW ARE YOU?
DON'T CALL ME DOC BOY!
OH, SORRY. HMMM WHAT ELSE DID I USED TO CALL YOU?...
OH, YEAH! IGUANA GUMS! HOW ARE YOU?
CALL ME DOC BOY
JIM DAVIS
7-11

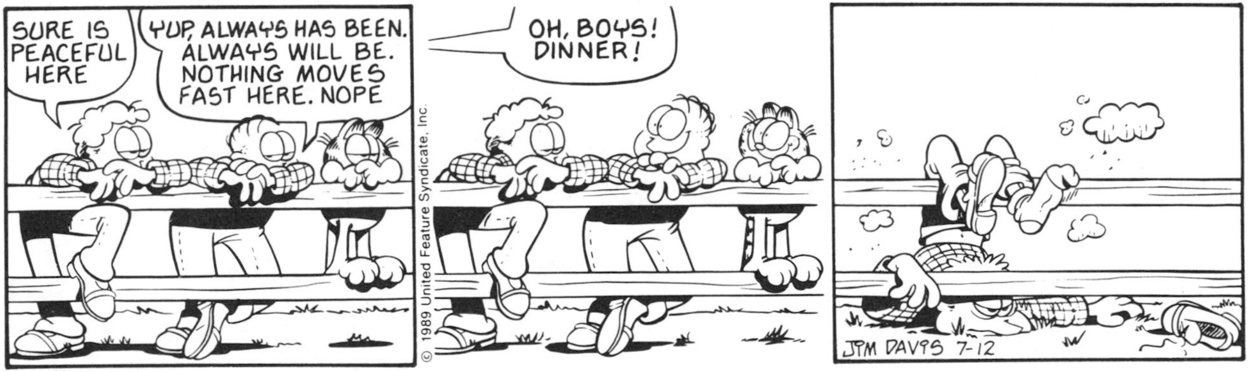
SURE IS PEACEFUL HERE
YUP, ALWAYS HAS BEEN. ALWAYS WILL BE. NOTHING MOVES FAST HERE. NOPE
OH, BOYS! DINNER!
JIM DAVIS 7-12
© 1989 United Feature Syndicate, Inc.

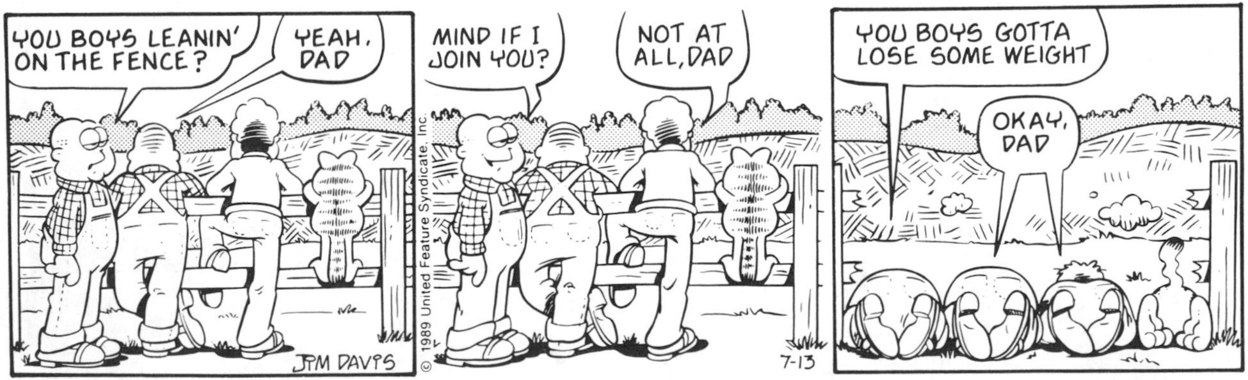
YOU BOYS LEANIN' ON THE FENCE?
YEAH, DAD
JIM DAVIS
MIND IF I JOIN YOU?
NOT AT ALL, DAD
7-13
YOU BOYS GOTTA LOSE SOME WEIGHT
OKAY, DAD
© 1989 United Feature Syndicate, Inc.

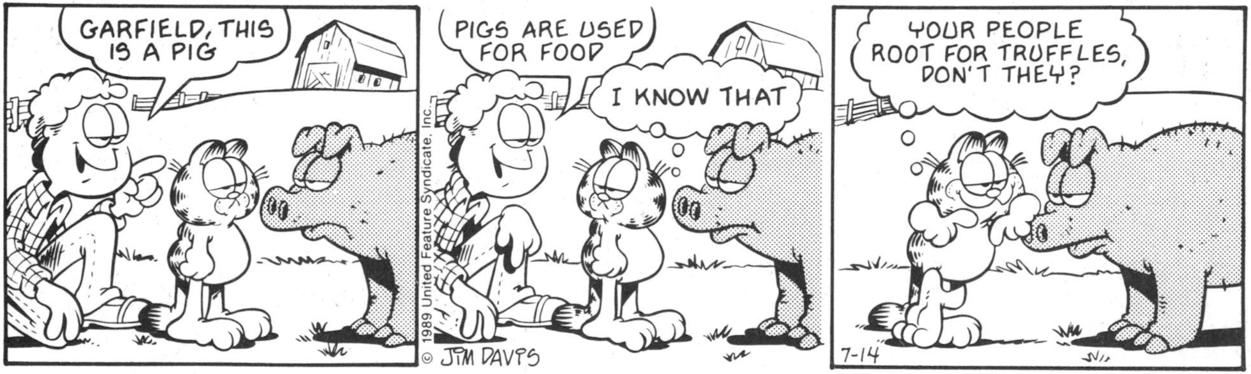
GARFIELD, THIS IS A PIG
PIGS ARE USED FOR FOOD
I KNOW THAT
YOUR PEOPLE ROOT FOR TRUFFLES, DON'T THEY?
© 1989 United Feature Syndicate, Inc.
JIM DAVIS
7-14

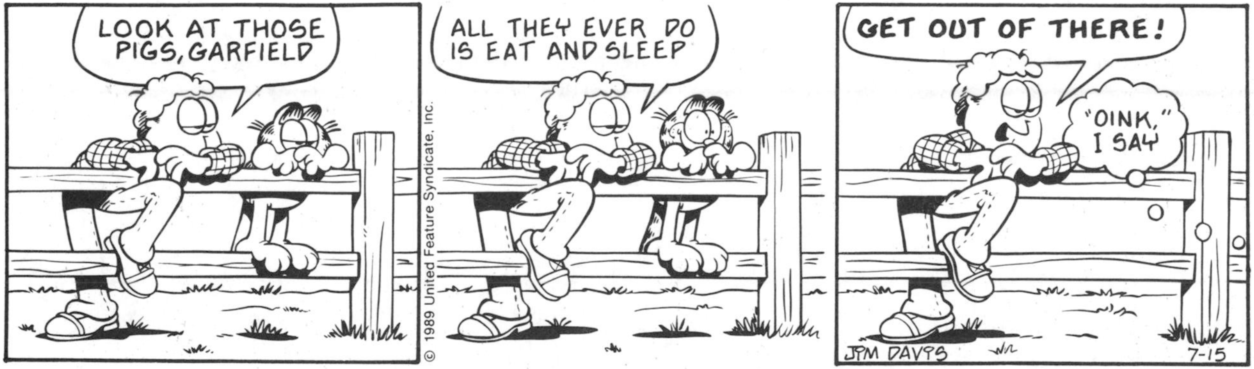
LOOK AT THOSE PIGS, GARFIELD
ALL THEY EVER DO IS EAT AND SLEEP
GET OUT OF THERE!
"OINK," I SAY
© 1989 United Feature Syndicate, Inc.
JIM DAVIS
7-15

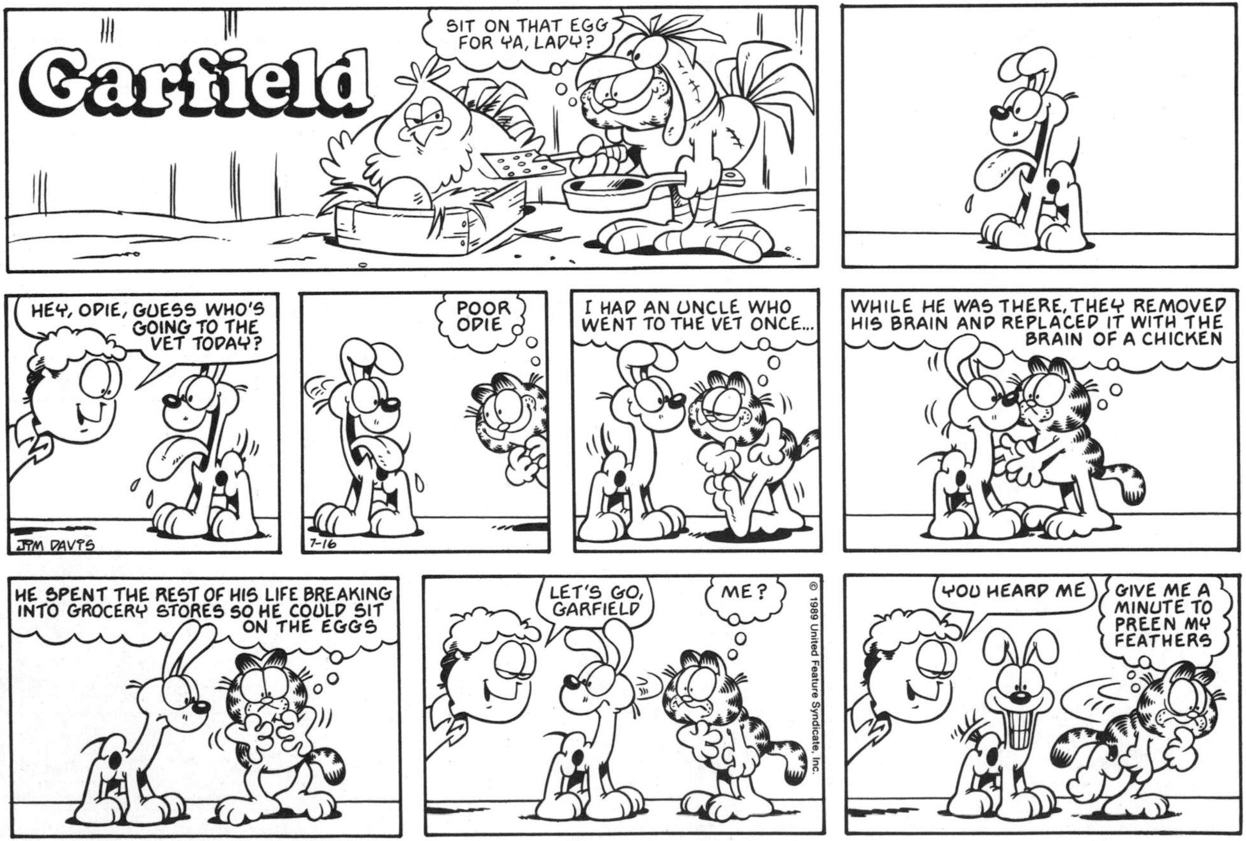
Garfield
SIT ON THAT EGG FOR YA, LADY?
HEY, ODIE, GUESS WHO'S GOING TO THE VET TODAY?
JIM DAVIS
POOR ODIE
7-16
I HAD AN UNCLE WHO WENT TO THE VET ONCE...
WHILE HE WAS THERE, THEY REMOVED HIS BRAIN AND REPLACED IT WITH THE BRAIN OF A CHICKEN
HE SPENT THE REST OF HIS LIFE BREAKING INTO GROCERY STORES SO HE COULD SIT ON THE EGGS
LET'S GO, GARFIELD
ME?
© 1989 United Feature Syndicate, Inc.
YOU HEARD ME
GIVE ME A MINUTE TO PREEN MY FEATHERS

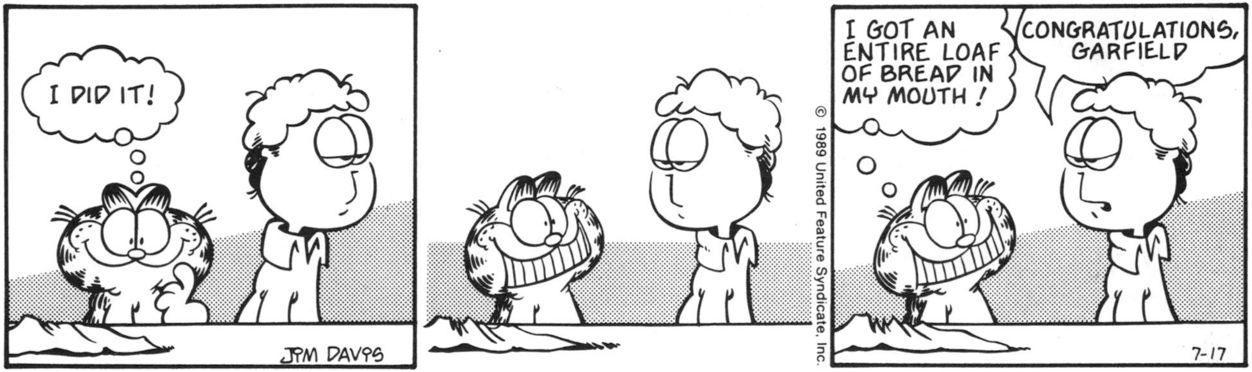
I DID IT!
JIM DAVIS
© 1989 United Feature Syndicate, Inc.
I GOT AN ENTIRE LOAF OF BREAD IN MY MOUTH!
CONGRATULATIONS, GARFIELD
7-17

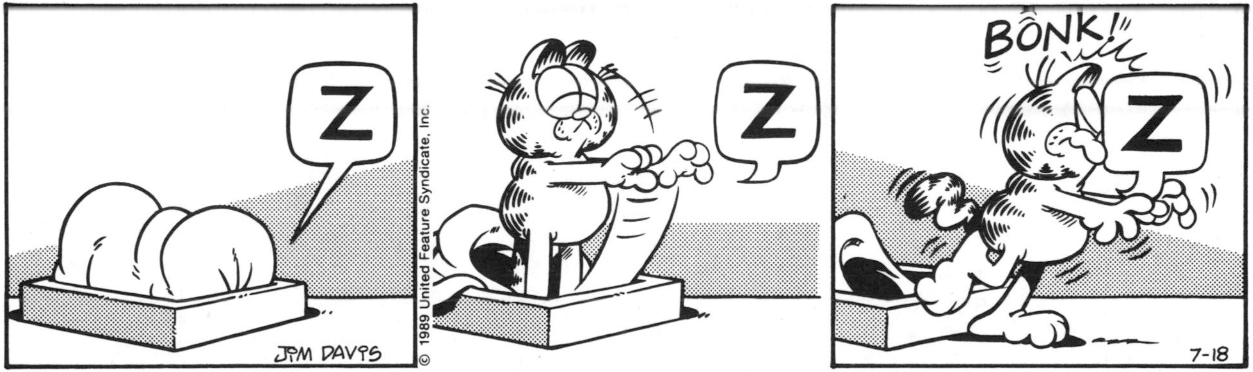
Z
JIM DAVIS
© 1989 United Feature Syndicate, Inc.
Z
BONK!
Z
7-18

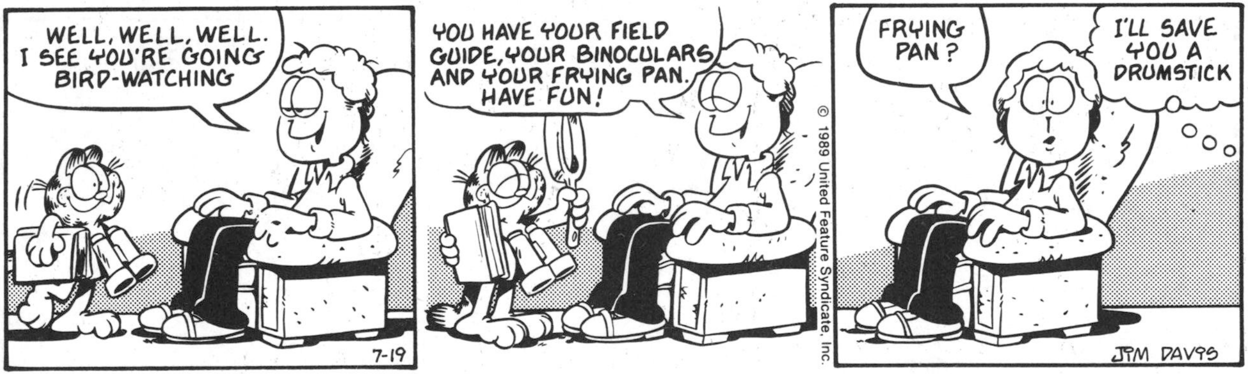
WELL, WELL, WELL. I SEE YOU'RE GOING BIRD-WATCHING
7-19
YOU HAVE YOUR FIELD GUIDE, YOUR BINOCULARS AND YOUR FRYING PAN. HAVE FUN!
© 1989 United Feature Syndicate, Inc.
FRYING PAN?
I'LL SAVE YOU A DRUMSTICK
JIM DAVIS

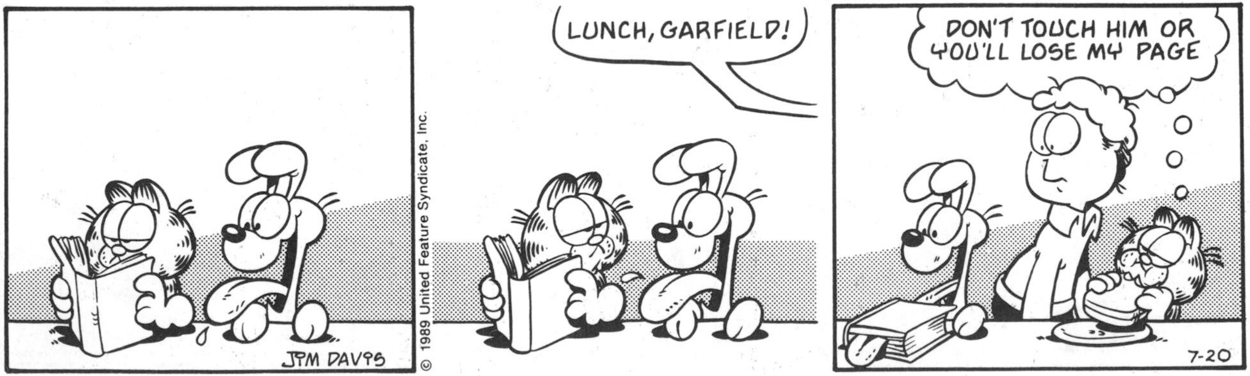
JIM DAVIS
© 1989 United Feature Syndicate, Inc.
LUNCH, GARFIELD!
DON'T TOUCH HIM OR YOU'LL LOSE MY PAGE
7-20

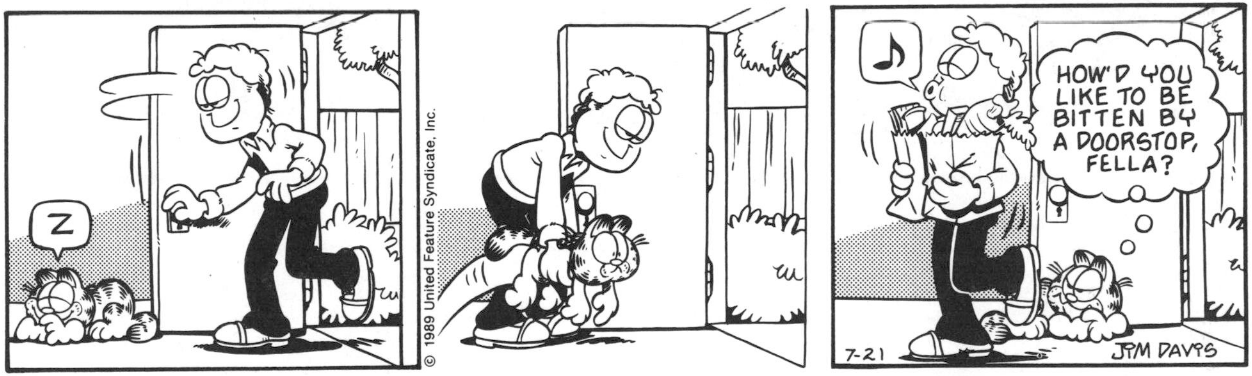
Z
© 1989 United Feature Syndicate, Inc.
♪
HOW'D YOU LIKE TO BE BITTEN BY A DOORSTOP, FELLA?
7-21
JIM DAVIS

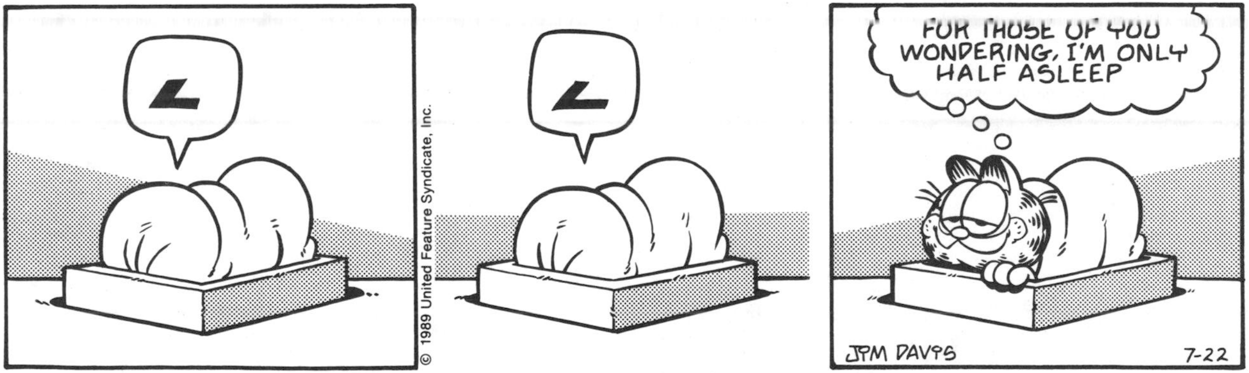
Z
© 1989 United Feature Syndicate, Inc.
Z
FOR THOSE OF YOU WONDERING, I'M ONLY HALF ASLEEP
JIM DAVIS
7-22

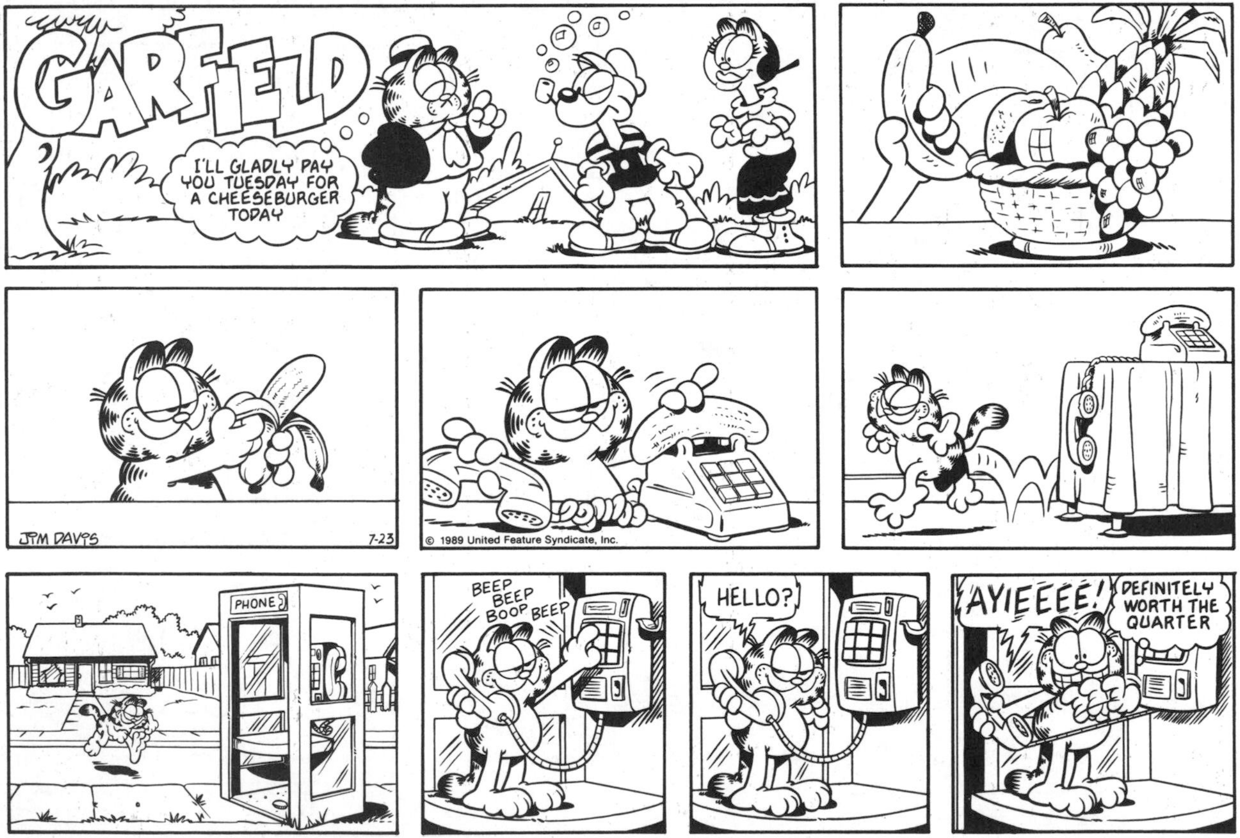
GARFIELD
I'LL GLADLY PAY YOU TUESDAY FOR A CHEESEBURGER TODAY
JIM DAVIS
7-23
© 1989 United Feature Syndicate, Inc.
PHONE
BEEP BEEP BOOP BEEP
HELLO?
AYIEEEE!
DEFINITELY WORTH THE QUARTER

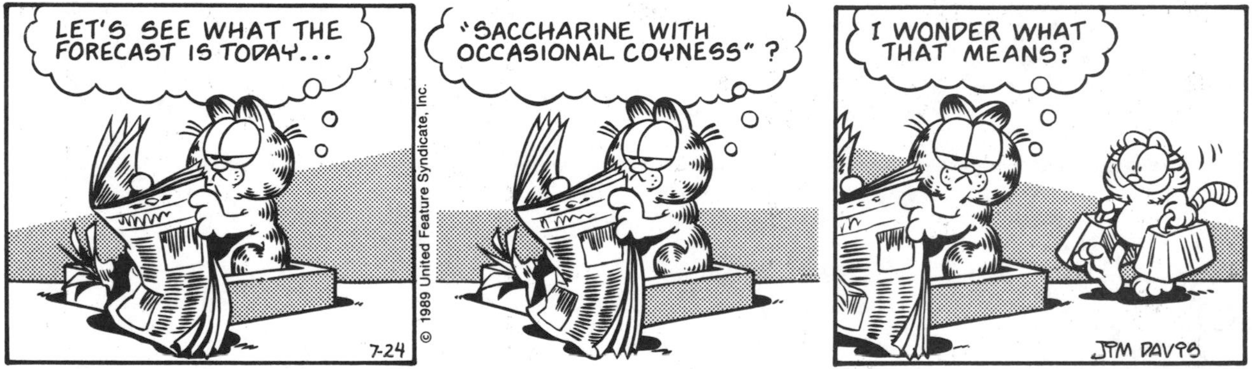
LET'S SEE WHAT THE FORECAST IS TODAY...
7-24
© 1989 United Feature Syndicate, Inc.
"SACCHARINE WITH OCCASIONAL COYNESS"?
I WONDER WHAT THAT MEANS?
JIM DAVIS

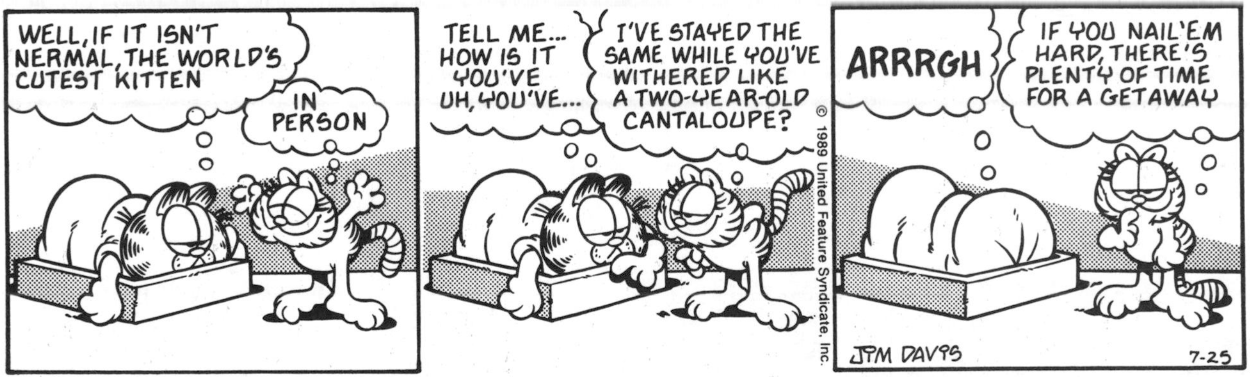
WELL, IF IT ISN'T NERMAL, THE WORLD'S CUTEST KITTEN
IN PERSON
TELL ME... HOW IS IT YOU'VE UH, YOU'VE...
I'VE STAYED THE SAME WHILE YOU'VE WITHERED LIKE A TWO-YEAR-OLD CANTALOUPE?
© 1989 United Feature Syndicate, Inc.
ARRRGH
IF YOU NAIL 'EM HARD, THERE'S PLENTY OF TIME FOR A GETAWAY
JIM DAVIS
7-25

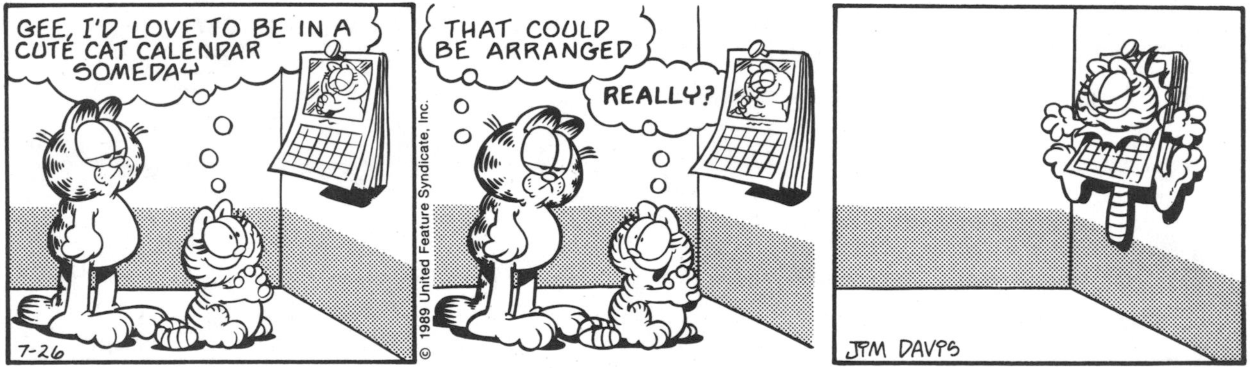
GEE, I'D LOVE TO BE IN A CUTE CAT CALENDAR SOMEDAY
7-26
© 1989 United Feature Syndicate, Inc.
THAT COULD BE ARRANGED
REALLY?
JIM DAVIS

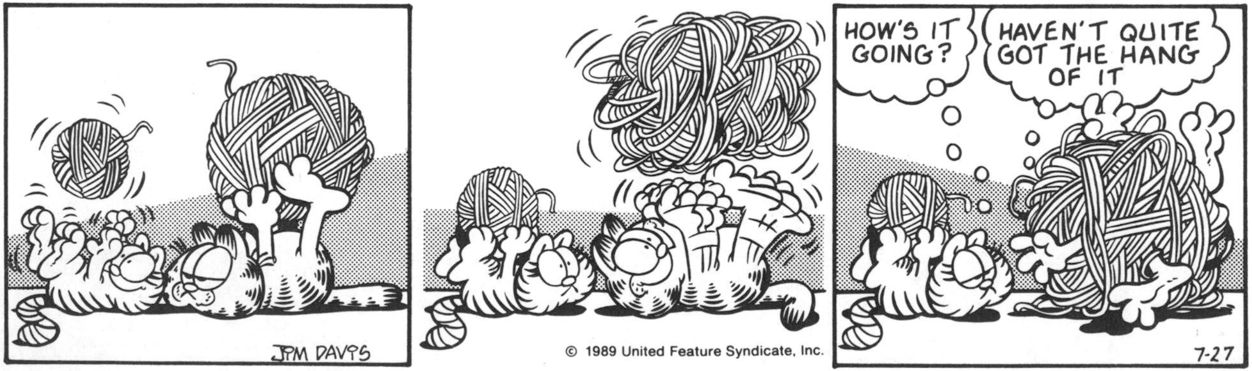
JIM DAVIS
© 1989 United Feature Syndicate, Inc.
HOW'S IT GOING?
HAVEN'T QUITE GOT THE HANG OF IT
7-27

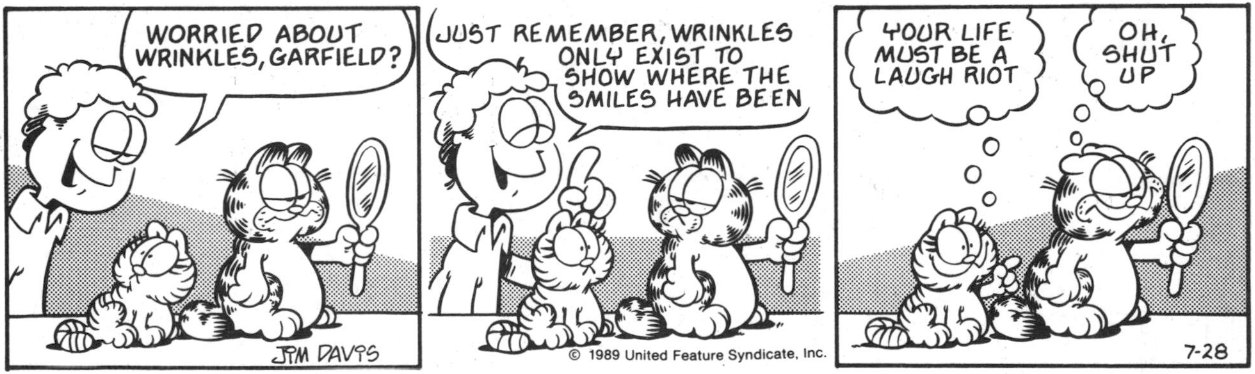
WORRIED ABOUT WRINKLES, GARFIELD?
JIM DAVIS
JUST REMEMBER, WRINKLES ONLY EXIST TO SHOW WHERE THE SMILES HAVE BEEN
© 1989 United Feature Syndicate, Inc.
YOUR LIFE MUST BE A LAUGH RIOT
OH, SHUT UP
7-28

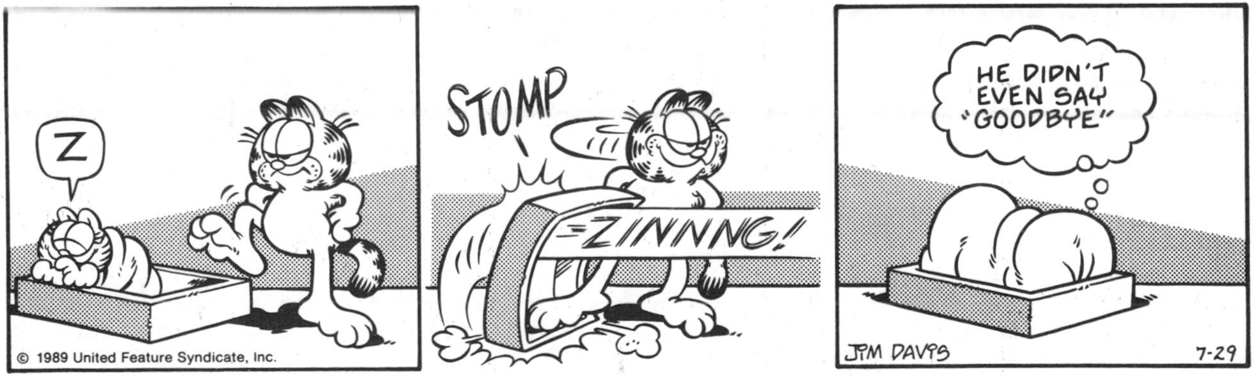
Z
© 1989 United Feature Syndicate, Inc.
STOMP
ZINNNG!
HE DIDN'T EVEN SAY "GOODBYE"
JIM DAVIS
7-29

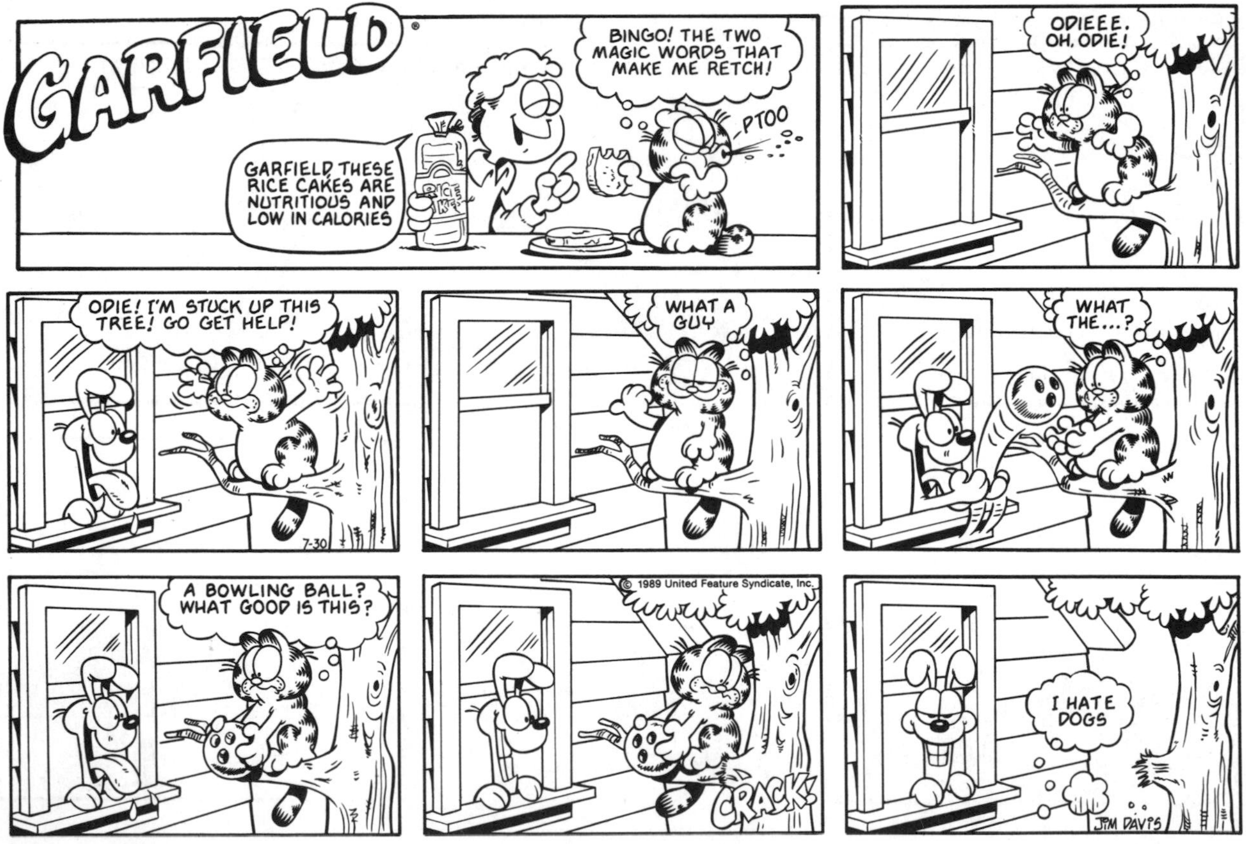
GARFIELD
GARFIELD THESE RICE CAKES ARE NUTRITIOUS AND LOW IN CALORIES
BINGO! THE TWO MAGIC WORDS THAT MAKE ME RETCH!
PTOO
ODIEEE. OH, ODIE!
ODIE! I'M STUCK UP THIS TREE! GO GET HELP!
7-30
WHAT A GUY
WHAT THE...?
A BOWLING BALL? WHAT GOOD IS THIS?
© 1989 United Feature Syndicate, Inc.
CRACK!
I HATE DOGS
JIM DAVIS

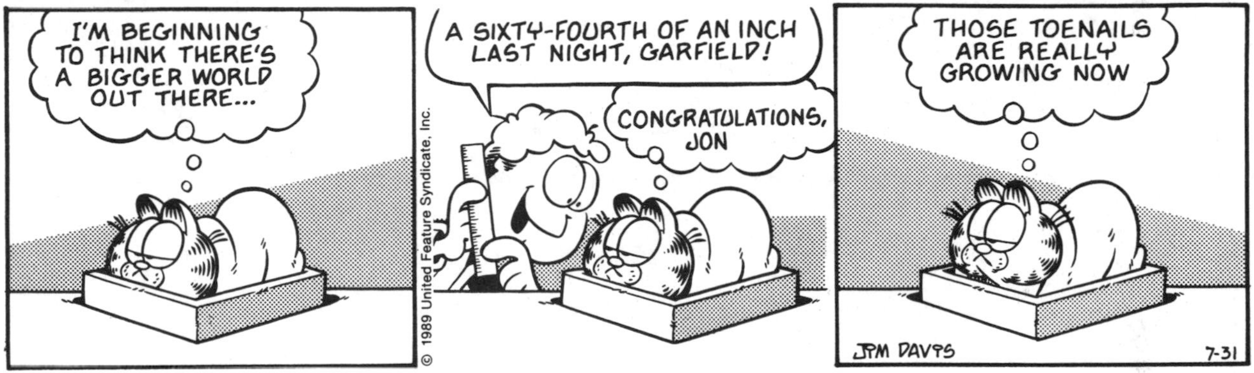
I'M BEGINNING TO THINK THERE'S A BIGGER WORLD OUT THERE...
A SIXTY-FOURTH OF AN INCH LAST NIGHT, GARFIELD!
CONGRATULATIONS, JON
THOSE TOENAILS ARE REALLY GROWING NOW
© 1989 United Feature Syndicate, Inc.
JPM DAVPS
7-31

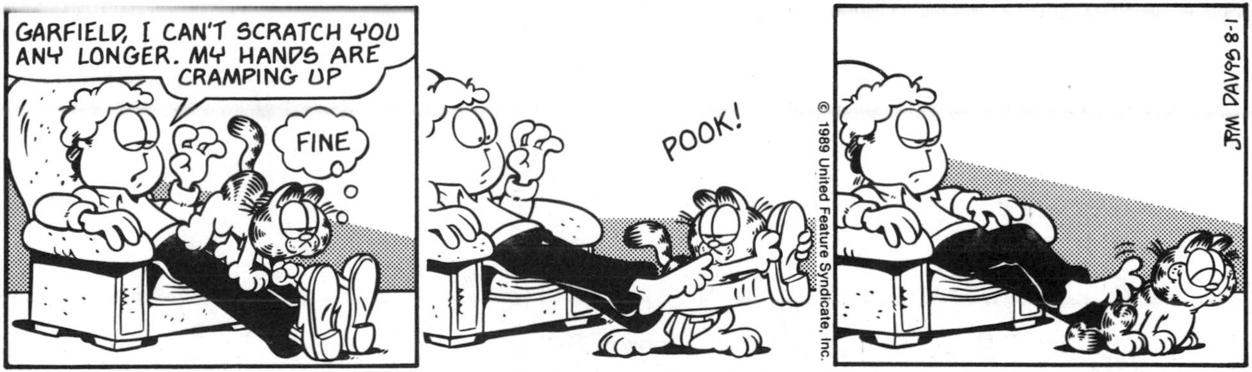
GARFIELD, I CAN'T SCRATCH YOU ANY LONGER. MY HANDS ARE CRAMPING UP
FINE
POOK!
© 1989 United Feature Syndicate, Inc.
JPM DAVPS 8-1

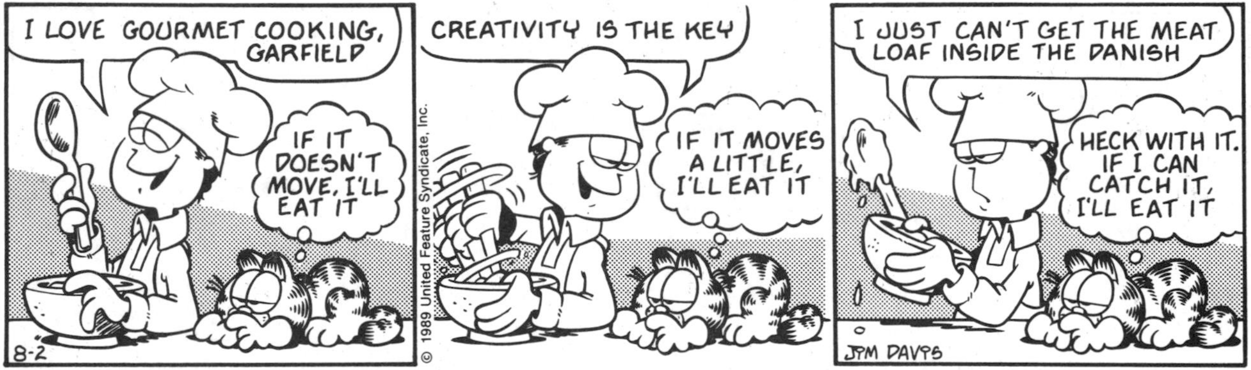
I LOVE GOURMET COOKING, GARFIELD
IF IT DOESN'T MOVE, I'LL EAT IT
8-2
© 1989 United Feature Syndicate, Inc.
CREATIVITY IS THE KEY
IF IT MOVES A LITTLE, I'LL EAT IT
I JUST CAN'T GET THE MEAT LOAF INSIDE THE DANISH
HECK WITH IT. IF I CAN CATCH IT, I'LL EAT IT
JIM DAVIS

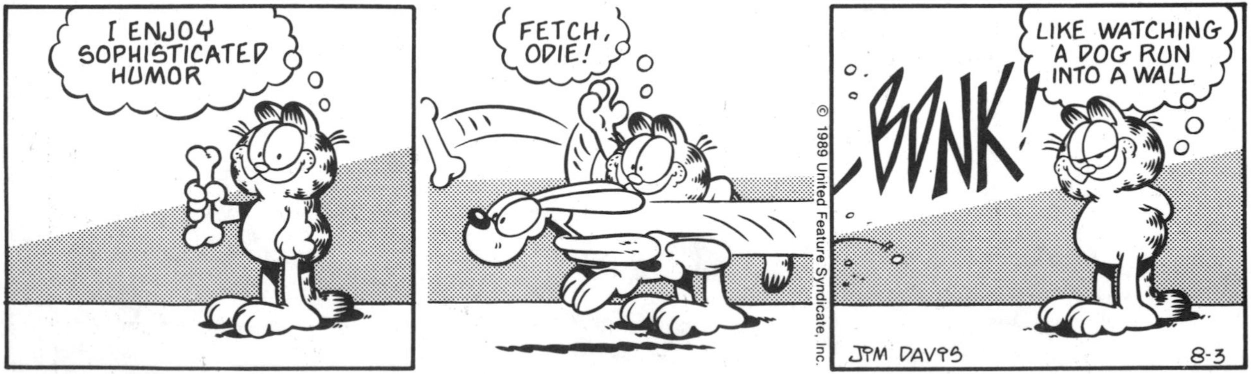
I ENJOY SOPHISTICATED HUMOR
FETCH, ODIE!
© 1989 United Feature Syndicate, Inc.
BONK!
LIKE WATCHING A DOG RUN INTO A WALL
JIM DAVIS
8-3

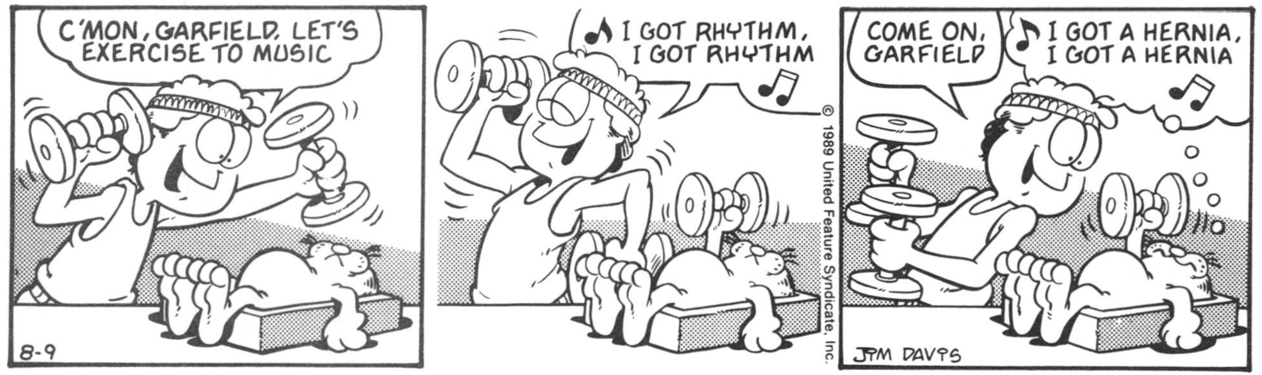
8-9
C'MON, GARFIELD. LET'S EXERCISE TO MUSIC
I GOT RHYTHM, I GOT RHYTHM
COME ON, GARFIELD
I GOT A HERNIA, I GOT A HERNIA
© 1989 United Feature Syndicate, Inc.
JIM DAVIS

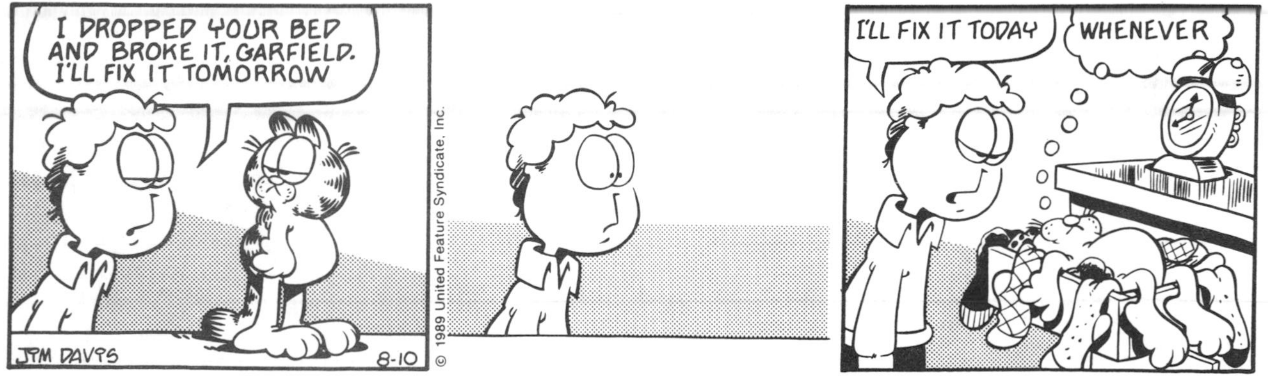
I DROPPED YOUR BED AND BROKE IT, GARFIELD. I'LL FIX IT TOMORROW
JIM DAVIS
© 1989 United Feature Syndicate, Inc.
8-10
I'LL FIX IT TODAY
WHENEVER

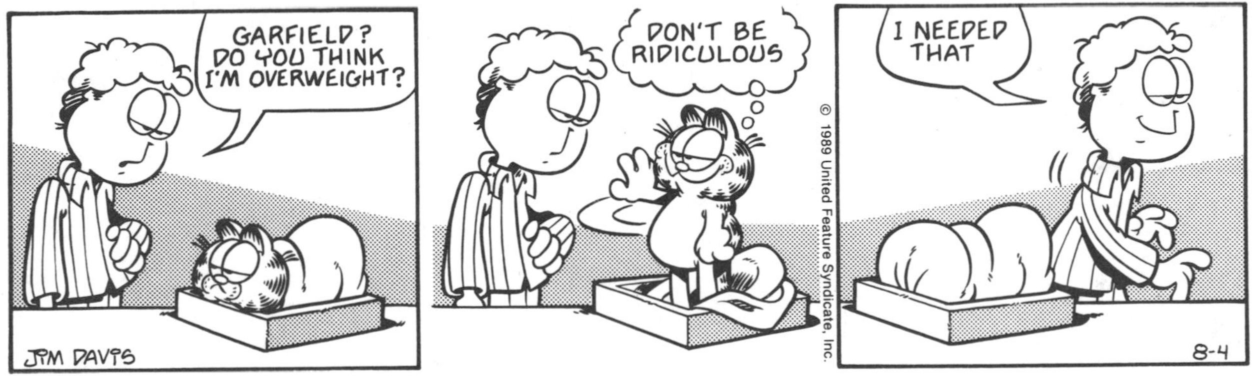
GARFIELD? DO YOU THINK I'M OVERWEIGHT?
JIM DAVIS
DON'T BE RIDICULOUS
© 1989 United Feature Syndicate, Inc.
I NEEDED THAT
8-4

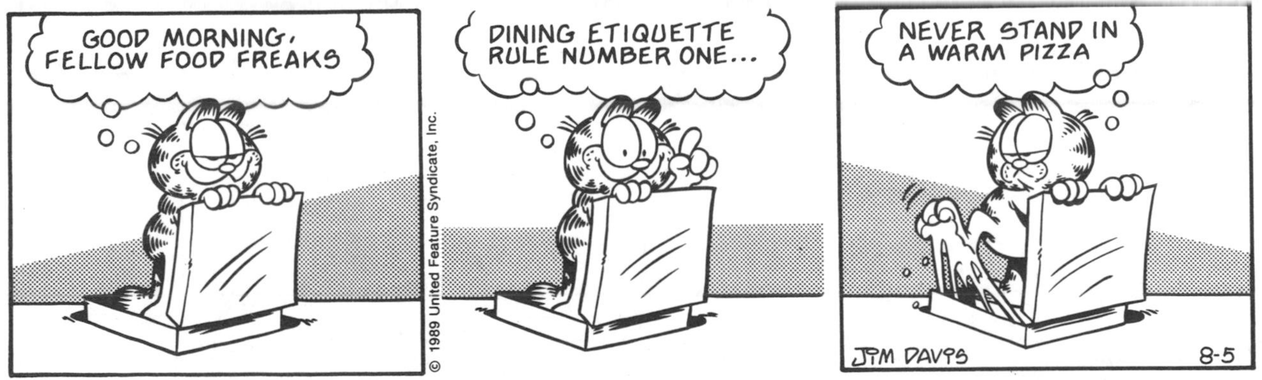
GOOD MORNING, FELLOW FOOD FREAKS
© 1989 United Feature Syndicate, Inc.
DINING ETIQUETTE RULE NUMBER ONE...
NEVER STAND IN A WARM PIZZA
JIM DAVIS
8-5

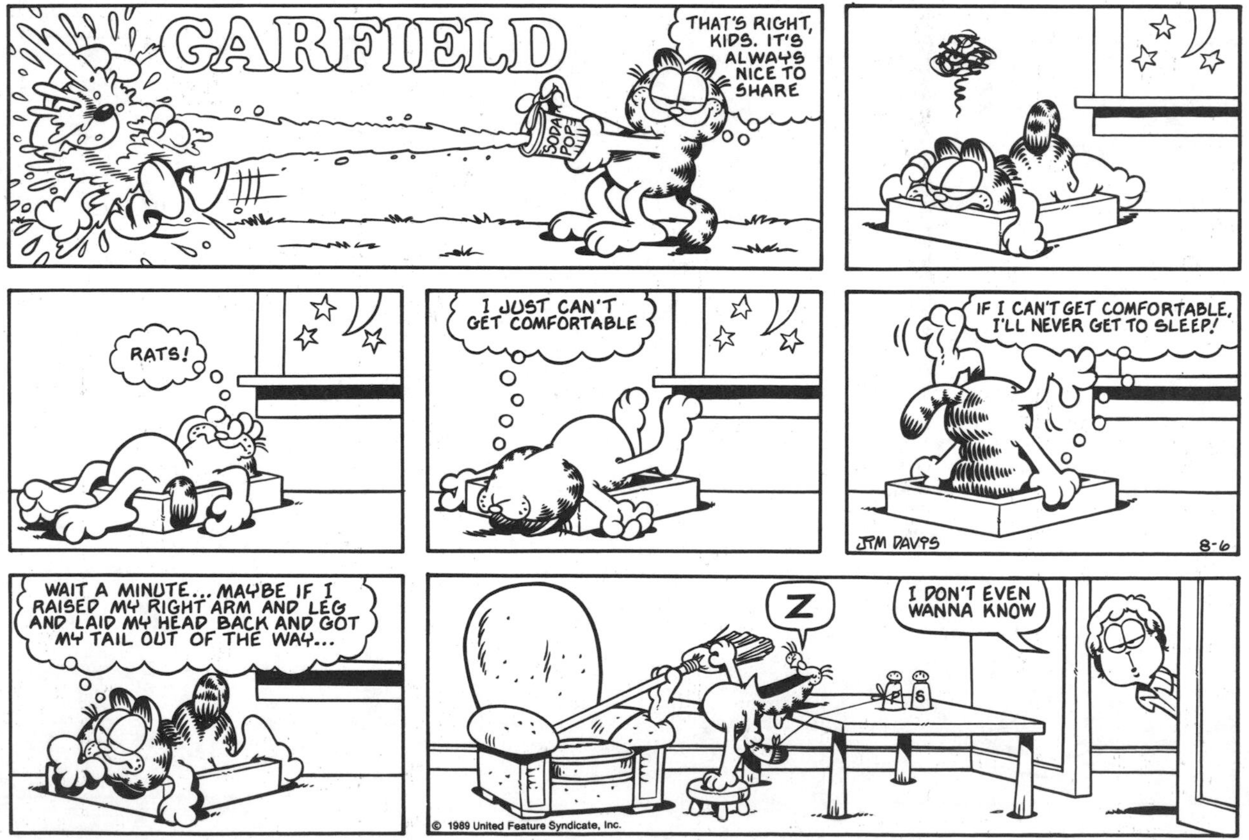
GARFIELD
THAT'S RIGHT, KIDS. IT'S ALWAYS NICE TO SHARE
SODA POP
RATS!
I JUST CAN'T GET COMFORTABLE
IF I CAN'T GET COMFORTABLE, I'LL NEVER GET TO SLEEP!
JIM DAVIS 8-6
WAIT A MINUTE... MAYBE IF I RAISED MY RIGHT ARM AND LEG AND LAID MY HEAD BACK AND GOT MY TAIL OUT OF THE WAY...
Z
I DON'T EVEN WANNA KNOW
© 1989 United Feature Syndicate, Inc.

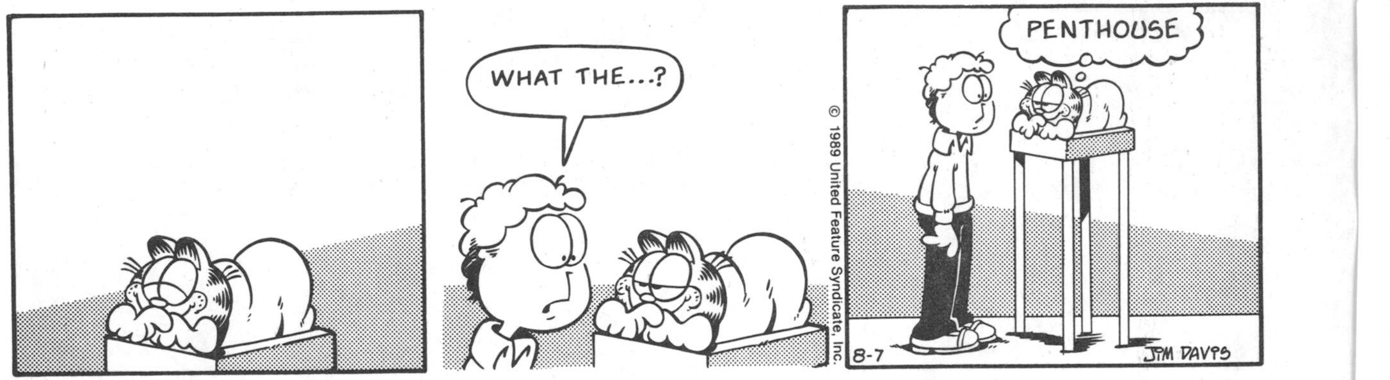
WHAT THE...?
PENTHOUSE
© 1989 United Feature Syndicate, Inc.
8-7 JIM DAVIS

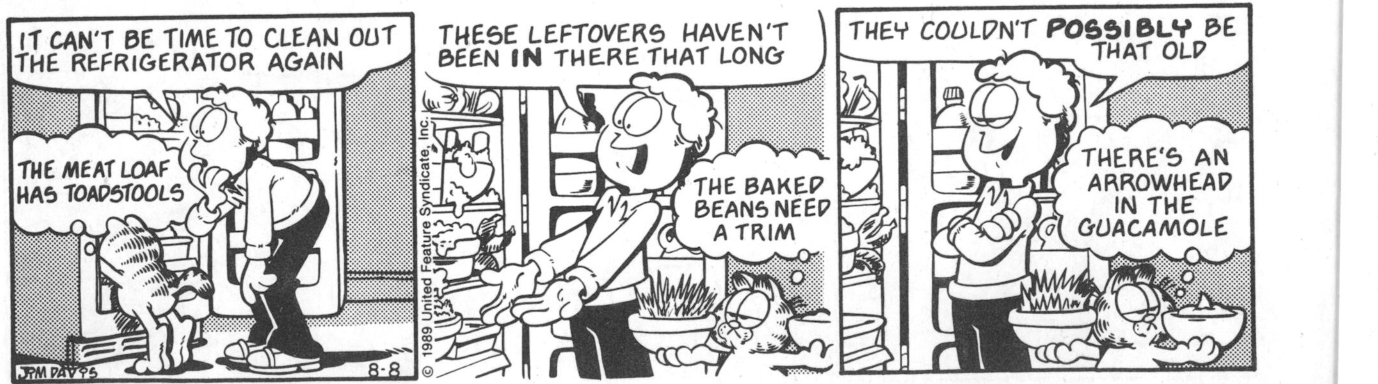
IT CAN'T BE TIME TO CLEAN OUT THE REFRIGERATOR AGAIN
THE MEAT LOAF HAS TOADSTOOLS
JIM DAVIS 8-8
© 1989 United Feature Syndicate, Inc.
THESE LEFTOVERS HAVEN'T BEEN **IN** THERE THAT LONG
THE BAKED BEANS NEED A TRIM
THEY COULDN'T **POSSIBLY** BE THAT OLD
THERE'S AN ARROWHEAD IN THE GUACAMOLE

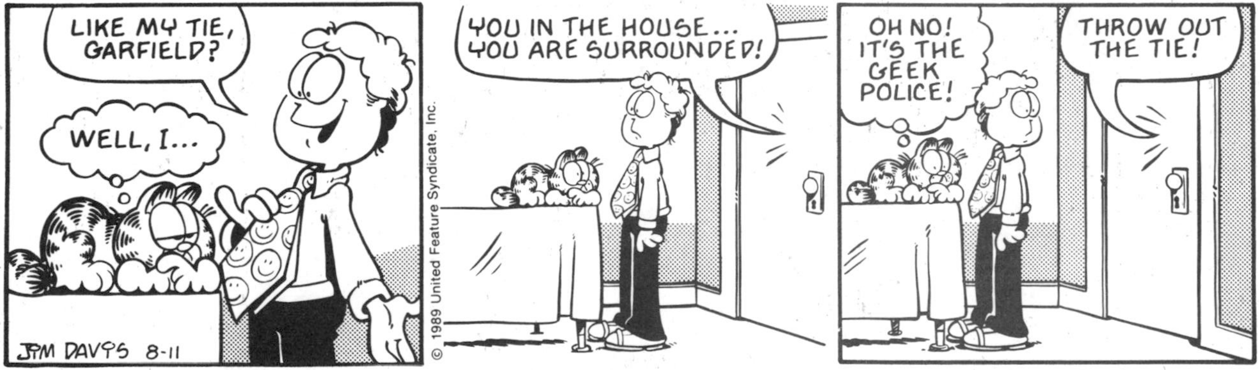
LIKE MY TIE, GARFIELD?
WELL, I...
JIM DAVIS 8-11
YOU IN THE HOUSE... YOU ARE SURROUNDED!
OH NO! IT'S THE GEEK POLICE!
THROW OUT THE TIE!

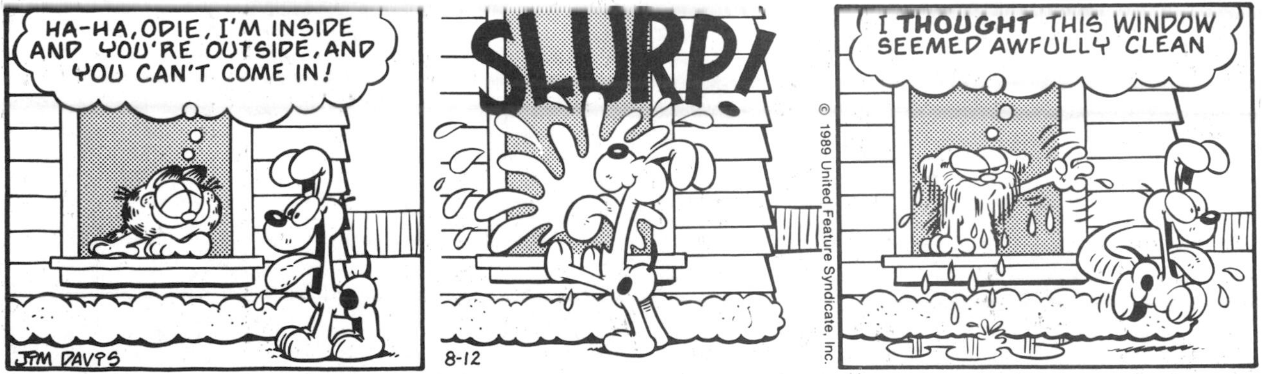
HA-HA, ODIE, I'M INSIDE AND YOU'RE OUTSIDE, AND YOU CAN'T COME IN!
JIM DAVIS
SLURP!
8-12
I **THOUGHT** THIS WINDOW SEEMED AWFULLY CLEAN

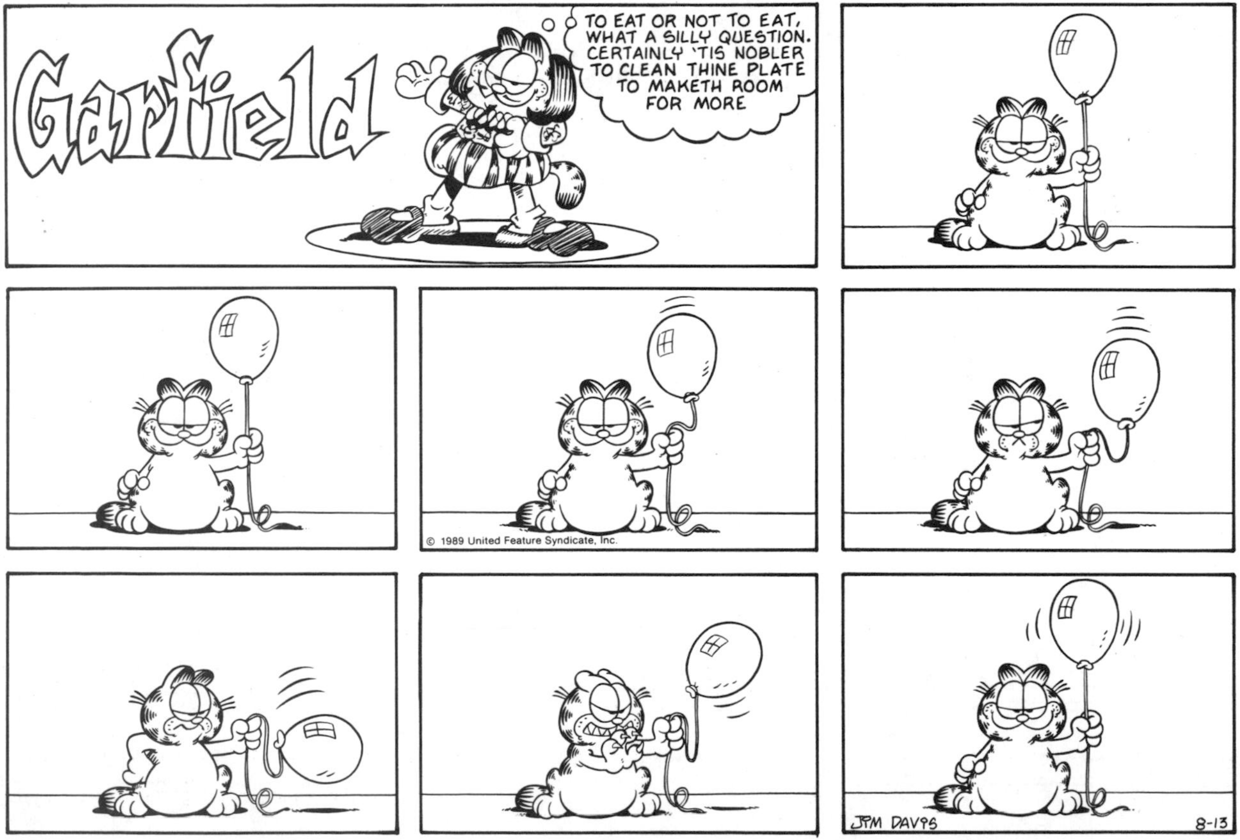
Garfield
TO EAT OR NOT TO EAT, WHAT A SILLY QUESTION. CERTAINLY 'TIS NOBLER TO CLEAN THINE PLATE TO MAKETH ROOM FOR MORE
© 1989 United Feature Syndicate, Inc.
JIM DAVIS
8-13

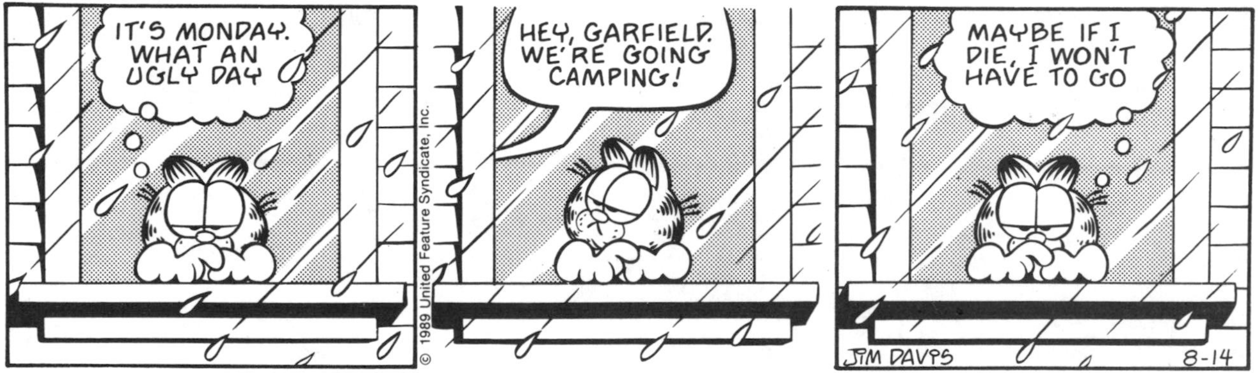
IT'S MONDAY. WHAT AN UGLY DAY
© 1989 United Feature Syndicate, Inc.
HEY, GARFIELD. WE'RE GOING CAMPING!
MAYBE IF I DIE, I WON'T HAVE TO GO
JIM DAVIS
8-14

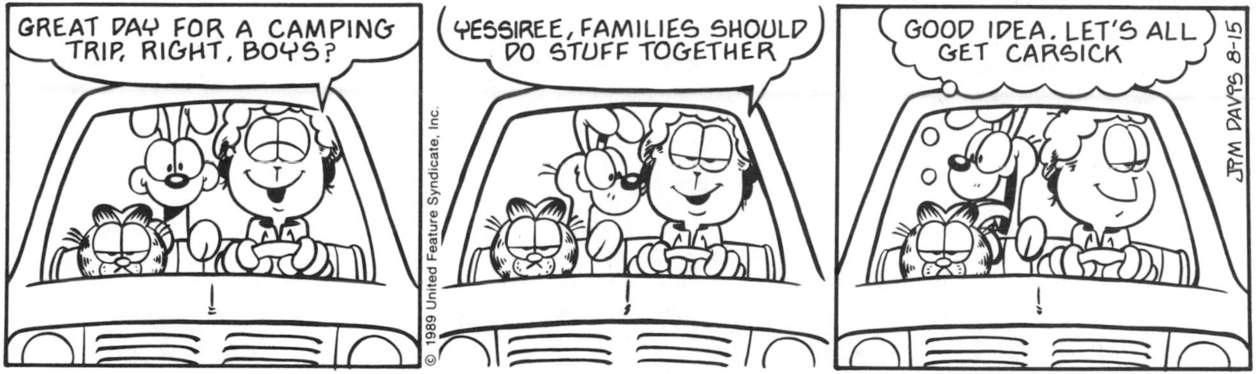
GREAT DAY FOR A CAMPING TRIP, RIGHT, BOYS?
© 1989 United Feature Syndicate, Inc.
YESSIREE, FAMILIES SHOULD DO STUFF TOGETHER
GOOD IDEA. LET'S ALL GET CARSICK
JIM DAVIS 8-15

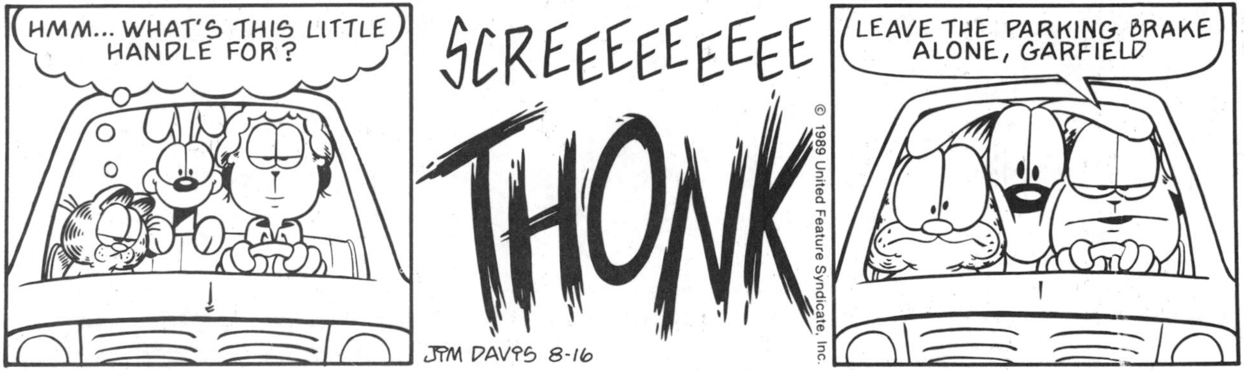
HMM... WHAT'S THIS LITTLE HANDLE FOR?
SCREEEEEEEEE
THONK
LEAVE THE PARKING BRAKE ALONE, GARFIELD
JIM DAVIS 8-16
© 1989 United Feature Syndicate, Inc.

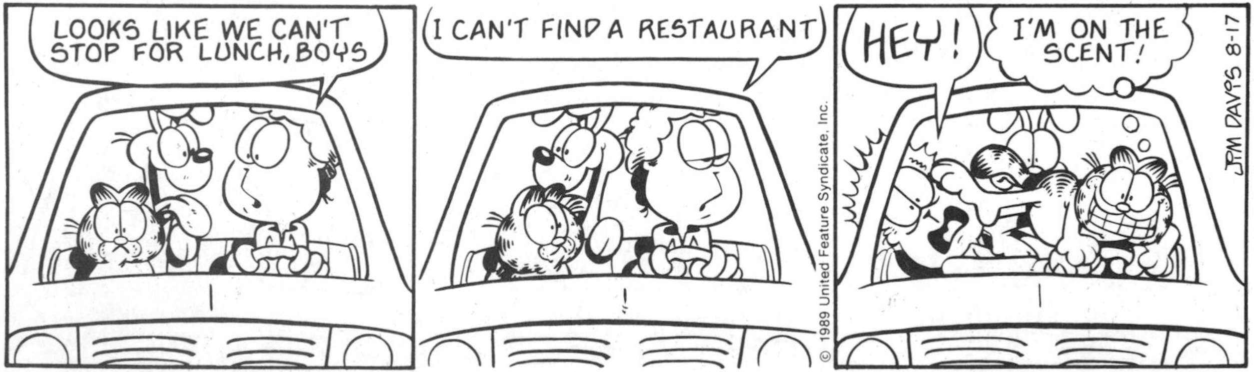
LOOKS LIKE WE CAN'T STOP FOR LUNCH, BOYS
I CAN'T FIND A RESTAURANT
HEY!
I'M ON THE SCENT!
JIM DAVIS 8-17
© 1989 United Feature Syndicate, Inc.

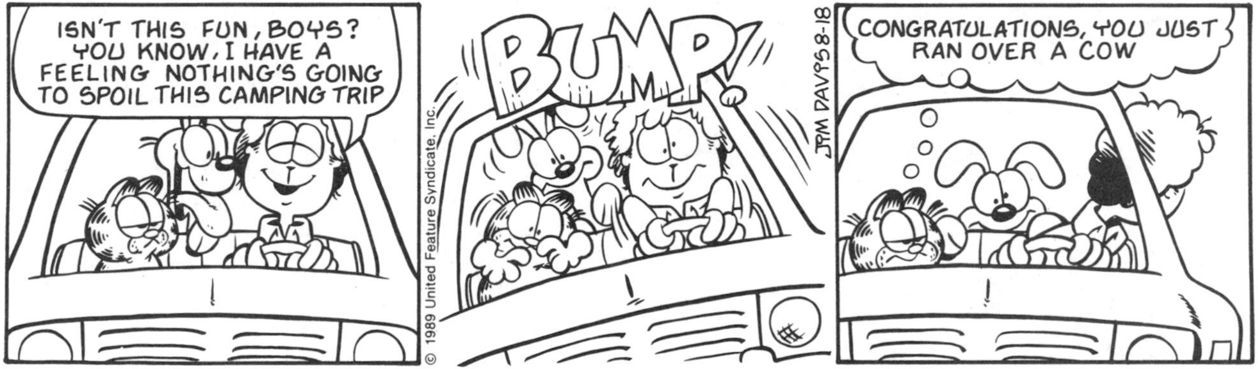
ISN'T THIS FUN, BOYS? YOU KNOW, I HAVE A FEELING NOTHING'S GOING TO SPOIL THIS CAMPING TRIP
© 1989 United Feature Syndicate, Inc.
BUMP
JIM DAVIS 8-18
CONGRATULATIONS, YOU JUST RAN OVER A COW

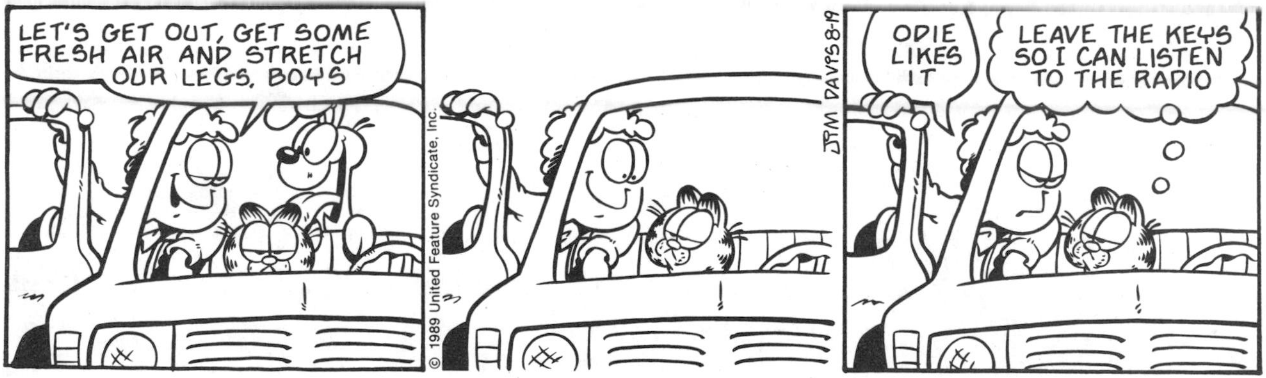
LET'S GET OUT, GET SOME FRESH AIR AND STRETCH OUR LEGS, BOYS
© 1989 United Feature Syndicate, Inc.
JIM DAVIS 8-19
ODIE LIKES IT
LEAVE THE KEYS SO I CAN LISTEN TO THE RADIO

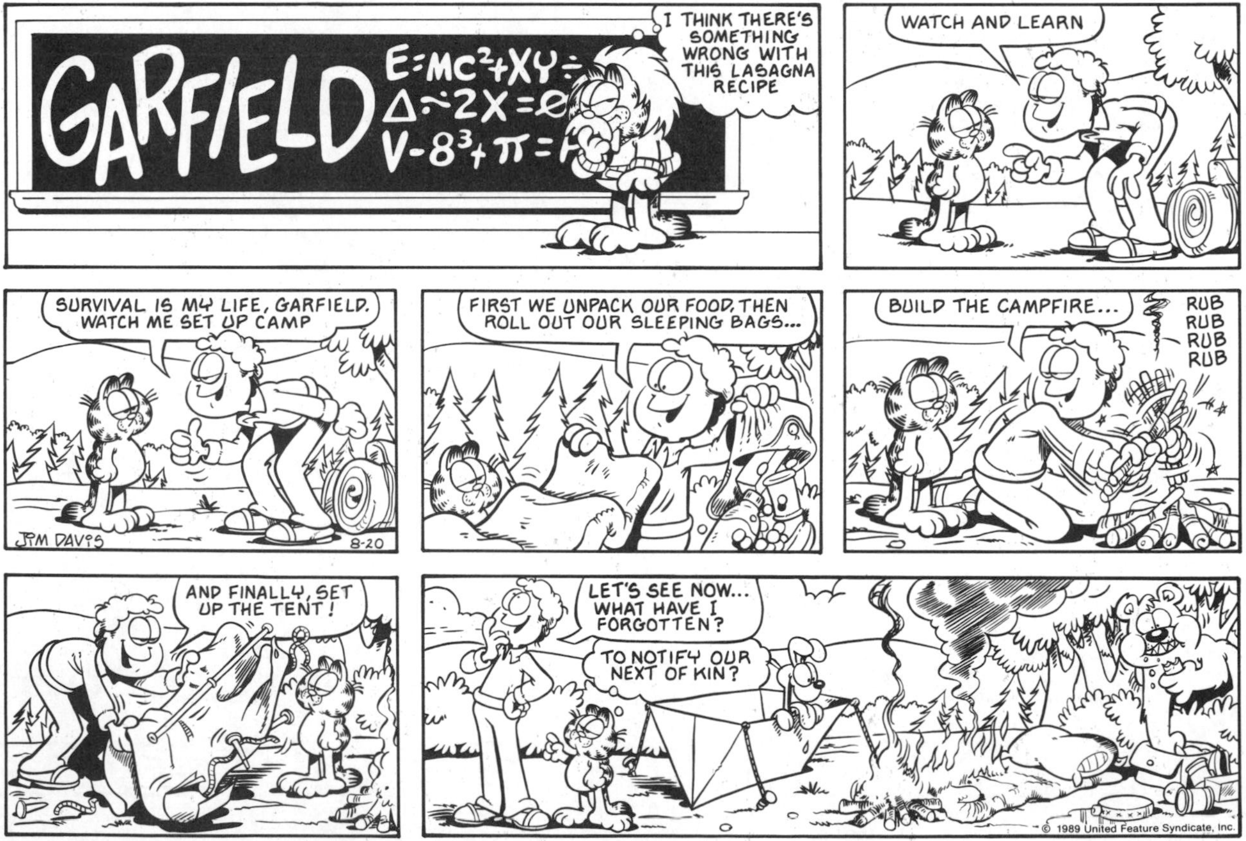
GARFIELD
E=MC²+XY÷
Δ≈2X=Ø
V-8³+π=
I THINK THERE'S SOMETHING WRONG WITH THIS LASAGNA RECIPE
WATCH AND LEARN
SURVIVAL IS MY LIFE, GARFIELD. WATCH ME SET UP CAMP
JIM DAVIS
8-20
FIRST WE UNPACK OUR FOOD, THEN ROLL OUT OUR SLEEPING BAGS...
BUILD THE CAMPFIRE...
RUB RUB RUB RUB
AND FINALLY, SET UP THE TENT!
LET'S SEE NOW... WHAT HAVE I FORGOTTEN?
TO NOTIFY OUR NEXT OF KIN?
© 1989 United Feature Syndicate, Inc.

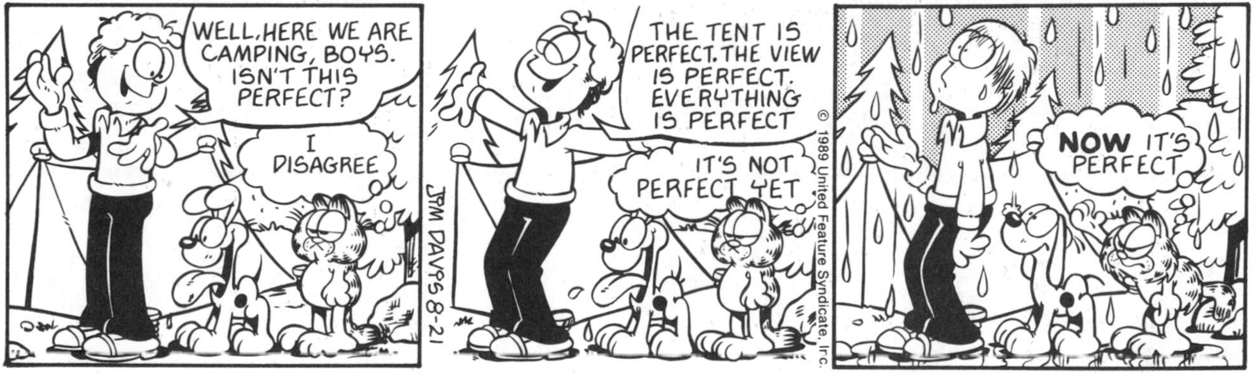
WELL, HERE WE ARE CAMPING, BOYS. ISN'T THIS PERFECT?
I DISAGREE
JIM DAVIS 8-21
THE TENT IS PERFECT. THE VIEW IS PERFECT. EVERYTHING IS PERFECT
IT'S NOT PERFECT YET
© 1989 United Feature Syndicate, Inc.
NOW IT'S PERFECT

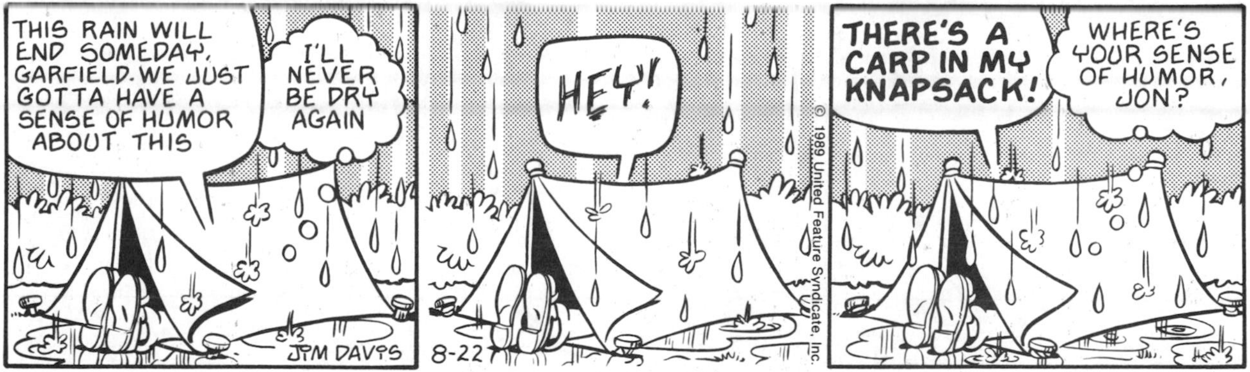
THIS RAIN WILL END SOMEDAY, GARFIELD. WE JUST GOTTA HAVE A SENSE OF HUMOR ABOUT THIS
I'LL NEVER BE DRY AGAIN
JIM DAVIS
8-22
HEY!
© 1989 United Feature Syndicate, Inc.
THERE'S A CARP IN MY KNAPSACK!
WHERE'S YOUR SENSE OF HUMOR, JON?

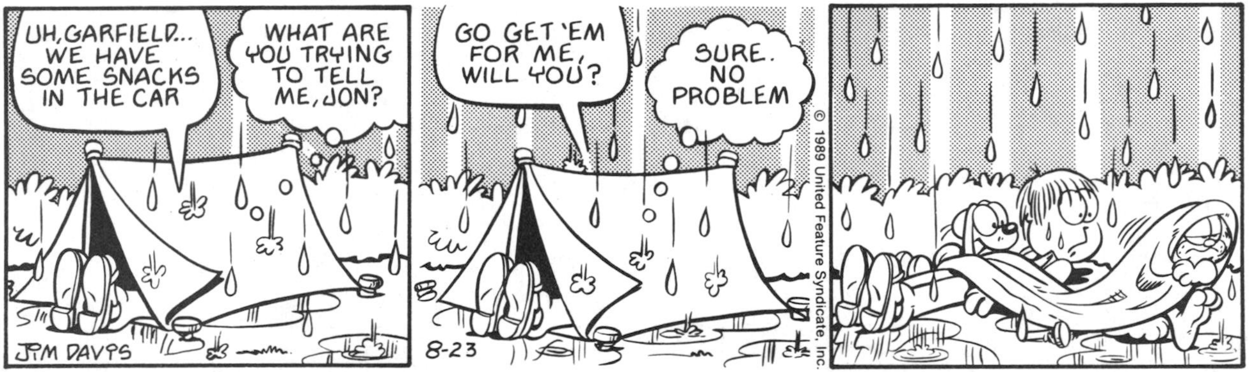
UH, GARFIELD... WE HAVE SOME SNACKS IN THE CAR
WHAT ARE YOU TRYING TO TELL ME, JON?
JIM DAVIS
GO GET 'EM FOR ME, WILL YOU?
SURE. NO PROBLEM
8-23
© 1989 United Feature Syndicate, Inc.

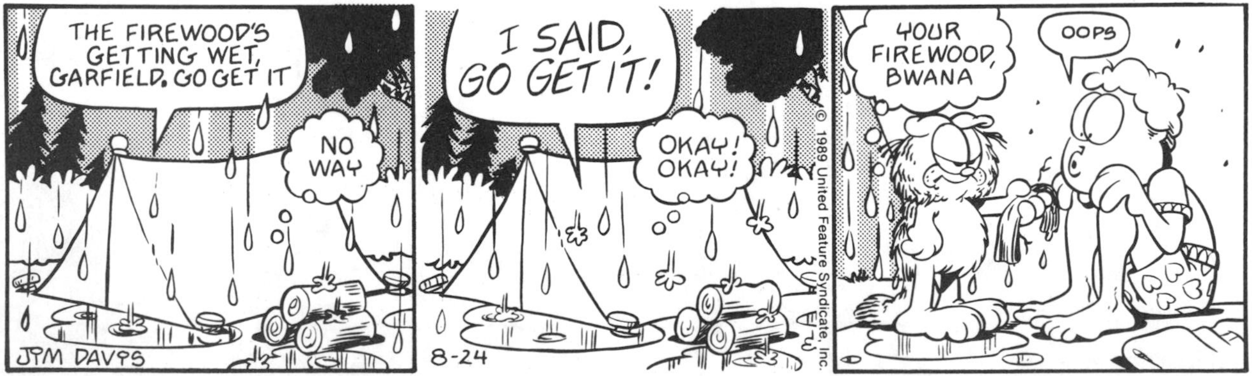
THE FIREWOOD'S GETTING WET, GARFIELD. GO GET IT
NO WAY
JIM DAVIS
I SAID, GO GET IT!
OKAY! OKAY!
8-24
© 1989 United Feature Syndicate, Inc.
YOUR FIREWOOD, BWANA
OOPS

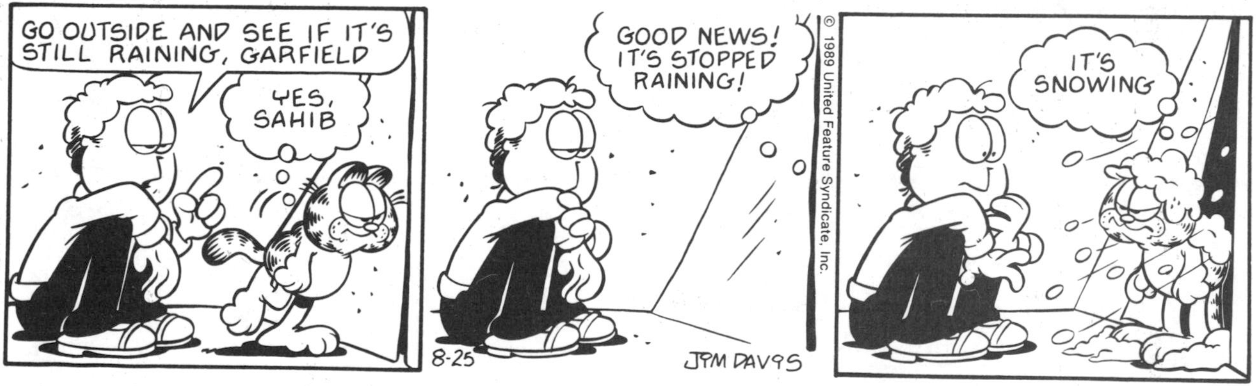
GO OUTSIDE AND SEE IF IT'S STILL RAINING, GARFIELD
YES, SAHIB
GOOD NEWS! IT'S STOPPED RAINING!
8-25
JIM DAVIS
IT'S SNOWING

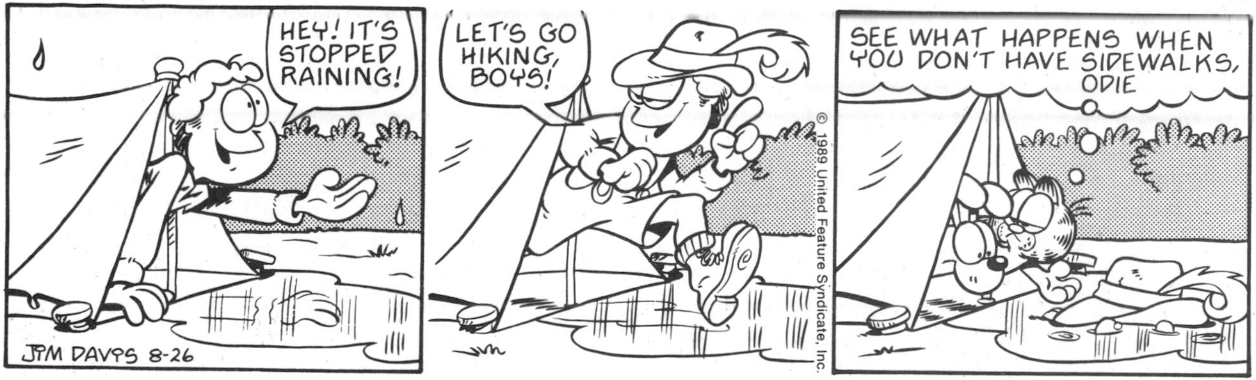
HEY! IT'S STOPPED RAINING!
JIM DAVIS 8-26
LET'S GO HIKING, BOYS!
SEE WHAT HAPPENS WHEN YOU DON'T HAVE SIDEWALKS, ODIE

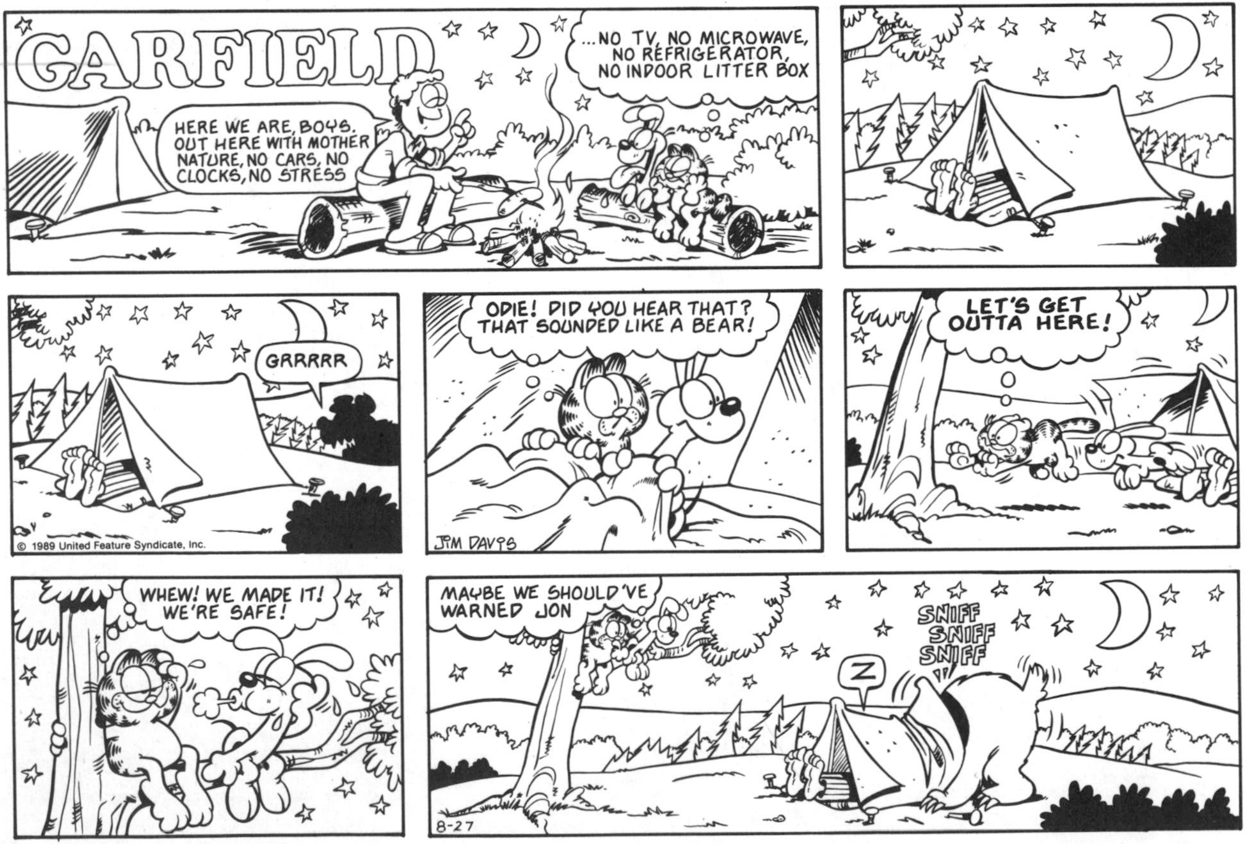
GARFIELD
HERE WE ARE, BOYS. OUT HERE WITH MOTHER NATURE, NO CARS, NO CLOCKS, NO STRESS
...NO TV, NO MICROWAVE, NO REFRIGERATOR, NO INDOOR LITTER BOX
GRRRRR
© 1989 United Feature Syndicate, Inc.
ODIE! DID YOU HEAR THAT? THAT SOUNDED LIKE A BEAR!
JIM DAVIS
LET'S GET OUTTA HERE!
WHEW! WE MADE IT! WE'RE SAFE!
MAYBE WE SHOULD'VE WARNED JON
Z
SNIFF SNIFF SNIFF
8-27

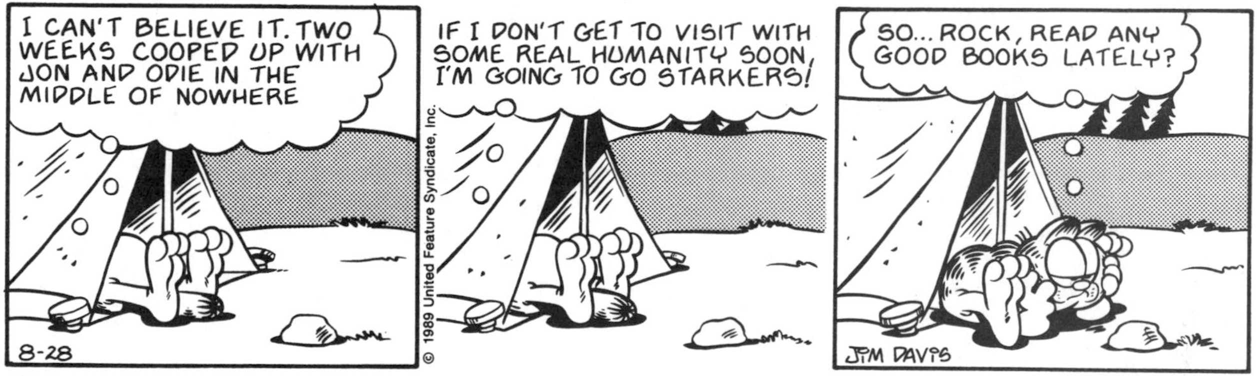
I CAN'T BELIEVE IT. TWO WEEKS COOPED UP WITH JON AND ODIE IN THE MIDDLE OF NOWHERE
8-28
© 1989 United Feature Syndicate, Inc.
IF I DON'T GET TO VISIT WITH SOME REAL HUMANITY SOON, I'M GOING TO GO STARKERS!
SO... ROCK, READ ANY GOOD BOOKS LATELY?
JIM DAVIS

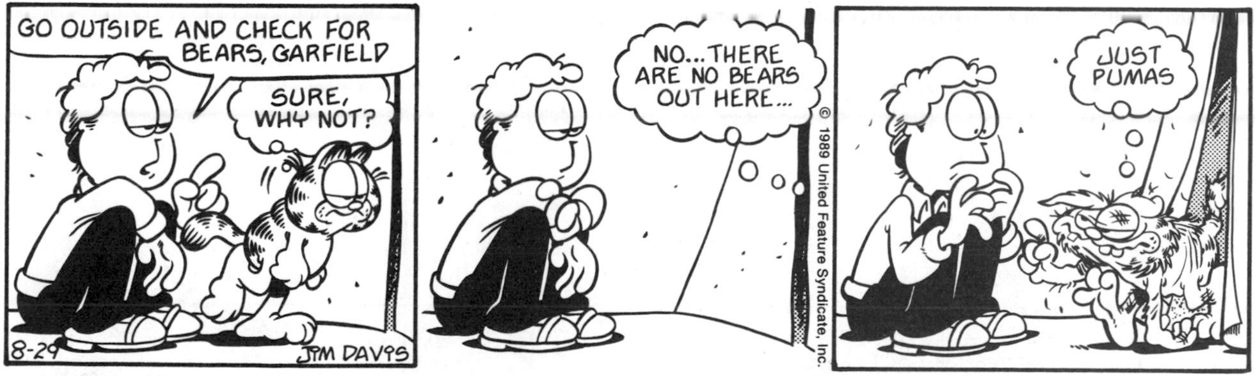
GO OUTSIDE AND CHECK FOR BEARS, GARFIELD
SURE, WHY NOT?
8-29
JIM DAVIS
NO... THERE ARE NO BEARS OUT HERE...
© 1989 United Feature Syndicate, Inc.
JUST PUMAS

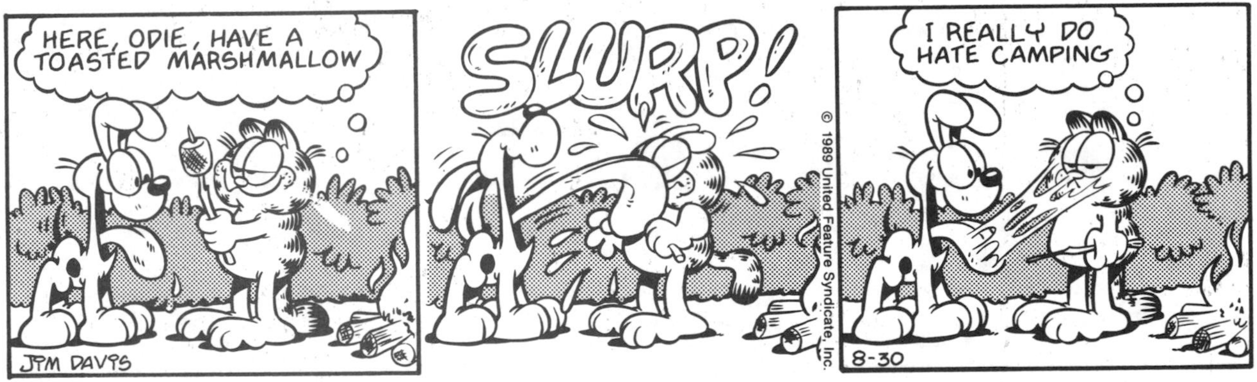
HERE, ODIE, HAVE A TOASTED MARSHMALLOW
JIM DAVIS
SLURP!
I REALLY DO HATE CAMPING
© 1989 United Feature Syndicate, Inc.
8-30

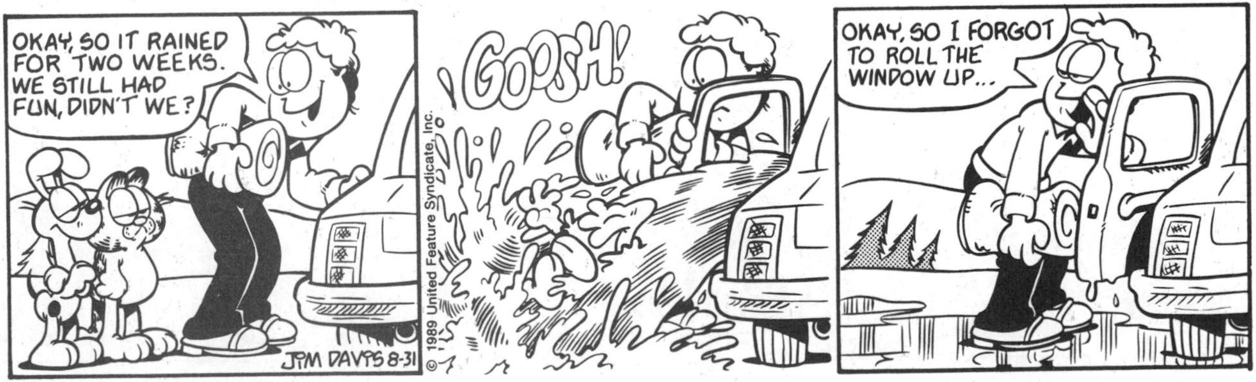
OKAY, SO IT RAINED FOR TWO WEEKS. WE STILL HAD FUN, DIDN'T WE?
JIM DAVIS 8-31
GOOSH!
© 1989 United Feature Syndicate, Inc.
OKAY, SO I FORGOT TO ROLL THE WINDOW UP...

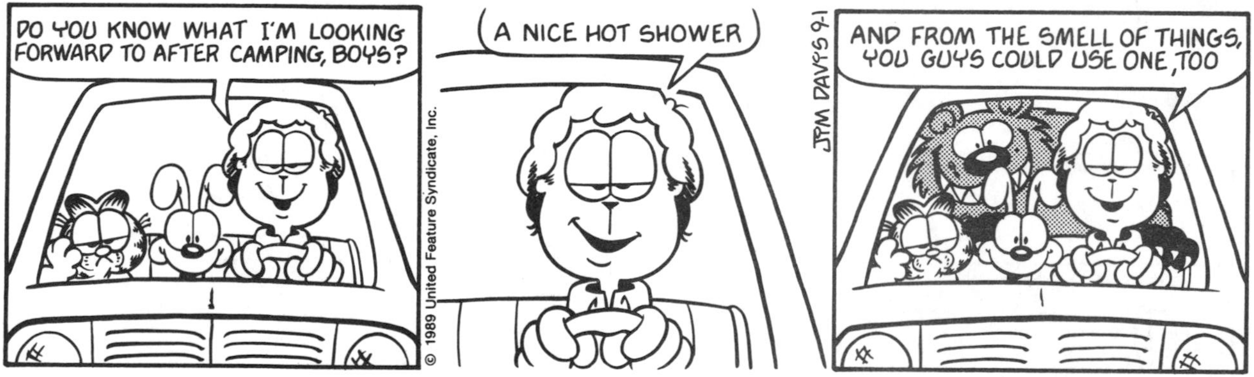
DO YOU KNOW WHAT I'M LOOKING FORWARD TO AFTER CAMPING, BOYS?
A NICE HOT SHOWER
AND FROM THE SMELL OF THINGS, YOU GUYS COULD USE ONE, TOO
JIM DAVIS 9-1
© 1989 United Feature Syndicate, Inc.

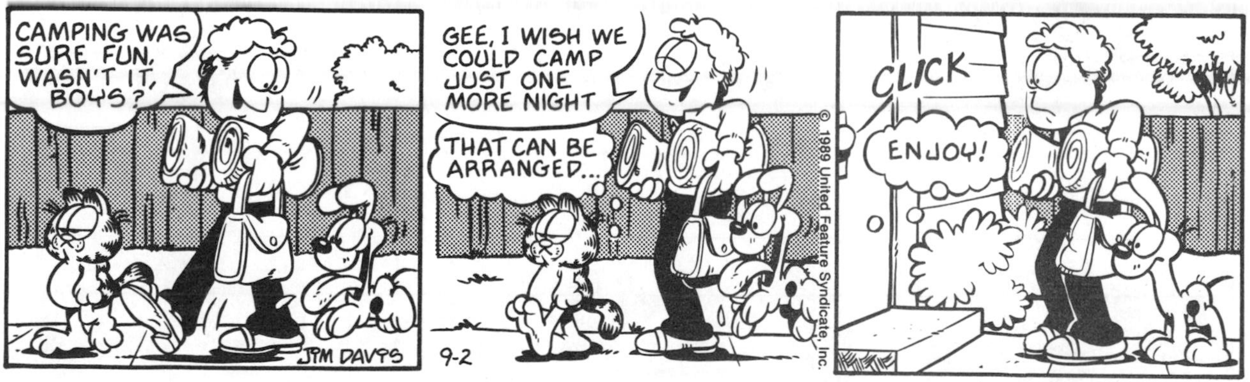
CAMPING WAS SURE FUN, WASN'T IT, BOYS?
JIM DAVIS
9-2
GEE, I WISH WE COULD CAMP JUST ONE MORE NIGHT
THAT CAN BE ARRANGED...
© 1989 United Feature Syndicate, Inc.
CLICK
ENJOY!

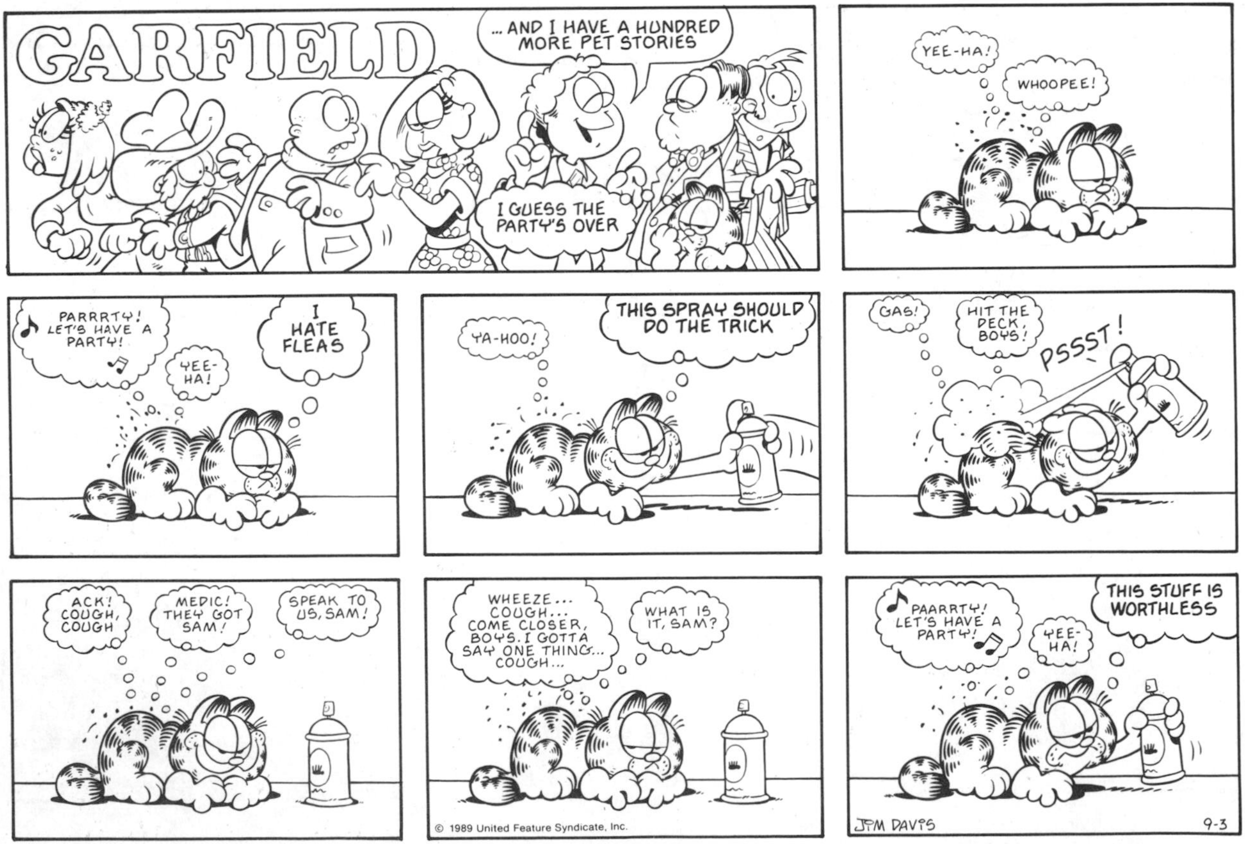
GARFIELD
... AND I HAVE A HUNDRED MORE PET STORIES
I GUESS THE PARTY'S OVER
YEE-HA!
WHOOPEE!
PARRRTY! LET'S HAVE A PARTY!
YEE-HA!
I HATE FLEAS
YA-HOO!
THIS SPRAY SHOULD DO THE TRICK
GAS!
HIT THE DECK, BOYS!
PSSST!
ACK! COUGH, COUGH
MEDIC! THEY GOT SAM!
SPEAK TO US, SAM!
WHEEZE... COUGH... COME CLOSER, BOYS. I GOTTA SAY ONE THING... COUGH...
WHAT IS IT, SAM?
PAARRTY! LET'S HAVE A PARTY!
YEE-HA!
THIS STUFF IS WORTHLESS
© 1989 United Feature Syndicate, Inc.
JIM DAVIS
9-3

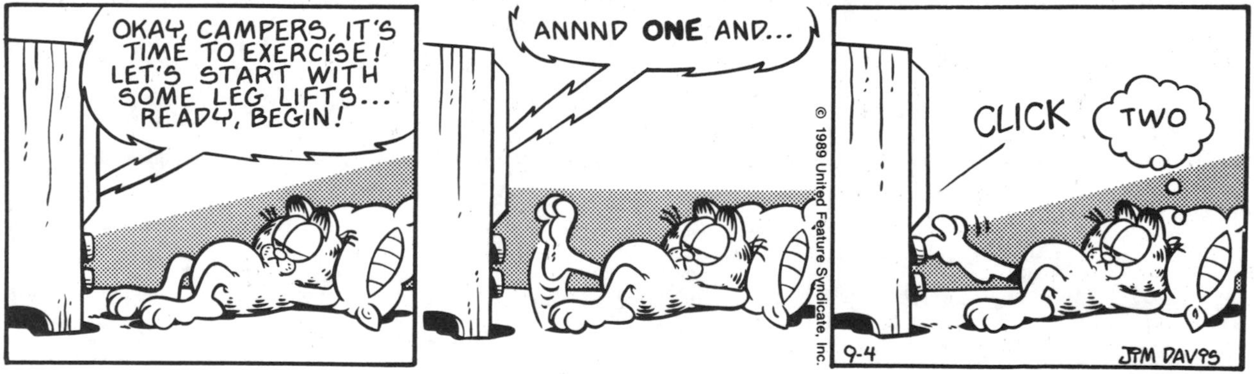
OKAY, CAMPERS, IT'S TIME TO EXERCISE! LET'S START WITH SOME LEG LIFTS... READY, BEGIN!
ANNND **ONE** AND...
CLICK
TWO
© 1989 United Feature Syndicate, Inc.
9-4
JIM DAVIS

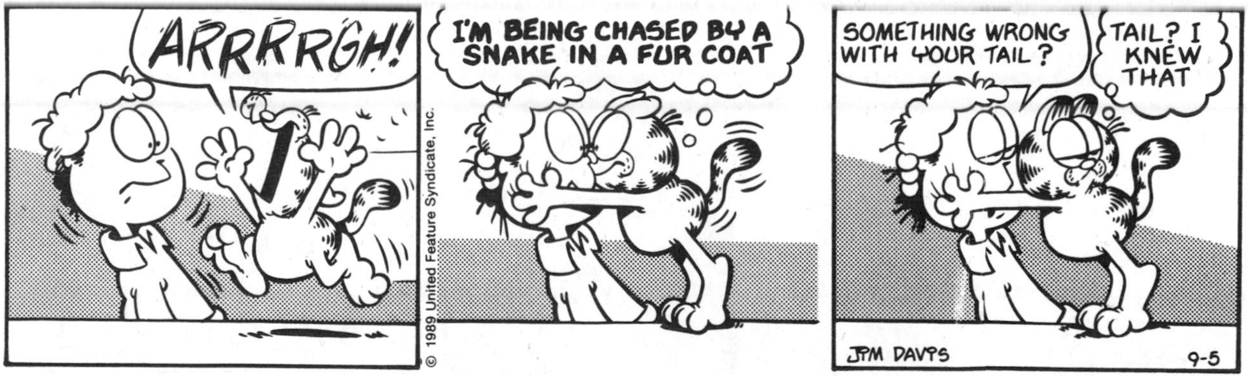
ARRRRGH!
I'M BEING CHASED BY A SNAKE IN A FUR COAT
SOMETHING WRONG WITH YOUR TAIL?
TAIL? I KNEW THAT
© 1989 United Feature Syndicate, Inc.
JIM DAVIS
9-5

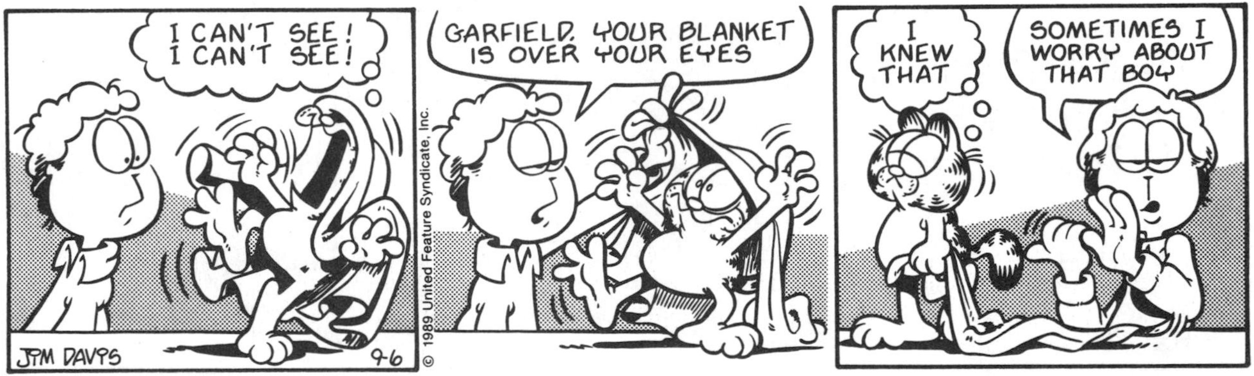
I CAN'T SEE! I CAN'T SEE!
JIM DAVIS
9-6
© 1989 United Feature Syndicate, Inc.
GARFIELD, YOUR BLANKET IS OVER YOUR EYES
I KNEW THAT
SOMETIMES I WORRY ABOUT THAT BOY

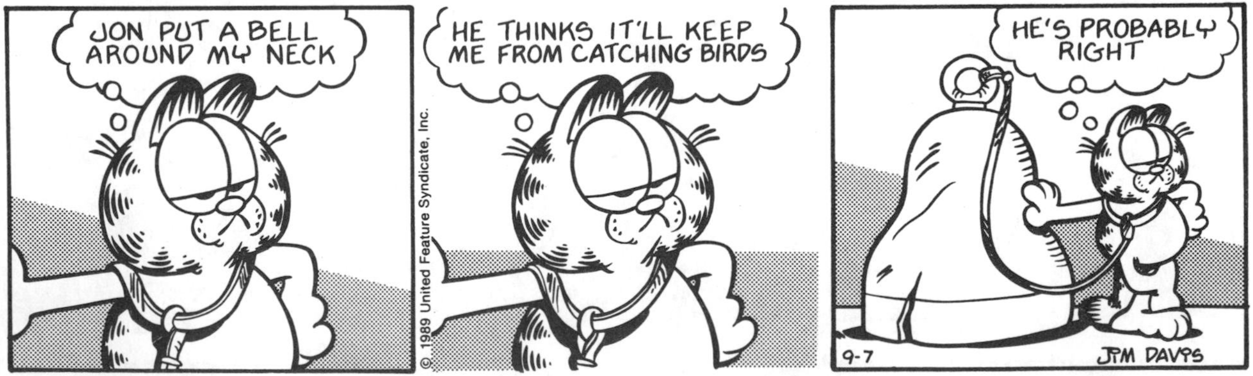
JON PUT A BELL AROUND MY NECK
© 1989 United Feature Syndicate, Inc.
HE THINKS IT'LL KEEP ME FROM CATCHING BIRDS
HE'S PROBABLY RIGHT
9-7
JIM DAVIS

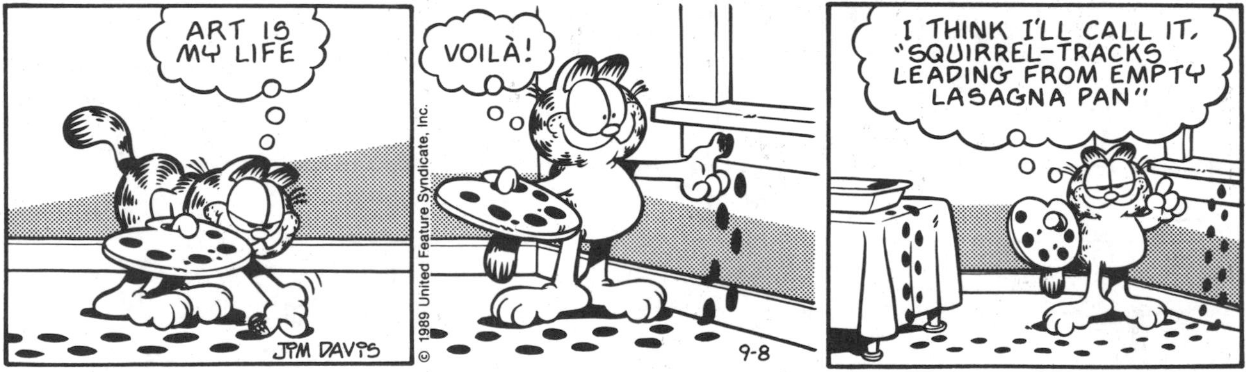
ART IS MY LIFE
JIM DAVIS
© 1989 United Feature Syndicate, Inc.
VOILÀ!
9-8
I THINK I'LL CALL IT, "SQUIRREL-TRACKS LEADING FROM EMPTY LASAGNA PAN"

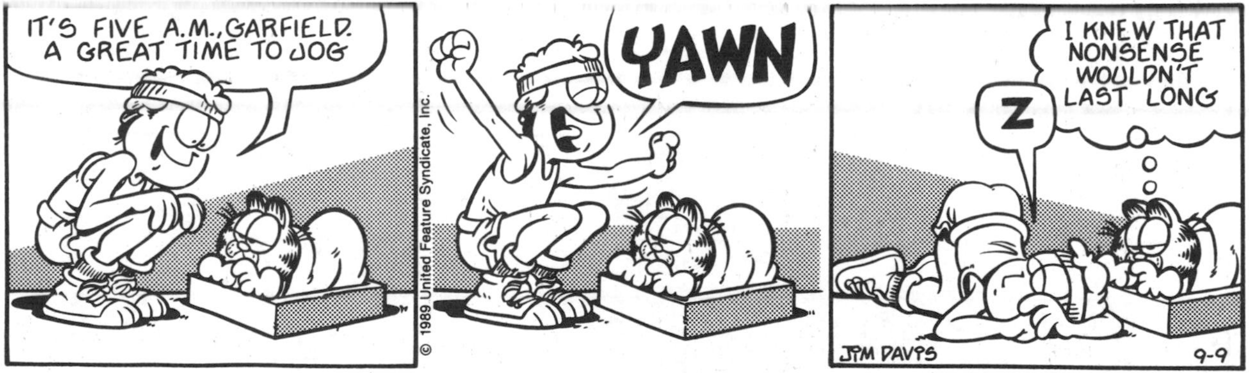
IT'S FIVE A.M., GARFIELD. A GREAT TIME TO JOG
© 1989 United Feature Syndicate, Inc.
YAWN
Z
I KNEW THAT NONSENSE WOULDN'T LAST LONG
JIM DAVIS
9-9

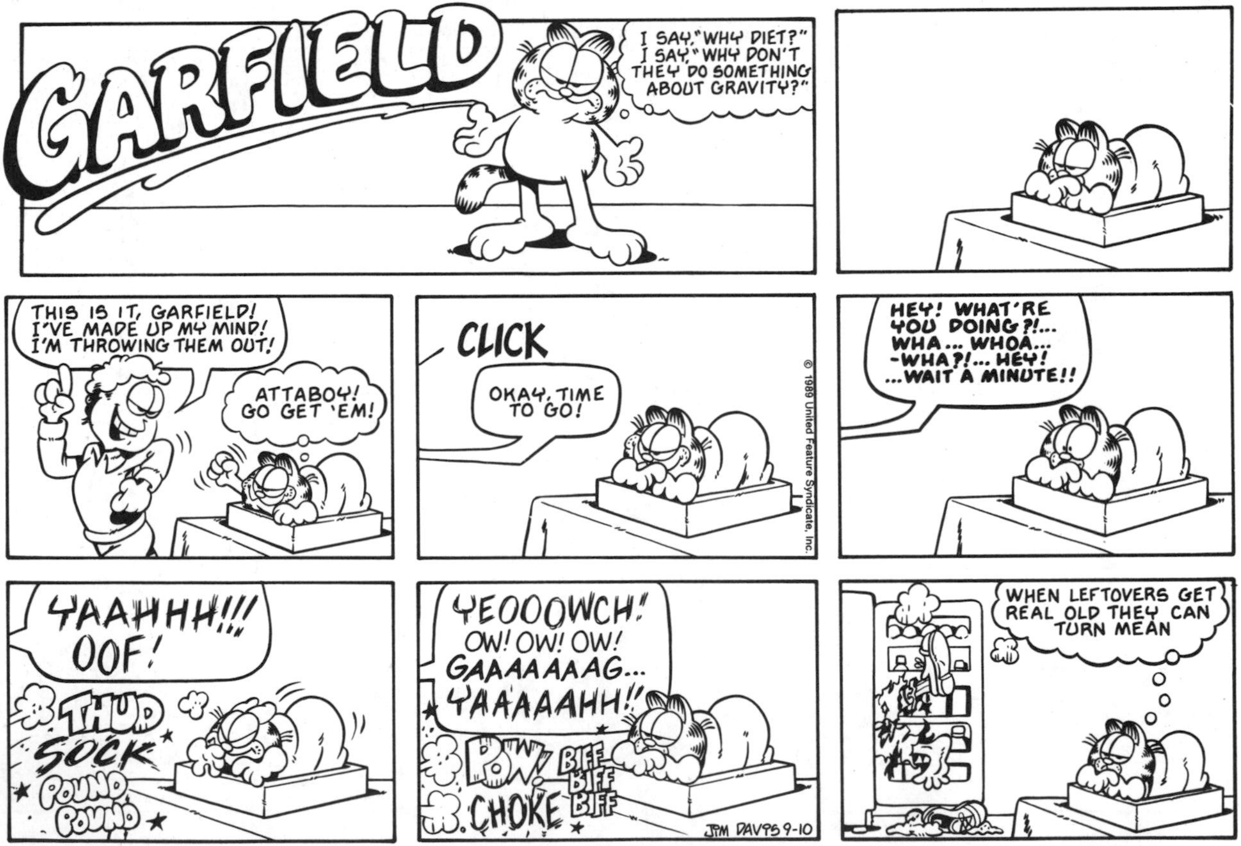
GARFIELD
I SAY, "WHY DIET?" I SAY, "WHY DON'T THEY DO SOMETHING ABOUT GRAVITY?"
THIS IS IT, GARFIELD! I'VE MADE UP MY MIND! I'M THROWING THEM OUT!
ATTABOY! GO GET 'EM!
CLICK
OKAY, TIME TO GO!
© 1989 United Feature Syndicate, Inc.
HEY! WHAT'RE YOU DOING?!... WHA... WHOA... -WHA?!... HEY! ...WAIT A MINUTE!!
YAAHHH!!! OOF!
THUD
SOCK
POUND
POUND
YEOOOWCH! OW! OW! OW! GAAAAAAAG... YAAAAAHH!!
POW!
BIFF
BIFF
BIFF
CHOKE
JIM DAVIS 9-10
WHEN LEFTOVERS GET REAL OLD THEY CAN TURN MEAN

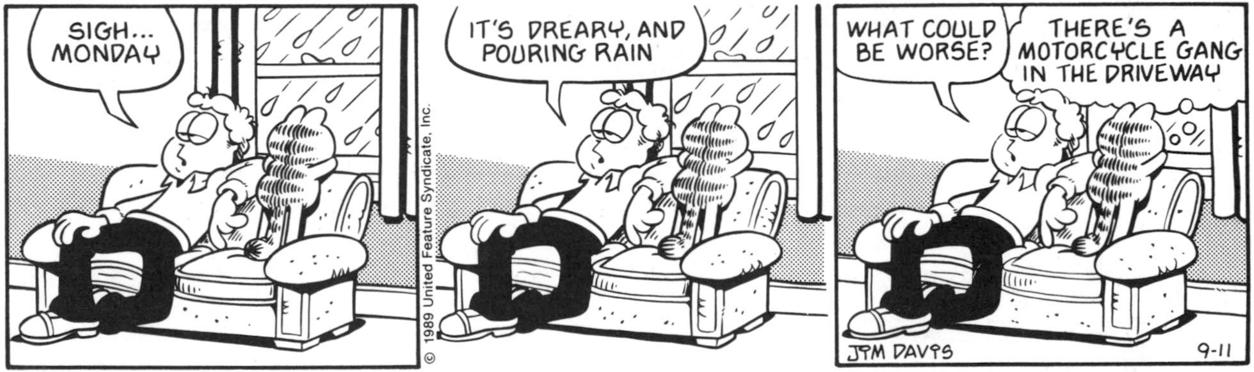
SIGH... MONDAY
IT'S DREARY, AND POURING RAIN
WHAT COULD BE WORSE?
THERE'S A MOTORCYCLE GANG IN THE DRIVEWAY
© 1989 United Feature Syndicate, Inc.
JIM DAVIS
9-11

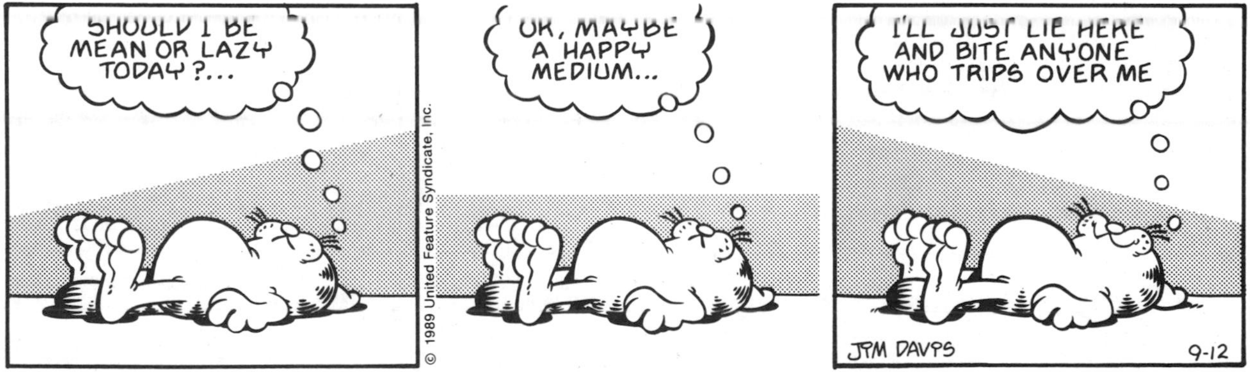
SHOULD I BE MEAN OR LAZY TODAY?...
OK, MAYBE A HAPPY MEDIUM...
I'LL JUST LIE HERE AND BITE ANYONE WHO TRIPS OVER ME
© 1989 United Feature Syndicate, Inc.
JIM DAVIS
9-12

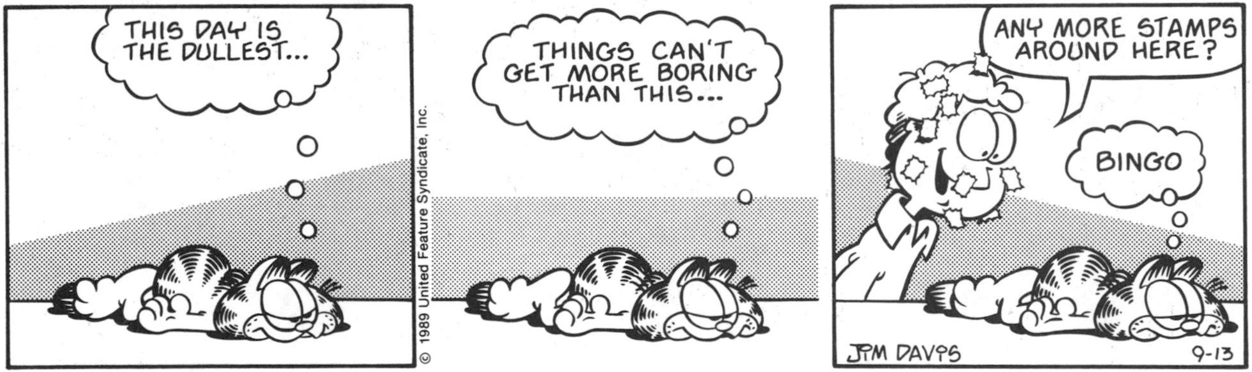
THIS DAY IS THE DULLEST...
THINGS CAN'T GET MORE BORING THAN THIS...
ANY MORE STAMPS AROUND HERE?
BINGO
© 1989 United Feature Syndicate, Inc.
JIM DAVIS
9-13

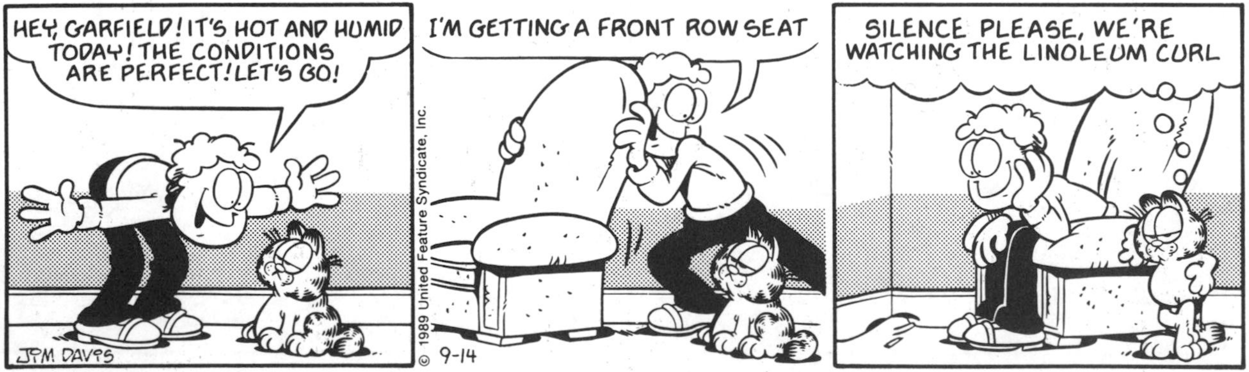
HEY, GARFIELD! IT'S HOT AND HUMID TODAY! THE CONDITIONS ARE PERFECT! LET'S GO!
I'M GETTING A FRONT ROW SEAT
SILENCE PLEASE, WE'RE WATCHING THE LINOLEUM CURL
© 1989 United Feature Syndicate, Inc.
JIM DAVIS
9-14

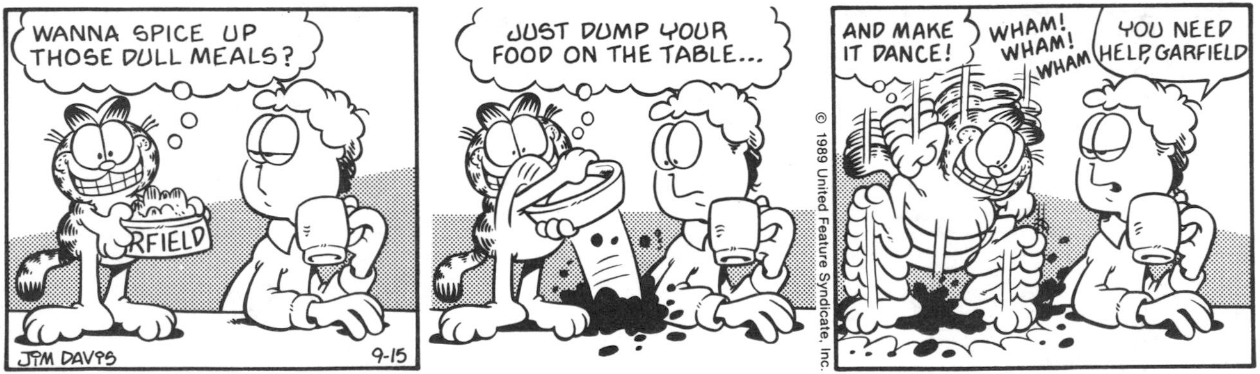
WANNA SPICE UP THOSE DULL MEALS?
RFIELD
JIM DAVIS
9-15
JUST DUMP YOUR FOOD ON THE TABLE...
© 1989 United Feature Syndicate, Inc.
AND MAKE IT DANCE!
WHAM! WHAM! WHAM
YOU NEED HELP, GARFIELD

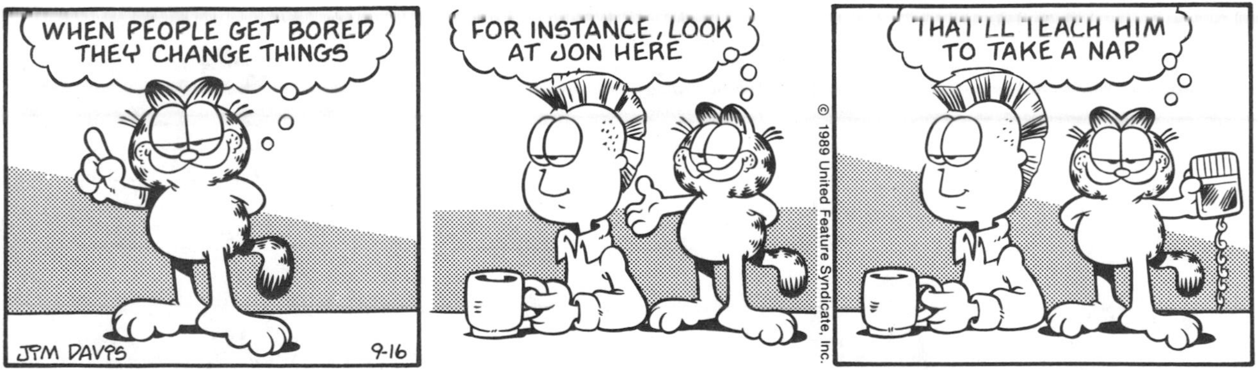
WHEN PEOPLE GET BORED THEY CHANGE THINGS
JIM DAVIS
9-16
FOR INSTANCE, LOOK AT JON HERE
© 1989 United Feature Syndicate, Inc.
THAT'LL TEACH HIM TO TAKE A NAP

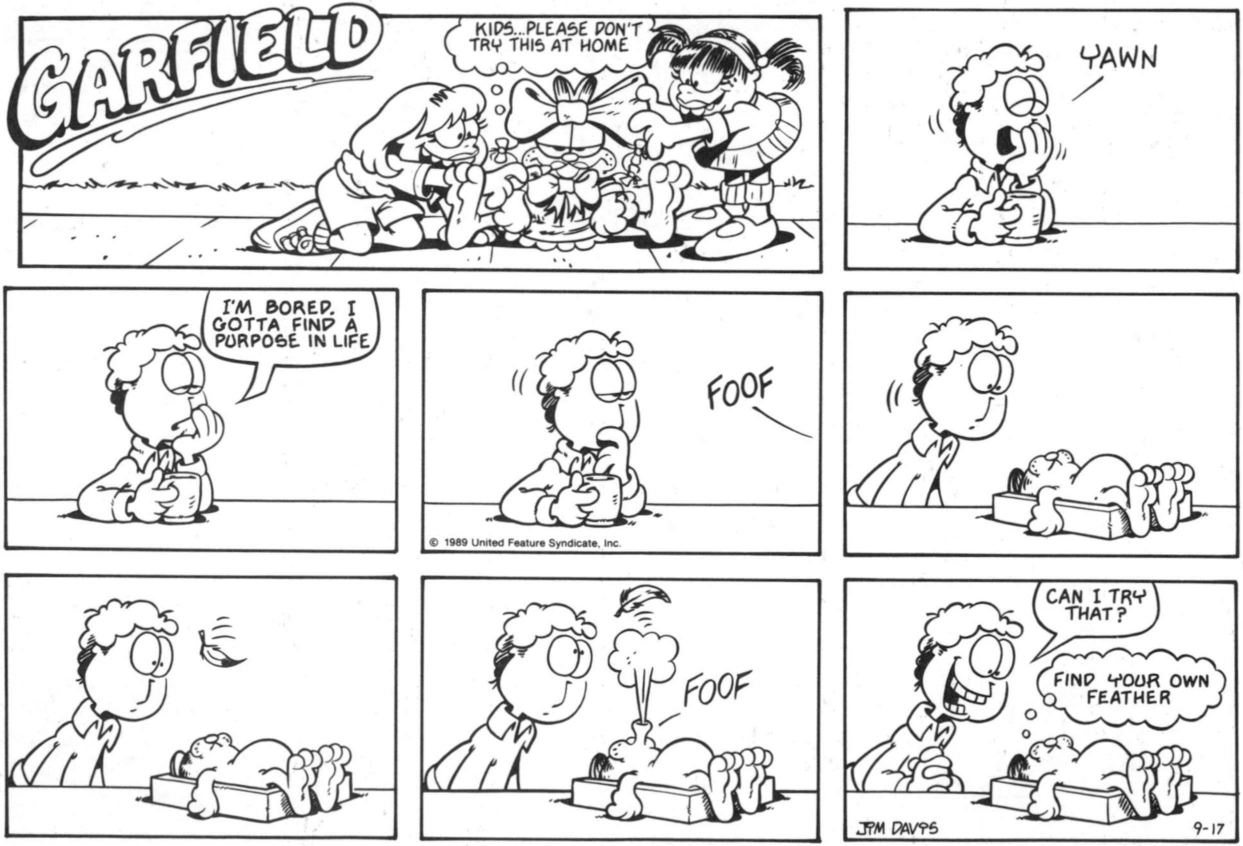
GARFIELD
KIDS...PLEASE DON'T TRY THIS AT HOME
YAWN
I'M BORED. I GOTTA FIND A PURPOSE IN LIFE
FOOF
© 1989 United Feature Syndicate, Inc.
FOOF
CAN I TRY THAT?
FIND YOUR OWN FEATHER
JIM DAVIS
9-17

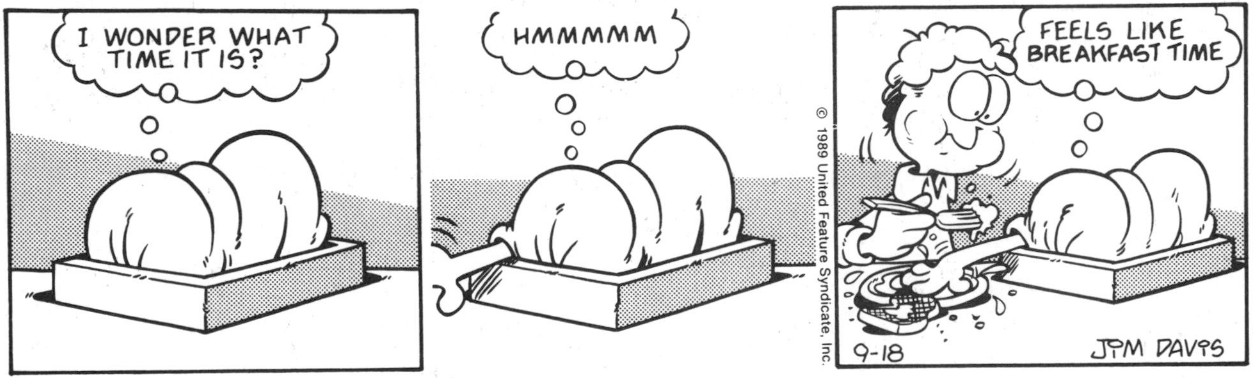
I WONDER WHAT TIME IT IS?
HMMMMM
FEELS LIKE BREAKFAST TIME
© 1989 United Feature Syndicate, Inc.
9-18
JIM DAVIS

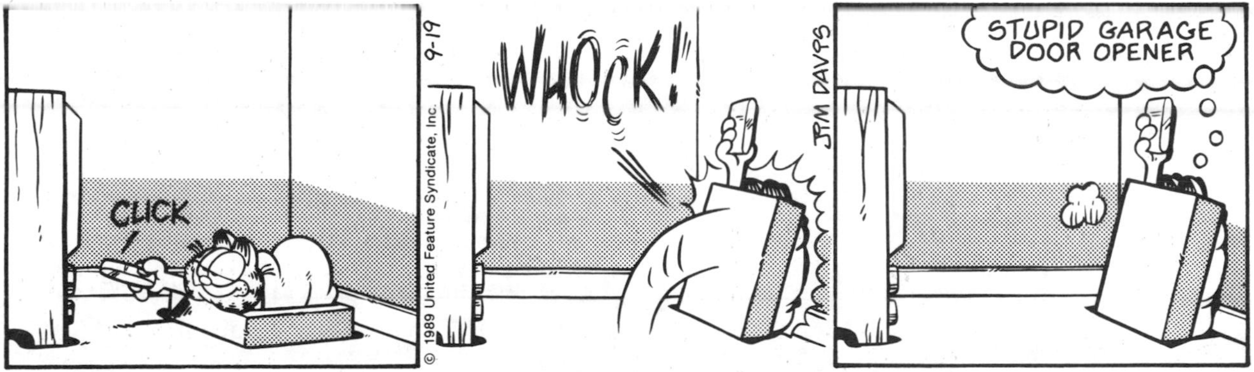
CLICK
9-19
© 1989 United Feature Syndicate, Inc.
WHOCK!
JIM DAVIS
STUPID GARAGE DOOR OPENER

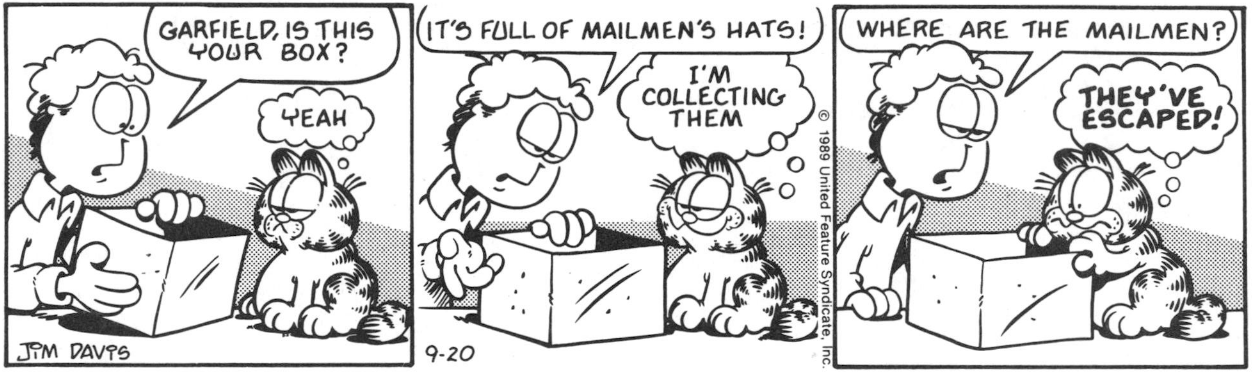
GARFIELD, IS THIS YOUR BOX?
YEAH
JIM DAVIS
IT'S FULL OF MAILMEN'S HATS!
I'M COLLECTING THEM
9-20
WHERE ARE THE MAILMEN?
THEY'VE ESCAPED!
© 1989 United Feature Syndicate, Inc.

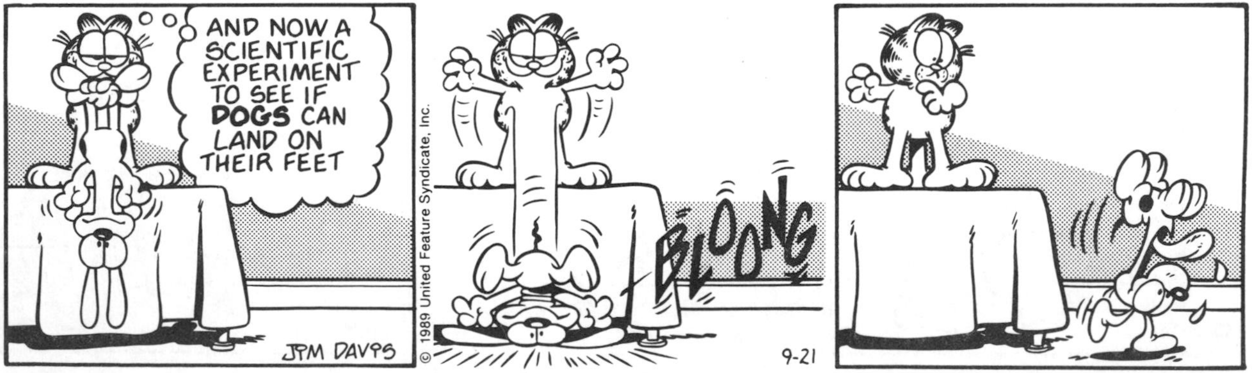
AND NOW A SCIENTIFIC EXPERIMENT TO SEE IF **DOGS** CAN LAND ON THEIR FEET
JIM DAVIS
© 1989 United Feature Syndicate, Inc.
BLOONG
9-21

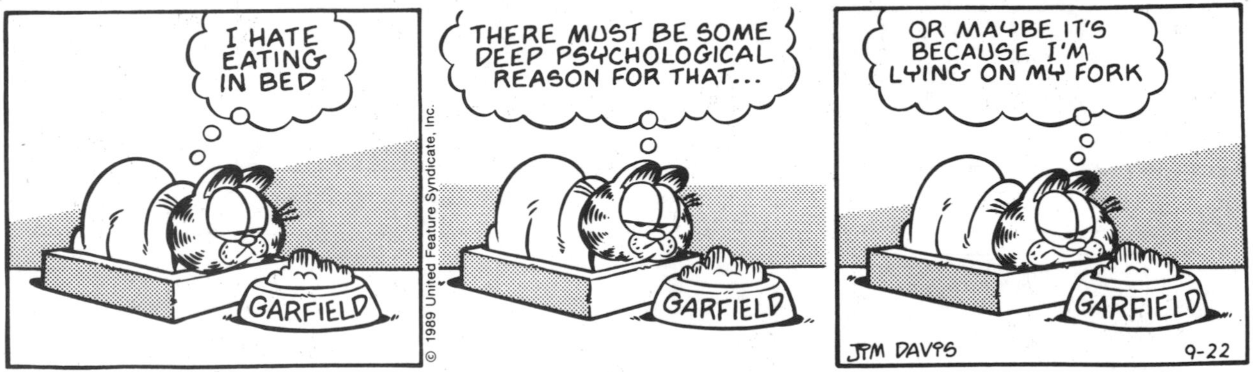
I HATE EATING IN BED
THERE MUST BE SOME DEEP PSYCHOLOGICAL REASON FOR THAT...
OR MAYBE IT'S BECAUSE I'M LYING ON MY FORK
GARFIELD
JIM DAVIS
9-22

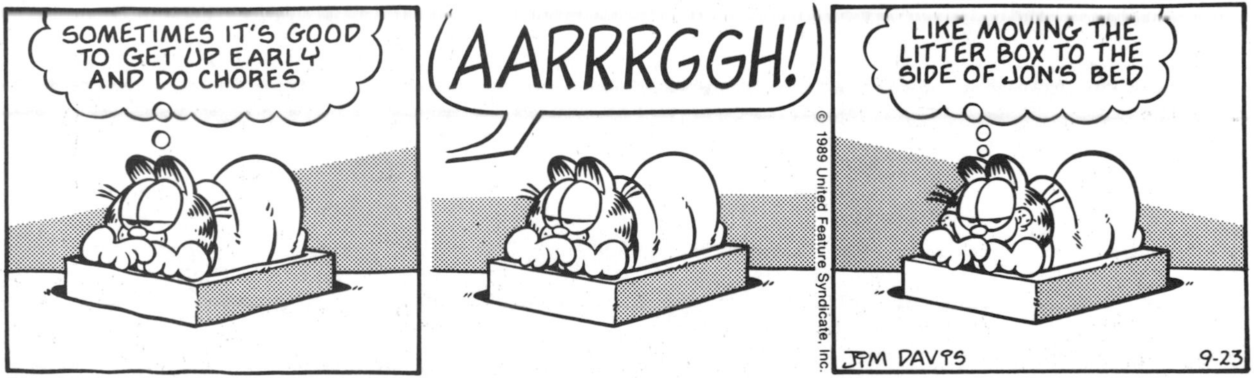
SOMETIMES IT'S GOOD TO GET UP EARLY AND DO CHORES
AARRRGGH!
LIKE MOVING THE LITTER BOX TO THE SIDE OF JON'S BED
JIM DAVIS
9-23

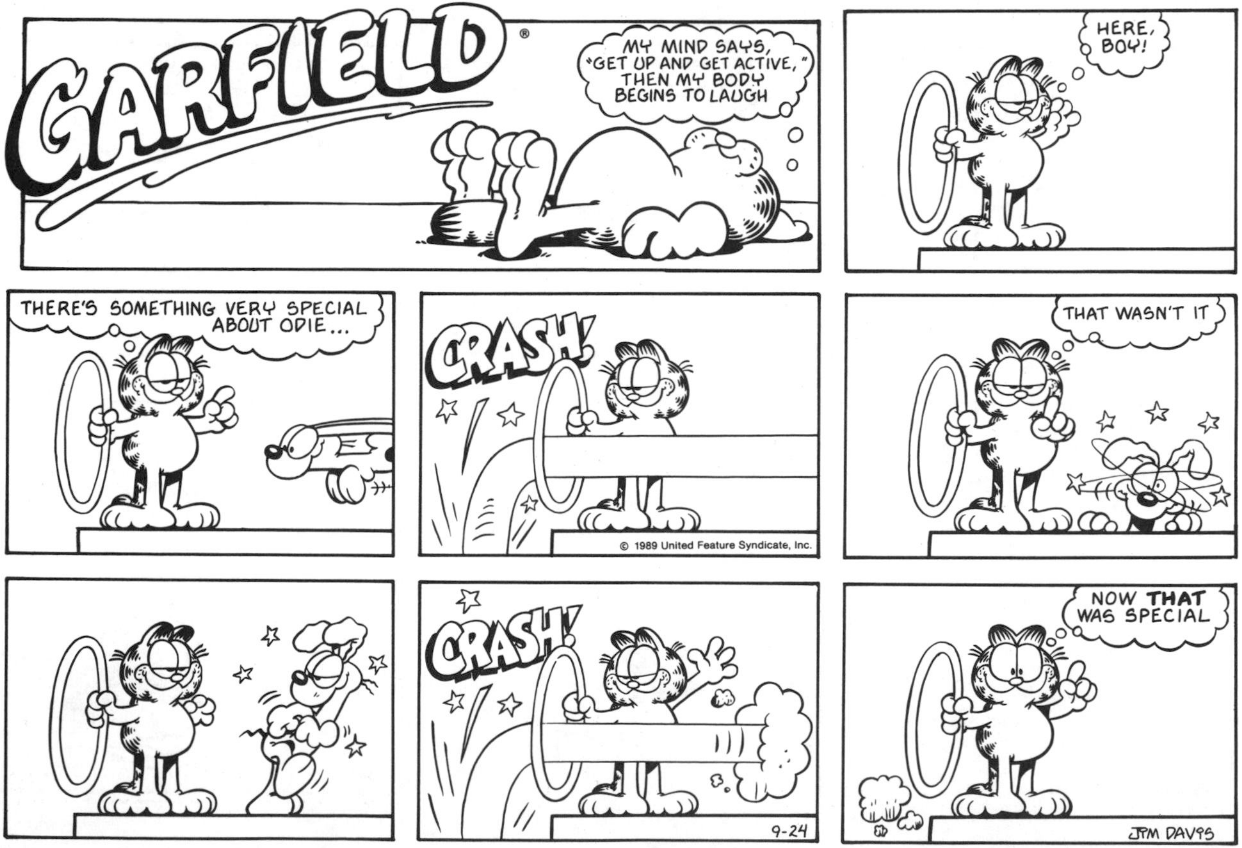
GARFIELD®
MY MIND SAYS, "GET UP AND GET ACTIVE," THEN MY BODY BEGINS TO LAUGH
HERE, BOY!
THERE'S SOMETHING VERY SPECIAL ABOUT ODIE...
CRASH!
© 1989 United Feature Syndicate, Inc.
THAT WASN'T IT
CRASH!
9-24
NOW THAT WAS SPECIAL
JPM DAVPS

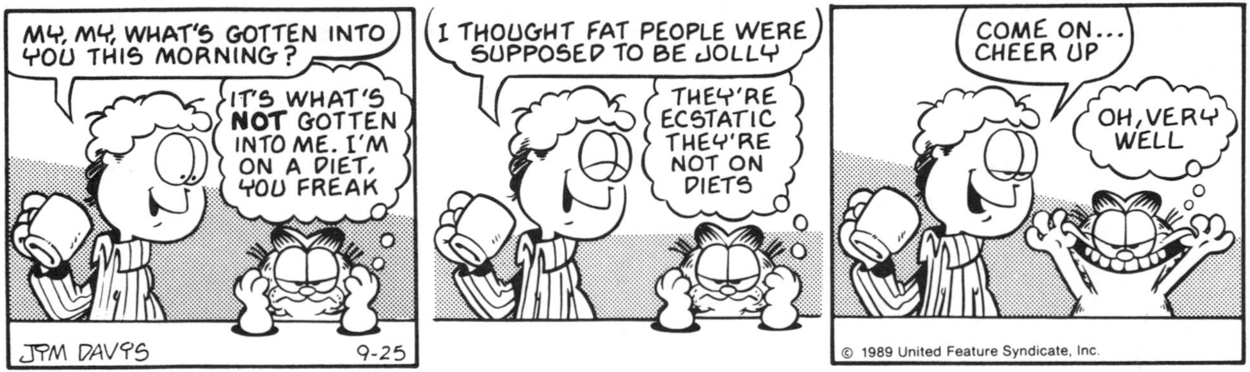
MY, MY, WHAT'S GOTTEN INTO YOU THIS MORNING?
IT'S WHAT'S NOT GOTTEN INTO ME. I'M ON A DIET, YOU FREAK
I THOUGHT FAT PEOPLE WERE SUPPOSED TO BE JOLLY
THEY'RE ECSTATIC THEY'RE NOT ON DIETS
COME ON... CHEER UP
OH, VERY WELL
JIM DAVIS
9-25
© 1989 United Feature Syndicate, Inc.

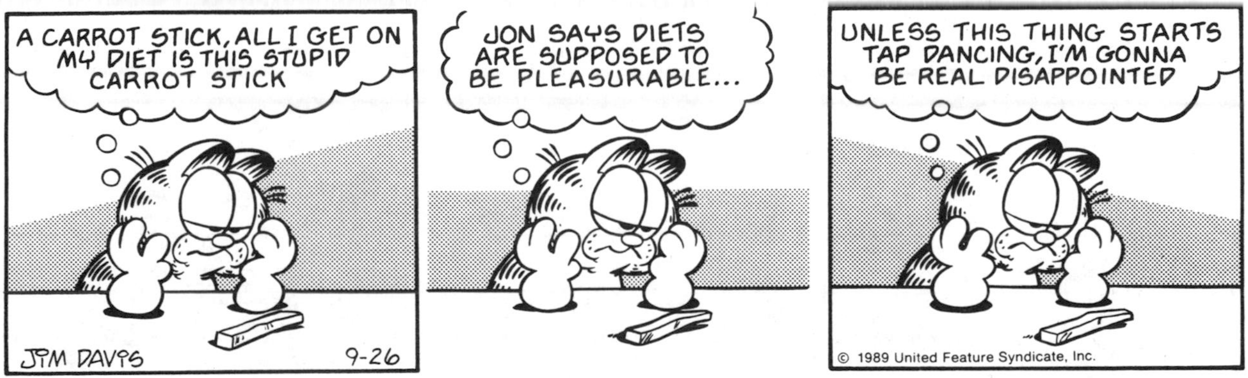
A CARROT STICK, ALL I GET ON MY DIET IS THIS STUPID CARROT STICK
JON SAYS DIETS ARE SUPPOSED TO BE PLEASURABLE...
UNLESS THIS THING STARTS TAP DANCING, I'M GONNA BE REAL DISAPPOINTED
JIM DAVIS
9-26
© 1989 United Feature Syndicate, Inc.

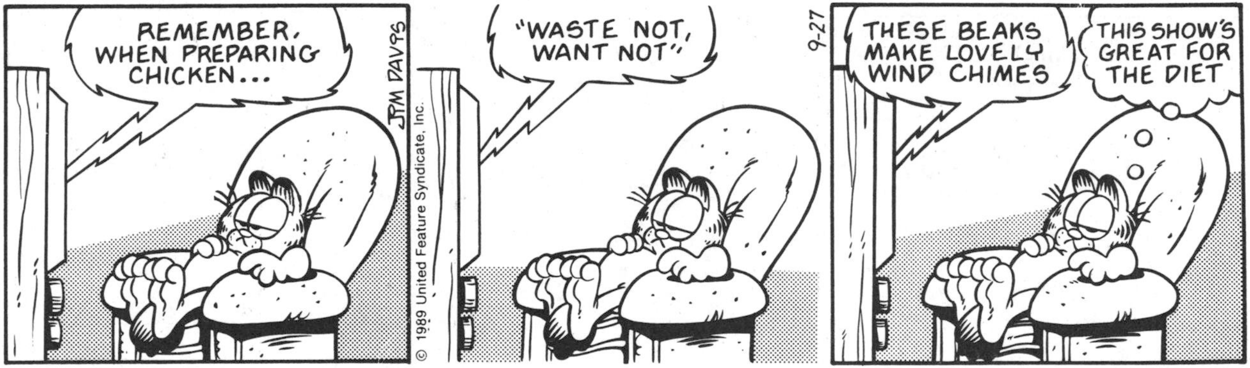
REMEMBER, WHEN PREPARING CHICKEN...
JIM DAVIS
© 1989 United Feature Syndicate, Inc.
"WASTE NOT, WANT NOT"
9-27
THESE BEAKS MAKE LOVELY WIND CHIMES
THIS SHOW'S GREAT FOR THE DIET

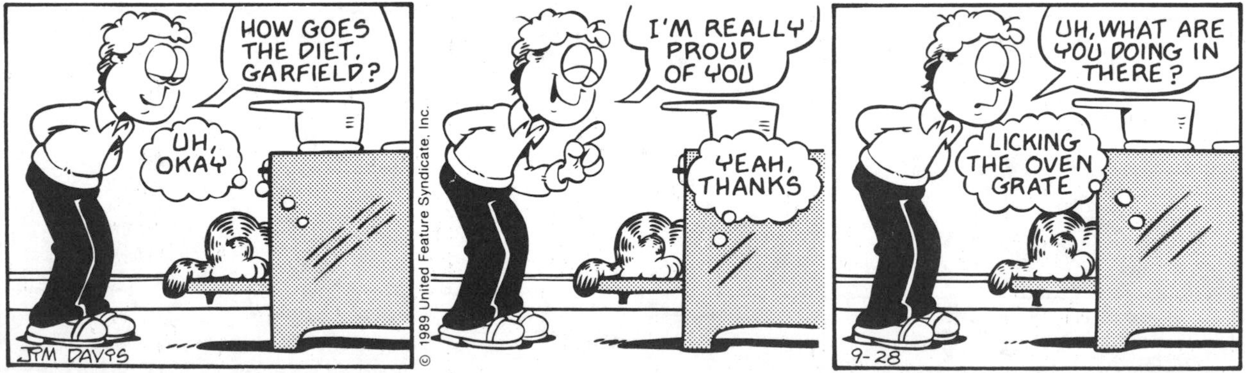
HOW GOES THE DIET, GARFIELD?
UH, OKAY
JIM DAVIS
© 1989 United Feature Syndicate, Inc.
I'M REALLY PROUD OF YOU
YEAH, THANKS
UH, WHAT ARE YOU DOING IN THERE?
LICKING THE OVEN GRATE
9-28

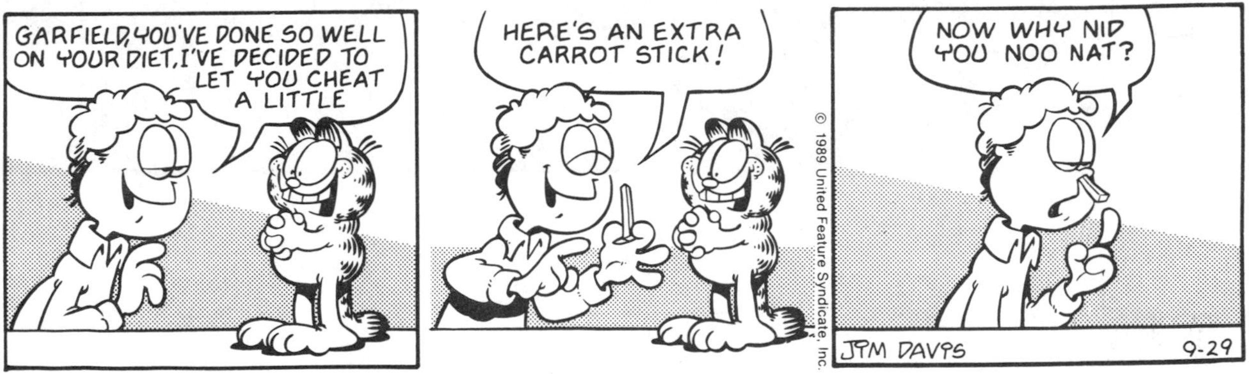
GARFIELD, YOU'VE DONE SO WELL ON YOUR DIET, I'VE DECIDED TO LET YOU CHEAT A LITTLE
HERE'S AN EXTRA CARROT STICK!
NOW WHY NID YOU NOO NAT?
© 1989 United Feature Syndicate, Inc.
JIM DAVIS
9-29

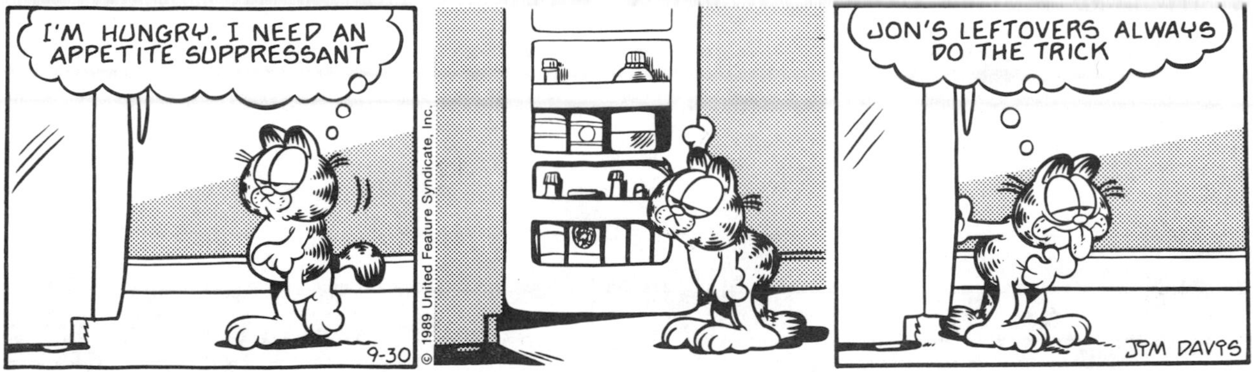
I'M HUNGRY. I NEED AN APPETITE SUPPRESSANT
9-30
© 1989 United Feature Syndicate, Inc.
JON'S LEFTOVERS ALWAYS DO THE TRICK
JIM DAVIS

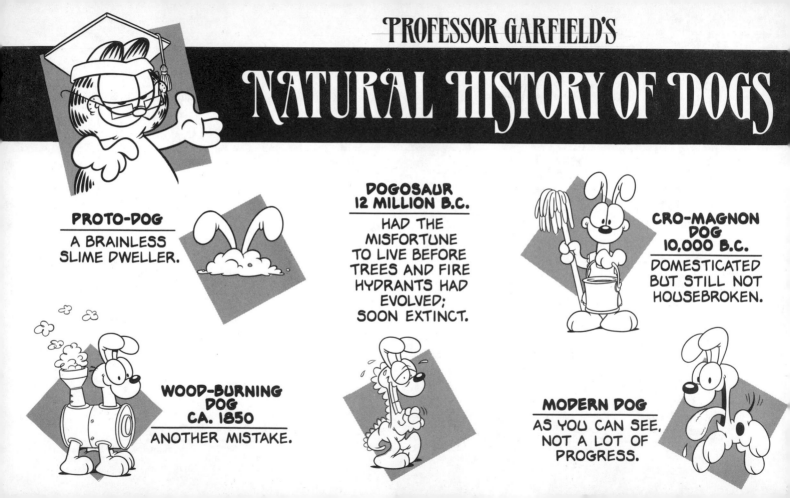

PROFESSOR GARFIELD'S NATURAL HISTORY OF DOGS

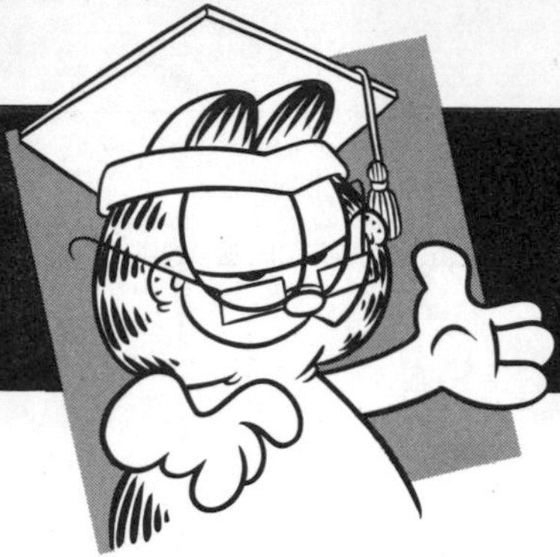

PROTO-DOG

A BRAINLESS SLIME DWELLER.

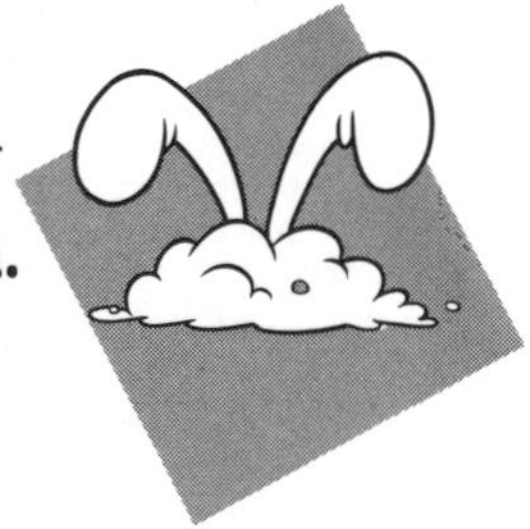

DOGOSAUR 12 MILLION B.C.

HAD THE MISFORTUNE TO LIVE BEFORE TREES AND FIRE HYDRANTS HAD EVOLVED; SOON EXTINCT.

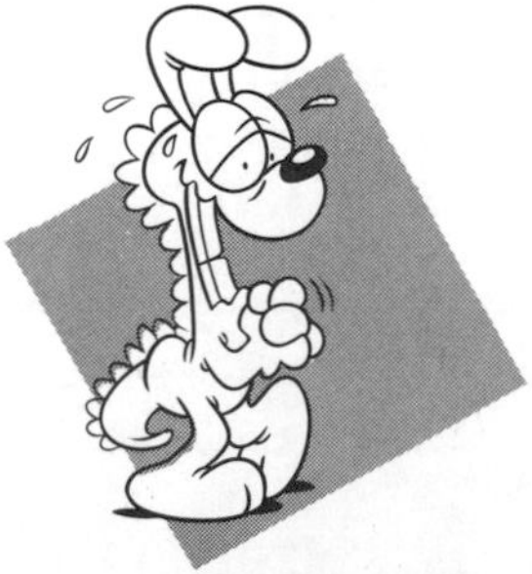

CRO-MAGNON DOG 10,000 B.C.

DOMESTICATED BUT STILL NOT HOUSEBROKEN.

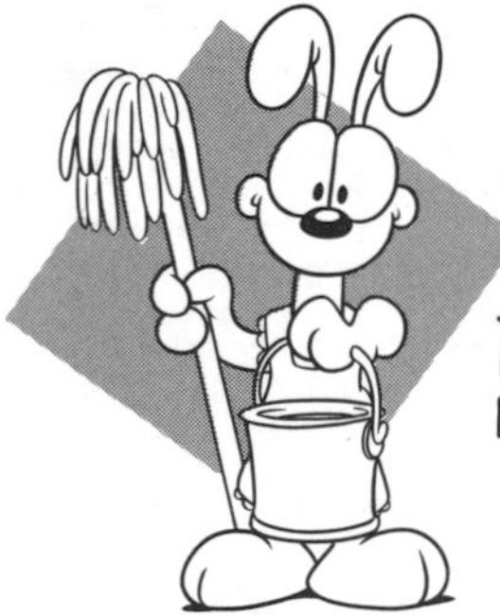

WOOD-BURNING DOG CA. 1850

ANOTHER MISTAKE.

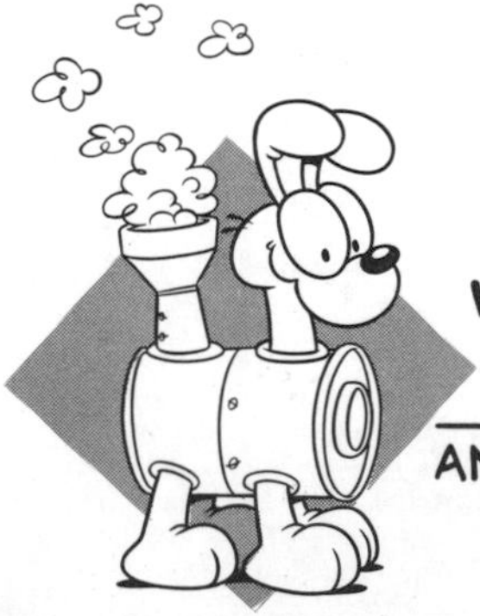

MODERN DOG

AS YOU CAN SEE, NOT A LOT OF PROGRESS.

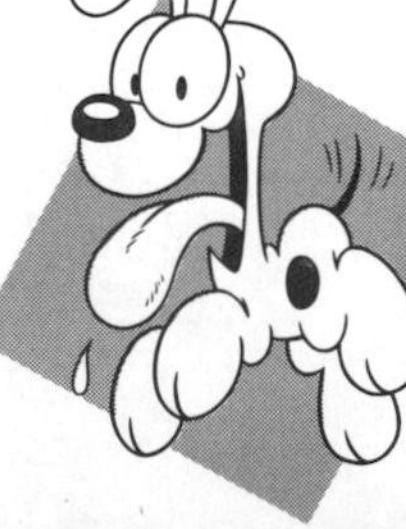